REINVENTING PINK FLOYD

REINVENTING PINK FLOYD

From Syd Barrett to The Dark Side of the Moon

Bill Kopp

ROWMAN & LITTLEFIELD
Lanham • Boulder • New York • London

Published by Rowman & Littlefield
An imprint of The Rowman & Littlefield Publishing Group, Inc.
4501 Forbes Boulevard, Suite 200, Lanham, Maryland 20706
www.rowman.com

Unit A, Whitacre Mews, 26-34 Stannary Street, London SE11 4AB

British Library Cataloguing in Publication Information Available

Library of Congress Cataloging-in-Publication Data

Names: Kopp, Bill, 1963– author.
Title: Reinventing Pink Floyd : from Syd Barrett to the Dark side of the Moon / Bill Kopp.
Description: Lanham, Maryland : Rowman & Littlefield, [2018] | Includes bibliographical references and index.
Identifiers: LCCN 2017046199 (print) | LCCN 2017046374 (ebook) | ISBN 9781538108284 (electronic) | ISBN 9781538108277 (hardcover : alk. paper)
Subjects: LCSH: Pink Floyd (Musical group) | Rock music—History and criticism.
Classification: LCC ML421.P6 (ebook) | LCC ML421.P6 K67 2018 (print) | DDC 782.42166092/2—dc23
LC record available at https://lccn.loc.gov/2017046199

Printed in the United States of America

For Annelise, Daniel, and Audrey.

CONTENTS

ACKNOWLEDGMENTS

The writing of *Reinventing Pink Floyd* would not have been possible without the dedicated and tireless contributions of my partner, Audrey Hermon Kopp. Audrey performed countless hours of research, and served as a wonderfully critical sounding board for the various ideas I set out to explore in this book. Audrey also patiently listened and commented as I read aloud each of the book's chapters.

When Jim Dougherty learned of the book project, he kindly purchased 2016's *The Early Years* box set, and handed it over to me on long-term loan for research purposes. Jim also welcomed me as a guest on his weekly radio program, "Closer to the Edge," allowing me to read selections from the manuscript many months before the book's publishing date.

Quite coincidentally, early in 2017 my friend Ian Reardon put in place plans for a concert to honor the fiftieth anniversary of *The Piper at the Gates of Dawn*. Taking place in July of that year, the concert featured a rotating cast of more than a dozen local musicians playing only pre–*The Dark Side of the Moon* Pink Floyd music. I am honored to have been a part of that project, playing keyboards on eighteen songs. The experience of band rehearsals and performance helped me develop a deeper insight and understanding into Pink Floyd's music of that era, one that no amount of careful listening alone could have achieved.

Were it not for the ongoing encouragement and mentoring of Cary Baker, my calling as a writer—one that began only in middle age—would not have developed. Over the past decade-plus he has gone from a favorite music journalist to a valued resource, then to a trusted associate, and finally (while retaining all of those descriptors) to a dear friend.

In 2016, my longtime friend Jerry Stubblefield encouraged me to speak at a monthly salon hosted by him and his wife Cindy; the positive reaction I received reading from my shorter published works inspired me to pursue the *Reinventing Pink Floyd* project.

I am forever in the debt of those individuals who agreed to be interviewed by me for this book: Craig Bailey, Scott Chasolen, Ron Geesin, Lon Goddard, Peter Jenner, Steve Howe, Robyn Hitchcock, Barney Kilpatrick, Yogi Lang, Steve Mac, Davy O'List, Joe Pascarell, Jason Sawford, Jerry Shirley, and John "Willie" Wilson.

Sincere thanks are also due to Steve Barker (BBC/On the Wire), André Cholmondeley, Bree Ishikawa, Billy James, Mushi Jenner, Bari Lieberman, Natalie Mandziuk and Katie O'Brien at Rowman & Littlefield, Cheryl Pawelski, Michelle Roche, John and Muriel Vitaglione, Kerstin Vohland, Katrin Weber, Ann-Marie Whitfield, and Andrew Yoder.

Last—but certainly not least—I am grateful for the support and encouragement of my sister Donna and my dad, Don Kopp. My mom, Geri, passed away in 2016, but I am sure she would have been very proud to see her son's work published in book form.

Bill Kopp, Asheville, NC, 2017

FOREWORD

Jerry Shirley

When I was barely sixteen years old, I was lucky enough to get a gig playing drums for a professional band called Wages of Sin, based in Cambridge, England. As a result, I had the good fortune to meet and play with many great musicians who have remained close friends to this day. Sadly, two of them, Syd Barrett and Richard Wright, are no longer with us. I am very pleased that the others—David Gilmour, Willie Wilson, Tim Renwick, and Rick Wills—are still alive and well.

When I was approached to be interviewed for Bill's book, my first reaction was to try and put him off, as I had grown tired of being interviewed about my involvement with Syd's brief recording career. Plus, I was always mistakenly credited with being the main drummer on both of Syd's solo albums when in fact my dear friend Willie Wilson played the bulk of the drums on Syd's first album, *The Madcap Laughs*.

So, I gave poor Bill a somewhat ridiculous list of wants that were intended to put him off, as I tend to stay away from discussing Syd Barrett with anybody. This I do out of respect to his family, who, when Syd died, gave me the impression that they wished his memory to be left to rest in peace. That, of course, would be next to impossible, as he was such an important part of Pink Floyd and their early days.

One of my requests was that Bill would put things straight and talk to Willie, as well as me, and therefore give my old flatmate Willie the credit he so deserves and often didn't get. To my utter joy and pleasant surprise, not only did Bill say yes to that wish, he had already planned to try to find and interview Willie. So right there, I knew he was not only well-intended but also was well-informed about his subject matter, where so many before him had not been.

As harrowing as working with Syd was, it was an extreme honor to be asked and I am forever grateful that I got to be part of what has become rock folklore.

I played in Humble Pie alongside rock 'n' roll legends Steve Marriott and Peter Frampton. I also played drums for B. B. King on his 1971 album, *B.B. King in London*; John Entwistle's first solo album, *Smash Your Head Against the Wall* (that same year); and, to top it all off, I played some percussion on George Harrison's *All Things Must Pass*. But in all my years, I have never been asked nearly as much about that incredible list of good musical fortune as I have about working with Syd Barrett. Such is the intrigue that continues to surround him and his music.

I have seen every stage of the Floyd's progression, from when Syd left all the way through to the very end. Much like all of us British bands, the more we toured the United States the better we got. Pink Floyd were no different in that respect. Plus, once David had found his place in the band after Syd left, he kept helping to improve their musicality. Along with Rick Wright, David provided the strong musical foundation of the band.

Whereas Roger was the ideas man and a great lyricist, he relied on the musical talent of the rest of the band—especially David and Rick—to make it all work. A listen to the music each of them makes in the post–Pink Floyd era proves what each brought to the band, and what some of them lacked. The success of the band is largely down to the cooperative, collaborative approach they had in those days.

What makes Bill's book stand apart from the rest—and what made me decide to contribute—is the fact that he is a musician himself. And with respect to Syd, that is what he wanted to write about: the musical experience of working with Syd, not "how weird was he since he took too much acid," etc.

Bill has written knowledgeable, well-informed, conscientious, and sensitive chapters about Syd's music and what it took to record it in somewhat difficult circumstances for us all. And it's nice for me personally to be able to get a considerate writer to include Willie, because the myth that I played all the drums on both of Syd's records has been going on for way too long.

In fact, the best drum track on either one of Syd's solo records was not played by me or Willie! It was played as an overdub by David Gilmour, on my favorite song, "Dominoes." My personal favorite moment of the sessions was when we were recording "Gigolo Aunt," but I didn't realize it until forty years after the fact when I was booked to do some work at EMI's Abbey Road Studios. As I walked through those famous white pillars that stand on each side of the gateway, I noticed that among the graffiti someone had written, "We shall miss Syd Barrett & Rick Wright. May they rest in peace." It then struck me that forty-plus years before, I had been granted the enormous honor of playing on what ended up as the only track on either of Syd's two albums that was recorded completely live in the studio. The lineup for that session was Syd Barrett on guitar and vocals, David Gilmour on bass, Rick Wright on Hammond organ, and little me on the drums.

Money can't buy that experience. Incredible amounts of luck are what got me there, and I am very grateful for it. Finally, that is what I wish Bill and his book: all the good fortune and luck in the world, because he deserves it. He has written about what really matters: Syd's talent, what it took to get it on record, and how it contributed to what ended up being one of the biggest bands the world has ever seen or heard. Don't forget that not only did Pink Floyd make some of the best records, they almost singlehandedly reinvented the visual side of rock 'n' roll. Bill's book is a great read and well worth the price of admission . . . much like the tickets were for the band he has written about.

Well done, Bill.

Jerry Shirley
Cornwall, England
September 2017

WHY (ANOTHER BOOK ABOUT) PINK FLOYD?

Most every creative artist grows over time. He or she learns from mistakes and builds on successes. That fact is neither remarkable nor, on its face, especially interesting. But not every artist or group rallies after a major creative/career setback and then goes on to create *The Dark Side of the Moon*.

For a teenage rock fan such as myself in the 1970s, Pink Floyd was seemingly everywhere. Though the term "classic rock" had yet to be coined as an idea—much less a marketing concept—FM radio was filled with the sounds of the best-selling, London-by-way-of-Cambridge, England, group. The band's breakthrough album, *The Dark Side of the Moon*, had been released in early 1973, and several of its songs quickly became staples of rock deejays' playlists.

Sometime in the middle of the seventies, my parents had bought a 1900s-era upright piano, and I had been taking lessons. I recall a visit by our piano tuner. I hung around to watch him work, and we chatted about music as he tuned the piano by ear. My interest in Pink Floyd came up in the conversation, and he told me a quick story.

He and his wife led a band that performed original material. One of the songs they had written was in the 7/4 time signature. As he recounted, the other band members were having quite a difficult time learning the song, getting the meter right. Finally, he suggested a solution. "Go home and learn how to play Pink Floyd's 'Money,'" he told them. "Once you can do that, you'll be able to learn my song."

In those days, I was still learning how to play songs on the piano using sheet music; alongside my Bach, Bizet, and Beethoven, my teacher would allow me to learn the occasional pop song. I quickly discovered there was something very wrong with those written arrangements: they were rarely—if ever—put together by the songwriter (who likely didn't read music to begin with) and were "arrangements" in the truest sense. The vocal melody was generally played by the right hand, and some gruesome combination of all the other instrumental parts was the function of the left hand. Played as written, the sheet music versions sounded nothing like the songs on the records. Worse yet, they were often in a key other than that of the recorded version. That conundrum would be my impetus to learn to play music by ear.

That goal was helped along when my piano teacher announced that she and her husband were moving to another city. She helpfully prepared a list of teachers with whom I might continue my studies. Instead, I discarded that slip of paper, gathered together my savings, and bought my first electronic keyboard, a primitive and somewhat limited synthesizer-of-sorts made by Elka, an Italian manufacturer. I played it through a Fender Deluxe Reverb amplifier; total investment for the gear plus a stand and cable was about $200. I set about learning to play all over again, this time without the aid of sheet music, and with my focus resolutely on rock music.

It was then that I discovered something special about the music of Pink Floyd. Because much of it was (at least in comparison to much of the era's popular rock music) somewhat slow, playing along was slightly less challenging than, say, sorting out an Elton John hit of the era. And because the Floyd's arrangements often (but certainly not always) involved holding a chord for several measures, there was time for my fingers to find their way to the right notes before the chord changed. That quality made the band's music ideal for learning, and for developing a faculty for playing by ear. So setting the phonograph to repeat-play, I would spend hours upon hours learning to play along with the second side of *The Dark Side of the Moon* and the first side of *Wish You Were Here*. Once I mastered (after a fashion) the keyboard parts on those songs, I never looked back.

But back to those songbooks: they were not without their advantages. I recall one in particular; I still have it today. Titled *Pink Floyd Anthology*, it contained sheet music for several of the band's most well-known numbers, along with several songs whose titles I did not recognize. My curiosity was thus piqued; like most of my generation, I knew Pink Floyd's music from *The Dark Side of the Moon* (1973), 1975's *Wish You Were Here*, and—later, and to a slightly lesser extent—*Animals* from 1977. I made a note to investigate further . . . someday.

A short, uncredited essay at the front of the songbook served as a kind of potted history of the band, with bit of critical analysis sprinkled about. For me, its final sentence summed up the appeal of Pink Floyd: "With a seemingly perfect blend of weirdness and melody *Dark Side of the Moon* provided fans with the kind of accessible tunes, such as the hit song 'Money,' that monstrously successful commercial records are made of."

In fact, *The Dark Side of the Moon* was—and remains—among the biggest-selling albums in the history of the recorded medium. While estimates vary, on a global scale *DSOTM* is widely believed to be the third-biggest-selling album ever—with claimed sales in excess of 45 million copies—bested sales-wise only by Michael Jackson's *Thriller* and AC/DC's *Back in Black*.

And for many years it was said that *The Dark Side of the Moon* was the audio standard by which to measure the quality of one's home stereo system. Even a kid like myself, with little more than a hand-me-down portable hi-fi, could tell that *Dark Side* was something special. But I didn't dig into the band's earlier work at that point; funds were limited, and there were other albums to be purchased, namely those by my favorite group, the Beatles. For me, Pink Floyd was in second place.

When I eventually laid hands on *Wish You Were Here* and then *Animals*, I couldn't help but be struck by the more abstract and textural—perhaps even "jazzy"—turn the band's music had taken. Neither of those albums felt as immediate to me as *Dark Side*, though in due time I would come to fully appreciate their many qualities.

Things turned downright weird in 1979, though. Pink Floyd had been very quiet for a couple of years, and then suddenly a new single appeared. "Another Brick in the Wall (Part 2)" had an undeniably disco/shuffling beat. To a rock fan in 1979, that was near blasphemy. But the tune was so infectious, I—like millions of others—was quickly won over. The single reached #1 on at least seventeen charts internationally, top-tenning in several others. Even more remarkable was the fact that Pink Floyd was as far as one could imagine from what was known as a "singles artist." The band had little interest in presenting its work in the 45rpm format, and—with the exception of two singles off *The Dark Side of the Moon*—the last time Pink Floyd had scored a chart single in the United States was 1967. And the 1967 band had nearly nothing in common sonically with the group's music circa *The Wall*.

The Wall—a sprawling double album—was a massive seller itself, and it renewed popular interest in the band. But as I would discover reading the popular music magazines of the day (*Rolling Stone, Musician*), Pink Floyd had all but ceased to function as a band by the time of its release. Following on from a trend that had been gathering momentum after the release of *The Dark Side of the Moon*, bassist Roger Waters was assuming a larger role in the direction of the band. With each successive release, Waters had a greater share of songwriting credits; beginning with *Animals*, each album's entire thematic concept came from him.

Meanwhile, I realized that drummer Nick Mason and keyboardist Richard Wright were involving themselves less and less in the creative process. The situation continued to the point at which Waters—effectively considering himself the band's leader—dismissed Wright from the band; Pink Floyd's founding keyboardist would stay on for *The Wall* sessions and its limited-engagement tour as a paid employee.

By most reports, guitarist David Gilmour was less than enchanted with the band's late 1970s musical direction. Though some of the most musically fulfilling moments on *The Wall* come courtesy of Gilmour's trademark lead guitar and mellifluous vocals, *The Wall* was never his project.

The Wall would be performed live by Pink Floyd in only three cities: New York, Los Angeles, and London. The massive stage setup made regular touring impossible, and in any event the band wasn't getting along very well. *The Wall* dates included four extra musicians—masked doppelgangers for Waters, Wright, Mason, and Gilmour—which meant that those lucky few who *did* witness Pink Floyd in concert on that tour could never really be sure of who they were watching and hearing.

In 1982, a film version of *The Wall* was released. A nightmarish film with no dialogue, *The Wall* brought Waters's terrifying vision to the big screen. I recall seeing it upon its theatrical release; my then-girlfriend was so emotionally distraught by the onscreen images that she vomited. In the film, the dark themes that had increasingly been at the center of Pink Floyd's music were taken to their extremes, often stripped of subtlety and nuance. Without a doubt, Waters's musical narrative had a great deal to recommend it, primarily in his addressing concepts like fascism, totalitarianism, and (not for the first time) mental illness. But musically, *The Wall* could be a bit ponderous; many of the songs were built around a single three-note motif. While that compositional method is impressive in its own way, as a listening experience, it can occasionally border on the dull.

In 1983, Pink Floyd released *The Final Cut*. That portentous title signaled many things, few of which were good news for longtime fans of the group. Waters had assumed total control of the band; Wright was completely absent; Mason allowed session drummers to play his parts while he concerned himself with the album's (admittedly stunning) three-dimensional "holophonics" soundscape. And Gilmour's contribution to *The Final Cut* was limited to a co-write on one song, the somewhat dire "Not Now John," a tune that—pointedly or not—contained the memorable line (sung by Gilmour), "Fuck all that." Not unsurprisingly, the "classic" lineup of Pink Floyd ceased operations not long thereafter.

Like me, many of those who followed Pink Floyd in the years between *The Dark Side of the Moon* and *The Final Cut* were largely unaware of what the band had done before that period. And that fact highlights a remarkable feature of Pink Floyd's popularity: casual fans knew of the band's work from *The Dark Side of the Moon* onward; more serious students of the group were familiar with the band's 1967 debut, *The Piper at the Gates of Dawn*, made when Pink Floyd was led by its founder, Roger Keith "Syd" Barrett.

But only the hardest of hardcore Pink Floyd fans—a label with which I began to identify by the end of the seventies—had more than a passing knowledge of the music made after *Piper* and before *Dark Side*. Which raises a compelling question: how did Pink Floyd make the journey from early 1968—when Barrett left, and the band's management departed with him—to spring 1973 when they released *The Dark*

Side of the Moon? Syd Barrett had been the founder, the leader, the public face, the primary (nearly exclusive) songwriter of Pink Floyd since its start. With him gone, the band suddenly found itself adrift creatively.

In the short space of just over five years, the Pink Floyd lineup of David Gilmour (taking over for Barrett on guitar), Roger Waters, Nick Mason, and Richard Wright would embark upon numerous experiments, follow many musical blind alleys, and pursue myriad creative directions, all in search of their collective musical expression.

The Dark Side of the Moon didn't create itself out of nothing. The seeds for most every enduring quality found in the Pink Floyd experience—the lyrics, the musical textures, the overall presentation—all developed across the six albums, related tours, and other projects that the band worked on in the years between *Piper* and *Dark Side*. At various points in their history, the band members have admitted as much.

The goal of *Reinventing Pink Floyd* is to explore that little-known period, uncovering clues to the band's eventual direction by examining what Pink Floyd did in those years. Happily, the band's activities during 1968–1973 are surprisingly well-documented, if one knows where to look. The collectors' community has amassed a huge trove of live Pink Floyd concert recordings; all of these are unauthorized, it should be noted. But taken together, those recordings provide a running chronicle of the band's development as a creative, performing unit. Fans recorded approximately one hundred Pink Floyd concerts in the period after Barrett's departure and before the band began presenting material that would see release as *The Dark Side of the Moon*.

2016's *Pink Floyd—The Early Years* box set (with all of its volumes—save one—released individually in 2017) helped fill many gaps in the band's story; it included some of the bootlegged material in better quality, along with a heretofore unexpected cache of material that had not already made its way into the hands of collectors of ROIOs ("Recordings of Indeterminate Origin," a term coined by hardcore Pink Floyd fans and collectors).

Pink Floyd experimented with long-form compositions, collaborations with outside composers, writing for film soundtracks, and even cobbling together a kind of musical narrative by sequencing already existing material. Some of these musical excursions were very successful, and suggested directions the band might take in future projects.

Others were seen by the band as failures, with Pink Floyd all but disowning the results. But with the benefit of nearly a half century's hindsight, and with the added context of *The Early Years* material and current-day interviews with many people connected in one way or another to the band, all can be recognized and appreciated as relevant pieces of the overall Pink Floyd picture. Nearly everything the band did would, in one way or another, provide clues to the band's eventual and wildly successful direction.

In a 1979 career-spanning critical review of Pink Floyd's catalog in the *Rolling Stone Record Guide*, reviewer Bart Testa made an astute observation: "Pink Floyd is a band that's never thrown away a single idea." While on its face that may seem a harsh assessment, there's truth in the assertion. Fans of *The Dark Side of the Moon* and the band's later work have reason to be thankful for that characteristic of Pink Floyd's modus operandi, as a dogged return to partly developed ideas—along with ongoing refinement of those ideas—culminated in the creation of one of the most popular and critically acclaimed albums in the history of recorded music. What's often forgotten—or at least overlooked—is the wealth of gems that Pink Floyd created in the run-up to making *DSOTM*.

Reinventing Pink Floyd aims to help correct that oversight.

Part I

Apples and Oranges (1966–1967)

I

LET'S ROLL ANOTHER ONE

On Friday, March 10, 1967, the debut single by Pink Floyd was released in the United Kingdom on Columbia Records. "Arnold Layne" and its B-side, "Candy and a Currant Bun," represented two slices of the nascent pop-psychedelic sounds coming into vogue in the British music scene. Both tunes were composed by Pink Floyd's leader, twenty-one-year-old Cambridge-born guitarist Syd Barrett.

The group had been together in one form or another for several years; various permutations of the band had gone by various other names, including The Tea Set, Leonard's Lodgers, Sigma 6, The Meggadeaths, the Abdads, and The Spectrum Five. As early as 1963, three original members of what would come to be known as Pink Floyd—Roger Waters and keyboardist Richard Wright (both born in 1943) and drummer Nick Mason (born 1944)—had played together in groups that performed in venues such as London's Marquee Ballroom. Notably, at that stage Waters was on guitar, not bass.

The first documented use of the Pink Floyd name came in March 1965 when the four-piece, Barrett-led group auditioned at London's Beat City Club; their bid to get on the venue's schedule failed. And while the band's fortunes with regard to securing live gigs would soon change, the group had already made its first foray into a recording studio more than two years before the release of the Columbia single.

Sometime between December 1964 and February 1965—perhaps on more than one occasion—the band visited Decca Studios in West Hampstead, London, where they recorded six songs. At that stage, the group was probably still going by the name The Tea Set; the band included lead guitarist Rado "Bob" Klose as well as guest vocalist Juliette Gale, later to become Rick Wright's first wife. Dubbed copies of two songs cut at that session—the Barrett original "Lucy Leave" and a cover of blues singer-guitarist Slim Harpo's 1957 B-side "I'm a King Bee"—circulated underground among Pink Floyd collectors as early as the 1990s; hardcore fans argued among themselves as to whether the tunes were indeed Barrett and company.

With Parlophone Records' November 2015 release—extremely limited at just over 1,000 copies—of a vinyl EP (Extended Play record) titled *1965: Their First Recordings*, the embryonic Pink Floyd's Decca session tapes received their first legal release. For those who had grown up on a sonic diet of Pink Floyd circa *The Dark Side of the Moon* and later albums, there would be little on *Their First Recordings* that would provide any kind of sonic continuity; the similarities between a slight tune like Barrett's "Remember Me" and, say, *DSOTM*'s "Brain Damage" are all but nonexistent. With its shouted rhythm and blues arrangement, "Remember Me" has more in common with early sides by the Rolling Stones.

Nonetheless, there are some clues to Pink Floyd's early sound contained on those 1965 sessions. While Rick Wright focuses primarily on playing a Wurlitzer electric piano, the guitar work—courtesy of Klose and Barrett—exhibits a slashing style that would become a feature of the Pink Floyd sound circa 1967. Four of the six tunes from the Decca sessions are Syd Barrett originals, and "Lucy Leave" bears the greatest resemblance to the style the four-man band would employ two years later. "Lucy Leave" is based upon a familiar R&B melodic line, and Barrett repeatedly wails "leave," extending the word across several measures. But what's most distinctive about the tune—which is for most of its three minutes little more than a two-chord vamp—are the start-and-stop sections of the melody that punctuate the verses and choruses, and the slightly nonstandard (by pop measures, anyway) chord choices.

Taken together, the seemingly out-of-place chords in "Lucy Leave" form the "Devil's interval"—also known as the Devil's tritone or flatted-fifth, a musical device employed since the Middle Ages to convey dread and doom. It's wholly open to conjecture whether Syd Barrett discovered the interval via old blues records—he would name his band after little-known American blues artists Pink Anderson and Floyd Council, after all—or hearing it in the tony academic environs of his native Cambridge. Or perhaps the musically self-trained guitarist came up with it—savant-like—completely on his own.

"Double O Bo" is a thin rewrite of any given tune from the catalog of Elias McDaniel (better known as Bo Diddley), but even it displays a few qualities that elevate the tune above being a faceless entry in the "shave and a haircut, two bits" rock style. Once again, Barrett inserts some unexpected chords to break up the musical monotony.

"Butterfly" is another R&B tune, but the song's arrangement presages Barrett's later tendency in songwriting toward bending song structure to fit his lyrics. Like American country bluesmen of old—musicians to whom he would acknowledge a clear debt—Barrett developed a style that often meant inserting or dropping a beat or two (or more) into a musical phrase to allow his wordplay to fit into the song's structure. While "Butterfly" is fairly conventional stuff, it is perhaps the earliest recorded example of Barrett moving in this direction, and—then as now—is somewhat unconventional by pop music standards.

While the February 1965 demo (demonstration recording) sessions are primarily a showcase of Syd Barrett's songwriting and vocals, bassist Roger Waters would place one of his original songs on the tape as well. Decidedly less prolific a songwriter than Syd, the twenty-one-year-old Waters nonetheless penned the chirpy "Walk With Me Sydney." With a Barrett lead vocal and Gale doubling the lead vocal in an upper register, "Walk With Me Sydney" is, more or less, a love song. That alone qualifies it as something of an anomaly among Waters's songwriting. And though humor is a rare—and under-recognized—part of Waters's lyrics, "Sydney" is positively silly. With its lyrical complaints of flat feet, fallen arches, meningitis, peritonitis, delirium tremens, and other maladies, the song showcases Roger Waters's love of the darker side of humor, all within the context of a melody that wouldn't be out of place on a Herman's Hermits record.

Taken as a whole, the recordings featured on *1965: Their First Recordings* are a flatly produced session, and represent little beyond a slice of Pink Floyd/Syd Barrett juvenilia. Their interest lies primary among Pink Floyd completists and those seeking to understand the group's complete body of work. The contents of *Their First Recordings* would receive widespread release in 2016 as part of the box set *The*

Early Years 1965–1972, and as part of a smaller break-out of that set, 2017's four-disc *1965–1967: Cambridge St/ation*. Viewed in context with the later "Arnold Layne," the six songs from the Decca sessions provide a kind of aural benchmark against which the group's subsequent work may be viewed.

Notwithstanding a mid-January 1967 session for the soundtrack of the film *Tonite Let's All Make Love in London*, the January 23 "Arnold Layne" session at London's Sound Techniques Studio would be Pink Floyd's studio debut. With American expatriate Joe Boyd—an early champion of the band—producing the sessions, Pink Floyd recorded Syd Barrett's song about a man who enjoyed stealing women's clothing off of wash lines and then wearing the clothing. Near the song's end, listeners learn Layne's sad fate: he is arrested and sent to jail.

The melody of "Arnold Layne" features descending chord progressions, a prominent feature of Barrett's songwriting. Like many of the tracks recorded in the band's first year under contract with EMI (Electrical and Musical Industries, parent company of Columbia, the label that would release the band's music in the UK), "Arnold Layne" sports an instrumental break that spotlights Richard Wright's Farfisa organ skills. While Barrett was the band's chief songwriter, his instrumental skills were no equal to the more classically trained Wright, so giving the solo spot over to the keyboardist—at least on pop recording dates— made good sense. For his part, Wright was a multi-instrumentalist; he was adept on vibraphone and some brass instruments as well.

In its original form, the B-side of "Arnold Layne" was controversial. The song's first title was "Let's Roll Another One," a clear reference to marijuana. But a decision was made during the session to retitle the song and change its lyrics; the phrase "Candy and a Currant Bun" fit neatly into place of the potentially offending lyrics. Writing enthusiastically some years later about the tune, *Creem*'s Dave Marsh described "Candy and a Currant Bun" as "somewhere between truly cosmic Beatles and truly powerful Who," and likened it to the best tracks on the Rolling Stones' 1967 LP, *Their Satanic Majesties Request*.

Not at all out of step with the prevailing practice of the music business in the mid 1960s, the band's management team of Andrew King and Peter Jenner paid to boost the single's chart placement; it would briefly reach #20 on the singles chart in the United Kingdom. Today, it is often mistakenly assumed that the staid "Auntie Beeb" (state-controlled BBC Radio) banned "Arnold Layne" because of its subject matter; in truth, it was the more commercial-minded "pirate" radio station Radio London (broadcasting from a ship operating in the North Sea, ostensibly outside the UK government's jurisdiction), *not* the British Broadcasting Corporation, that would refuse to play the single.

While "Arnold Layne" would eventually appear on *Relics*, a compilation released on EMI's budget label Music For Pleasure in 1971, "Candy and a Currant Bun" was widely unavailable on album until it was included on *The Early Singles*, a CD available only as part of the 1992 *Shine On* box set. It would appear again on *The Early Years* box set on CD and on a replica 45-rpm single housed in a picture sleeve.

2

INTERSTELLAR OVERDRIVE

On February 1, 1967, Pink Floyd signed an exclusive contract with EMI, the same company with which the Beatles had signed. Less than a month after recording what would become their debut single, Pink Floyd commenced sessions for their debut album, *The Piper at the Gates of Dawn*. Sessions began at EMI's Abbey Road Studios in Southwest London under supervision of producer Norman Smith, and would continue—sandwiched between the band's live dates and other engagements—through the third week of May of that year. A generation older than the band he was producing, Smith (born in 1923) was by 1967 an experienced hand in the studio; he worked as recording engineer on all of EMI's studio recordings featuring the Beatles through their 1966 album *Rubber Soul*. As it happened, the Beatles were working variously in Studios One, Two, and Three, recording songs for *Sgt. Pepper's Lonely Hearts Club Band* while Pink Floyd worked at the same time with Smith in other rooms at Abbey Road. The sessions for *Piper* would be Smith's first as a producer. "Norman Smith had a lot to do with helping Syd and the band in the studio," says Peter Jenner, the band's manager from 1966 to 1968.

But mere days before the *Piper* sessions began at the Abbey Road Studios, Smith oversaw the recording of "See Emily Play," a song eventually released as the A-side of Pink Floyd's second single. Cut at Sound Techniques Studio in London, "Emily" was in many ways a distillation of all the qualities showcased on the subsequent *The Piper at the Gates of Dawn* album. Relying on its most accomplished musician, Pink

Floyd's "See Emily Play" features Richard Wright's keyboards as a prominent instrument. His four-note descending motif repeatedly punctuates the song's chorus. Norman Smith's tape-manipulation skills—likely developed during his tenure working with the Beatles—are showcased here, as Barrett's vocals are pitch-shifted down for a portentous feel. In contrast, a Wright piano solo is greatly sped up via tape, creating the ambience of a wind-up toy. Years after the song's release, the Rock and Roll Hall of Fame named "See Emily Play" among its "500 Songs That Shaped Rock and Roll."

Several of the eleven songs that would be recorded for *The Piper at the Gates of Dawn* had been in the group's set list since at least October 1966, and possibly earlier. While the band's live shows of the era were built around extended, often free-form musical excursions, the songs on *The Piper at the Gates of Dawn* are models of conventional, concise pop songwriting, albeit filtered through the musical sensibilities of Barrett and his band mates. In fact, when writing or speaking candidly on the subject, it's the rare artist or performer who does not characterize their first album as a document of their live set. In contrast, it's perhaps most accurate to suggest that *Piper* represented one side of the band. Syd Barrett seemed to understand this before the band was ever signed; in a January 1967 interview with Nancy Bacal of the Canadian Broadcasting Company, he admitted, "I think our records will be very different from our stage shows." He added, "Listening to a gramophone record in your home or on the radio is very different from going into a club or into a theater and watching a stage show. They're two different things that require a different approach." And he was emphatic: "We think we can do both."

"Astronomy Dominé" opens the album—and Pink Floyd's album catalog—in grand fashion. Voices effecting a "NASA Mission Control" vibe—actually Peter Jenner reading off the names of constellations and such, his voice filtered through effects—introduce the tune while Barrett lays down a stuttering, repetitive guitar figure. "I did the intro on the megaphone," Jenner recalls. "That was just an excerpt from half a page of an encyclopedia-type thing about space." Waters initially doubles the guitar part on his bass guitar. Richard Wright enters, mimicking Morse code on his Farfisa organ, and Nick Mason follows, hitting his floor toms with mallets instead of the more common (in rock context) drum sticks. After the dramatic introduction, dual lead vocalists (and co-composers) Barrett and Wright sing the tune's space-themed lyrics in a deliberately icy manner.

That dispassionate demeanor is merely the setup for the song's chorus-after-a-fashion, a descending chord progression adorned by some near-falsetto, wordless vocalizing. As a template for the so-called space rock associated with Pink Floyd, "Astronomy Dominé" is a glorious introduction. The beginning moments of "Astronomy Dominé" are remarkably similar to a song by American psychedelic rock group the Electric Prunes. The B-side of a 1966 single, "Are You Lovin' Me More (But Enjoying It Less)" reached #42 on the UK charts in 1966, so it's reasonable to assume that Barrett heard the song before entering the studio to record *Piper* with Pink Floyd. Both songs feature an ethereal, foreboding introduction built around a single repeated note, and both songs build to a crescendo after the introduction.

Curiously, when EMI's American subsidiary Harvest Records reissued *The Piper at the Gates of Dawn* (packaged in a two-LP set with the band's second album, *A Saucerful of Secrets*, as *A Nice Pair*), the studio version of "Astronomy Dominé" was replaced by a live version taken from *Ummagumma*, Pink Floyd's hybrid live/studio double LP released in 1969; the studio version would thus be largely unavailable to American consumers until the CD reissue of *The Piper at the Gates of Dawn* in 1987.

A Syd Barrett song about his cat, "Lucifer Sam" again employs a descending guitar riff. It also features a keening Farfisa solo courtesy of Rick Wright. It's among the most conventionally hard-rocking songs on the LP. Had Pink Floyd gotten a commercial foothold in the United States—and followed the American practice of releasing album tracks as singles—the catchy "Lucifer Sam" might have done well there.

The first song recorded for *The Piper at the Gates of Dawn*, "Matilda Mother" is among its most tuneful. Yet again, Barrett builds his verses upon a foundation of a repeated phrase of descending notes; in those verses, Wright's Farfisa plays sustained chords that preview the approach he would develop more fully in the post-Barrett years. Close harmony vocals from Barrett and Wright add a dreamlike ambience to a song that already makes explicit mention of "wondering and dreaming." Barrett's lyrics combine idyllic images of childhood—fables of ancient kings—with something vaguely more sinister and foreboding: the fear and loneliness of perceived abandonment.

The instrumental break in "Matilda Mother" features some impressive, almost bluesy organ work from Wright, while Barrett provides wordless vocalization that previews "Pow R. Toch H.," a song that would also appear on *The Piper at the Gates of Dawn*. Though he holds off at the beginning of the song, Waters's nimble bass work adds significant interest to Barrett's rather simple melody. Mason's drums are atypically low in the mix throughout "Matilda Mother." Cutting the tempo in half, the song's "outro" features some lovely three-part "ahh" harmonies, more single-note work from Wright, and—somewhat frustratingly—the opening strains of a lead guitar solo from Barrett as the song fades into silence.

An LSD-laced version of a childlike sense of wonder is among the most oft-remarked attributes of *The Piper at the Gates of Dawn*. (Though by most accounts, Barrett was the only member of Pink Floyd to take the drug.) Perhaps nowhere are those qualities so vividly showcased as on "Flaming." With an opening that borders on the abstract, initially the song seems to be heading in a particularly dark direction. But a mere fifteen seconds in, the sound changes radically. While Wright plays a see-saw melody, Barrett trills his lyrics about blue clouds, unicorns, lying in fields of eiderdown, and games of hide-and-seek. (Childhood games were favored lyrical fodder for Barrett, who had explored the theme on "See Emily Play," released two months before *Piper*.)

If "Flaming" is a textbook example of anything, it's Syd Barrett's happy refusal to be constrained by the normal rules of pop song convention: the song has no chorus. Instead, it's a series of vaguely poetic lyrical lines wherein the only rhymes are internal. After about one minute and forty seconds, "Flaming" dissolves into a collage of impressionist aural images, taking the place of what—in a "normal" song—would be the solo or instrumental break. After one more verse, "Flaming" resolves with a melodic ending, one so conventional that it seems almost to belong to another song.

Sequencing of songs on a finished album is an important task; the manner in which tracks flow from one to the next is a critical part of achieving a unified effect. With that in mind, "Flaming" serves as the ideal musical gateway to "Pow R. Toc H.," which opens upon a wild cacophony of whooping and other vocal effects set against a malevolent instrumental backing. Once that madness subsides, Richard Wright's single-note piano excursions are laid atop an arrangement that feels like a theme to an American cowboy western. Mid-song the freakout returns—against some trademark descending note figures—and then the song fades into abstract, hall-of-horrors sounds. Barrett's guitar works as an effect, while Wright adds spooky organ and piano lines. Waters's hypnotic bass figure joins Mason's tom-tom work—cymbals are all but absent on the song—and as the tune reaches its end, all of the instruments dissolve into a hazy oneness. In many ways, the wordless "Pow R. Toc H." is the track on *The Piper at the Gates of Dawn* most representative of Pink Floyd's live set; that the song's composition is credited to all four band members underscores this fact.

"Take Up Thy Stethoscope and Walk" is Roger Waters's sole composition credit on *Piper*, and it displays a marked improvement in the bassist's songwriting abilities over "Walk With Me Sydney." With Barrett's repeated "doctor, doctor" phrase serving as a kind of percussive device that aids and abets Nick Mason's insistent, tribal drumming, "Stethoscope" is, for lack of a better phrase, one of the most conventionally psychedelic songs on the album. The lyrics are an early example of Waters's growing fascination with medical and biological matters, themes he'd explore in greater detail on a collaborative 1970 album with Ron Geesin. And the band's instrumental attack borders on the sinister, an approach Pink Floyd would also develop more fully on their albums right up to Waters's departure in the mid-1980s. The title of "Take Up Thy Stethoscope and Walk" is an oblique reference to the New Testament (John 5:8); Waters would mine Bible texts once again—Ecclesiastes this time—for a new, extended Pink Floyd work in 1972 initially known as *Eclipse*. That project—minus the Biblical recitations—would eventually be retitled *The Dark Side of the Moon*.

"Interstellar Overdrive" is, along with "Pow R. Toc H.," the spot in which *The Piper at the Gates of Dawn* comes closest to Pink Floyd's live shows. The band recorded more studio versions of this song than any other, including at least two for film soundtracks, one for *Piper*, and at least one for broadcast on the BBC. In perhaps another case in which Barrett drew influence not from American bluesmen of old but from current-day American West Coast rock groups, Syd Barrett was inspired to write "Interstellar Overdrive" after hearing the Burt Bacharach–Hal David song "My Little Red Book" in a hard-rocking, proto-punk cover version released in 1966 by the hip Los Angeles group Love.

Pink Floyd manager Peter Jenner had heard Love's version some-where—"maybe a record shop," he suggests—and mentioned it to Bar-rett. "I said, 'I heard this great new record.' So, I started singing out a tune incompetently, and Syd picked up a guitar and said, 'Oh, like this?' and played his version of that. And that became 'Interstellar Overdrive,' which was just that one riff, really," Jenner says. "And then they impro-vised it from there on in. That was the absolute backbone of their initial year or eighteen months."

A largely improvisational work, "Interstellar Overdrive" varies great-ly in its many versions. The recording made for *Piper* runs nearly ten minutes, an eternity for an album track in 1967. Barrett's descending riff serves as the basis for free-form musical excursions on the part of all four members, guaranteeing a unique reading each time it would be played. Only by refraining that descending phrase could Barrett pull his band mates back into the structured part of the song. Though Pink Floyd would never be considered a jazz group (their tune "Biding My Time," discussed in a future chapter, possibly excepted), the practice of playing a "head" (basic melodic theme), improvising at length, and then returning to the head is a common practice among jazz players. In the rock idiom, perhaps only the Grateful Dead would explore this ap-proach in any kind of detail.

Syd Barrett's playful track "The Gnome" brings *Piper* back to its regular state: whimsical songs with fairytale-like lyrics. The story of one Grimble Gromble, "The Gnome" is perhaps the most dated track on *Piper*. It's an exemplar of Barrett's style, and shows a direction he would follow on his fractured solo albums. Notably, however, it would also represent a style from which Pink Floyd would distance itself once Barrett departed.

Equally psychedelic yet more creatively successful is "Chapter 24." Again dispensing with formal verse-chorus structure, Barrett's fanciful tune features a hypnotic piano figure from Richard Wright (plus an overdubbed countermelody on Farfisa organ), with minimal guitar, and little or no drumming from Nick Mason. Roger Waters's bass figure provides linkage between the song's sections.

"The Scarecrow" is built upon a growing set of clip-clop percussive figures, with free-form verses by composer Barrett. The singer rushes certain vocal phrases to make them fit into his (still quite nonstandard) melody. The brief song's second half is given over to another Wright solo on Farfisa.

The Piper at the Gates of Dawn ends as it began, in remarkable fashion. "Bike" is another instance in which Syd Barrett dispenses with rules pertaining to phrasing, meter, and melody. The song's deeply textured production is easily producer Norman Smith's finest contribution to the album. The song itself runs under two minutes; the remaining minute and a half is filled with countless clocks being wound and chiming—yet another sonic idea that would be resurrected five years later on *The Dark Side of the Moon*'s "Time"—and truly bizarre treated vocals that presage Roger Waters's "Several Small Species of Furry Animals Gathered Together and Grooving on a Pict" on Pink Floyd's 1969 double LP, *Ummagumma*.

According to research by Pink Floyd historian Glenn Povey, EMI session notes suggest that a Barrett song called "She Was a Millionaire" was recorded in April; no further evidence of the song exists. A few months later, a similarly titled song *did* appear briefly in the group's live set: a September 1967 bootleg recording of a Copenhagen concert includes a song possibly titled "One in a Million." Sung by Roger Waters, the six-minute tune did not surface as part of *The Early Years*.

Pink Floyd would quickly return to the studio in late October 1967, beginning sessions for what would eventually become *A Saucerful of Secrets*, once again with Norman Smith producing. But the results of the initial sessions would take the form of "Apples and Oranges," released as Pink Floyd's third UK single. A relatively slight and self-consciously psychedelic number, "Apples and Oranges" would fail to chart in England, nor—despite the band gamely supporting it via multiple television performances—in the United States.

No more successful was its B-side, "Paint Box." But "Paint Box" would be significant as the first released Pink Floyd track with a sole Richard Wright songwriter's credit. Wright's tack piano is the song's defining instrumental characteristic; the unique effect is achieved by pressing thumbtacks into the felt-covered hammers inside an acoustic piano; the resulting "metallic" effect recalls the feel of saloons in the American west of the late 1800s.

Critical reaction to *Piper* was generally positive, though more than a few writers expressed their thinly veiled bewilderment at the music. "If you must call a group 'psychedelic'—and admittedly labels are convenient—then it should be the Pink Floyd," wrote a reviewer for the *Detroit Free Press* in November 1967. "This English group has gotten deep into the electronics of pop music and uses feedback and other effects knowledgeably. The album isn't easy to listen to and you may not like it, but it shows you the far reaches of pop." Reviewing the album somewhat belatedly, the February 1968 issue of American music magazine *Hit Parader* singled out "Interstellar Overdrive" and called it "dazzling" yet "two-dimensional," and ultimately "about three and a half minutes too long."

Taken as a whole, the eleven songs on *The Piper at the Gates of Dawn* and the other singles recorded and released in 1967 are very much of their time. Released during the so-called Summer of Love when psychedelia was in full bloom—and before some of that scene's darker elements would manifest themselves—it has nonetheless worn quite well in the more than half a century since its release. Speaking in a 2016 NPR radio interview (with *All Songs Considered* host Bob Boilen) about the "Arnold Layne" sessions he produced, Joe Boyd described the tune as playful and "almost folk, nineteenth-century . . . almost like schoolkids' rhyming songs." Boyd could have just as easily been commenting on Syd Barrett's songwriting in general.

Avowed Syd Barrett fan Robyn Hitchcock started making records with his first professional group, the Soft Boys, near the end of the 1970s. While he's a wholly original artist with more than twenty albums to his credit, Hitchcock's style owes an acknowledged debt to Barrett. "I think Syd Barrett was a magician," he says. "Not just [his] words, but his way of writing a song with this very natural, almost nursery-rhyme [quality] . . . but also very unlikely."

Hitchcock remarks on Barrett's unconventional use of melody. "He'd start a song in [the key of] E, and then he'd realize it was in A," he chuckles, "but it didn't sound forced." And he turns a bit wistful when he thinks about Barrett's relatively brief time in the spotlight. "While he was still 'there,' there was an incredible character personality coming off Barrett's work, one which was more intense than most other people's," Hitchcock observes. "It's almost as if he was just compressing all his life into two years. So it had a density like dark matter." Hitchcock believes that Syd Barrett's peculiarly original songwriting stood apart from other artists, who would tend to "write what they think they ought to write."

Along with the singles released in 1967, the songs on *Piper* sharply defined the music of Pink Floyd as having a particular nature and style; that style was undoubtedly the product of creative collaboration among the group's four members, but the indelible and unmistakable fingerprints of Syd Barrett were perhaps the most enduring quality of the music Pink Floyd would make in this period. With only minor exceptions—and though the band didn't quite realize it as 1967 drew to a close—Pink Floyd would never again produce studio work with the creative input of its leader. Instead, the group would begin a new chapter in its creative journey, one that was both a reaction to and an attempt to follow on with the work created with Syd Barrett.

3

HAPPENINGS AND UFOS

Like most every other band of their era (and most others), the musicians who would eventually call themselves Pink Floyd started as a group playing "covers," songs written by others. Various pre-Floyd aggregations included songs as varied as the jazz standard "How High the Moon" and "Long Tall Texan," the latter recorded by the Beach Boys and others. But once Pink Floyd signed a recording contract, the band would never again play a cover. In a January 1967 interview with the Canadian Broadcasting Company, Roger Waters summed up the change in the band's approach: "It stopped being sort of third-rate academic rock; it started being sort of an intuitive groove, really."

In 1966, Lon Goddard was an American expatriate living in London. He ran what he describes as a "sandwich and lager bar" and recalls walking to Middle Earth, a nearby club in London's Covent Garden. There, he saw Pink Floyd for the first time. "There was a lot of incomprehensible noise coming from a very small stage," he says. "Because at that time, Pink Floyd was so experimental that I think [the music] was mostly within their heads."

The free-form music bore little resemblance to the short songs the band would soon record for *The Piper at the Gates of Dawn*. "There was no conventional structure to what they were doing," Goddard says.

Peter Jenner recalls his first encounter with Pink Floyd, in March 1966. Then twenty-one, Jenner was a lecturer at the London School of Economics. After a long day of grading exams, he decided he needed a break. "Some acquaintances of mine were putting on a 'happening' in the Marquee, which was then a jazz club in Oxford Street," he says. "And so I thought I could get on the guest list, which I did." Once there, he found a somewhat unusual scene. In addition to poets reading their works, he witnessed "girls who were highly naked or scantily clad in colored jelly or something. It wasn't like a standard gig where you have a beer, and one band comes on, and then you have a few records, and then another band comes on."

Eventually the group—then billing itself as The Pink Floyd Sound—came on to perform. Jenner says that at first the band played a few standard blues numbers, like "Dust My Broom" ("I don't know if they actually played that," says Jenner, "but they played things *like* that"). He does recalls that the band definitely played "Louie, Louie."

But Jenner was nonetheless intrigued because some of the familiar tunes didn't have the then-obligatory guitar solo. "Instead," Jenner explains, "there were these strange noises going on. And I wandered around the stage trying to work out how and where they were coming from." He eventually sorted out that what he was hearing was the combined sound of Richard Wright's Farfisa organ and Syd Barrett's electric guitar, both sounds processed through a device called a Binson Echorec, with incredible amounts of sustain.

"Instead of there being a blues break," Jenner says, "there was this sort of instrumental sound thing going on." At the time, he suspected—but wasn't sure—that much of what he was hearing was improvised. "In hindsight, it was probably just a sort of one chord thing, just sort of waffling on one chord," Jenner says, noting that what Barrett and Wright were doing was similar to the sounds the Doors were making more than 5,000 miles away in Los Angeles.

But at the time, the London music scene was still somewhat insular; Jenner explains that while people in Great Britain might have heard *about* underground acts like the Grateful Dead and Country Joe and the Fish, they were far less likely to have actually heard their music. So while the then-new idea of "psychedelic" music was understood to mean that the bands "wore psychedelic clothes and took drugs," Jenner still felt that the music he was hearing from Pink Floyd was itself psychedelic.

By this time, Jenner and some of his friends—among their number John "Hoppy" Hopkins, Felix Mendelssohn, and American expatriate producer Joe Boyd—had decided to start a record label. "I decided this band playing this weird improvisation stuff was something that we should have on our label." He decided to pay the band a visit. "I went out to find them in their house in Highgate, knocked on the door, and I said, 'Are you the Pink Floyd Sound?'" One of them—probably Roger Waters, Jenner recalls—said yes. "I said, 'Well, I would like to have you all on a label. I have an underground label and I'm very interested in what you're doing.' And they said, 'Well, great, but we're going on holiday now. See you when we get back.' They slammed the door."

Jenner returned a month later, again finding Waters. He made his pitch, but Waters replied that the band wasn't interested in signing to a label. But they were looking for a manager. Jenner was interested, so he contacted another friend, Andrew King. "I said to him, 'Why don't we manage this band?' He said, 'All right,' because he was just leaving his job. He also had a little bit of money that an aunt had left him. I still had my job at the LSC."

Jenner and King began the work of lining up live dates for the band. Jenner's father was a clergyman in London's working-class districts, so Jenner knew a thing or two about fund-raising events featuring live music. He and his friends were supporters of another underground venture, the London Free School. "It needed money for the new autumn term coming up," he recalls, "so we should do a fundraiser." Pink Floyd was booked to perform at a church hall in London's Notting Hill, and Jenner says that Hoppy "somehow got a hold of some draft-dodging Americans who had a light show."

"We did a gig, and it was really successful," says Jenner. "So we did another one, and people were being turned away." The now ongoing series of events was moved to a larger venue—"a ballroom, a sort of really old Irish bar/dance hall," Jenner recalls—dubbed by the event's organizers as UFO. "And that's where things took off," he says.

Thanks in large part to the success of the Beatles, it was becoming less fashionable for groups to play "covers." Original material was a mark of quality for performing bands. "I knew that Syd had written some songs," Jenner says. "I said, 'Do you know any more songs?' Syd said yes, and from that point on, they started doing their own songs." Jenner believes that Barrett's new focus on songwriting would enhance Pink Floyd's ability to land a recording contract with a record label. And though in subsequent years it would become a non-issue, the band's visual style circa 1967 was a selling point—part of the whole package—

as well. "The key was Syd writing songs and singing them," Jenner says. "He was also the one who had the best taste in clothes, which was becoming very important. But Roger had appalling taste in clothes, and we all were embarrassed by that."

Jenner makes an important distinction between Barrett being the face (and songwriter) of the band and being Pink Floyd's guiding force. "It was his band," Jenner says, "but in no way was he the band leader." He strives to clarify his point. "Creatively, he *was*. But not in any organizational things, you know, 'What gig are we doing tomorrow?' He was more, 'Just pick me up, tell me what we're doing,' and then he'd do it. Roger was always the most organized one."

That quality of Pink Floyd's bassist would prove essential to the band's survival in a few months. But for the time being, the band was at the peak of its powers with Syd Barrett as its front man.

4

REACTION IN G

While set lists of the earliest Pink Floyd live performances are all but nonexistent, it is known that by October 1966 the group was performing songs that would eventually surface months later in studio versions on *The Piper at the Gates of Dawn*. And though popular lore among fans holds that Pink Floyd's live sets of 1967 bore little sonic resemblance to the music on *The Piper at the Gates of Dawn*, in fact the band performed every song from *Piper* live onstage at least once.

A set list from an October 14, 1966, concert at All Saints Church Hall featured at least six songs destined for *Piper*, including "The Gnome," the group composition "Interstellar Overdrive," Roger Waters's "Take Up Thy Stethoscope and Walk," "Matilda Mother," "Pow R. Toch H.," and "Astronomy Dominé," all Syd Barrett compositions except as noted. Curiously, the nearly two-year-old tune "Lucy Leave" (from the Decca sessions) was included in the set as well. "Let's Roll Another One" was also performed, as were some other titles: "Pink," "Gimme a Break," "Stoned Alone," "I Can Tell," "Snowing," and "Flapdoodle Dealing." While no songs with those titles would be recorded by Pink Floyd, the band's early—and long-held—practice of changing song titles as they went along may well mean that the songs from the All Saints gig appeared on *The Piper at the Gates of Dawn* under other names.

Recording sessions for "Lucifer Sam"—originally called "Percy the Rat Catcher"—had only begun around April 11, 1967, but within days the song became part of Pink Floyd's live set; the first documented performance dates from an April 15 concert at the Kinetic Arena on the West Pier in England's seaside resort city of Brighton.

In fact, some time after Barrett's departure, portions of at least two of the songs from *The Piper at the Gates of Dawn* would be reworked and incorporated into a larger thematic work, the 1969 live presentation known as "The Man and the Journey."

But seemingly as quickly as *Piper* songs were added to the group's live set, most were dropped. The only tunes from Pink Floyd's debut album to remain in the band's live set for more than a short while were the more atmospheric cuts like "Pow R. Toc H.," "Interstellar Over-drive," and "Astronomy Dominé."

By this time, Pink Floyd was attracting the notice of music critics and well-admired musicians. As of January 1967, guitarist Jimi Hen-drix—who had come to England to get his solo career started—hadn't yet seen or heard the group live. His impression of the band would seem to have been secondhand, but it still provides an insight into the skepticism that greeted Pink Floyd at most every turn. Speaking to Steve Barker, reporter for *West One*, a student publication of the Re-gent Street Polytechnic, where several members of the Floyd had at-tended, he said, "I've heard they have beautiful lights but they don't sound like nothing." Writing about Pink Floyd for *IT*, Barry Miles (usu-ally known simply as Miles) sniffed that "the melodic line has gone and been replaced by feedback."

That same month, a *Melody Maker* story with a Chris Welch and Nick Jones byline quoted Nick Mason. "We don't call ourselves a psy-chedelic group or say that we play psychedelic pop music," he said. "Let's face it, there isn't really a definition for the word 'psychedelic'. It's something that has all taken place around us—not within us."

For his part, in a January 1967 interview for the CBC, Syd Barrett admitted, "you can't sort of walk around the kitchen humming to The Pink Floyd." And if you did, he said, "you'd probably scream." He described the band's onstage approach this way: "We just sort of let loose a bit . . . sort of hitting the guitar a bit harder and not worrying quite so much about the chords." But in an April interview with *Melody Maker*, Barrett backpedaled just a bit, saying, "If we play well on stage I think most people understand that what we play isn't just a noise."

While in interviews, managers Peter Jenner and Andrew King would sometimes compare Pink Floyd to innovative artists like Albert Ayler and Ornette Coleman, the band members would only take the jazz references so far. Waters believed that what Pink Floyd was doing was even more free-form than jazz, though it's reasonable to assume he was thinking of "trad jazz" (known in the United States as Dixieland) when he contrasted Pink Floyd's music with jazz.

"If you're improvising on a jazz number," Waters explained in an interview, "if it's a 16-bar number, you stick to 16-bar choruses and you take 16-bar solos." But when Pink Floyd played live, they might play 17½ bars. "And then it will all stop happening when it stops happening: maybe 423 bars later, or 4."

In that same interview, Barrett and Mason expressed the difference in a much more down-to-earth fashion. "And it's not like jazz, because . . ." began Barrett, ". . . we all want to be pop stars," said Mason, finishing Syd's thought for him. "We don't want to be jazz musicians." Taking a cue from his band mates, Waters summed things up. "We don't really look upon ourselves as musicians as such."

An event billed as the "14 Hour Technicolor Dream" was an April 29, 1967, concert "happening" that would become the stuff of legends. A benefit concert to fund the counterculture publication *IT*, the event featured an eclectic lineup of nearly four dozen performers, including The Crazy World of Arthur Brown, former Moody Blues vocalist Denny Laine, Yoko Ono, The Move, Tomorrow (featuring guitarist Steve Howe, later of Yes), and a future Pink Floyd collaborator, Ron Geesin. Pink Floyd was the headlining performer at the event, staged at the Great Hall of the Alexandria Palace in London.

Pink Floyd wouldn't take the stage until early morning; the band had only just arrived straight from an engagement in Zandam, the Netherlands, where they had played "Arnold Layne" for a Dutch television program. Steve Howe was at the show from the beginning, but the specific details of the event are largely lost to time. "Let's not deny: everybody was pretty flipped out at that point," he explains. Howe does recall that since Pink Floyd was the headliner, use of the band's favored brand of amplifier, WEM, would be required of all performers. Howe notes that he "really, really didn't like" WEM gear. "It was 100 watts, and I was a 50-watt guy," he says. With little choice, he plugged in. "I guess I got some sort of noise I could recognize," he says.

In May 1967, the group staged its most high-profile performance to date. Dubbed "Games for May," the concert took place at the Queen

Elizabeth Hall in London. The show featured one of the first uses of some new audio technology. Nick Mason described it in an interview later that year with a *Record Mirror* reporter. "We worked out a fantastic stereophonic sound system whereby the sounds traveled 'round the Hall in a sort of circle, giving the audience an eerie effect of being absolutely surrounded by this music." He was forthright as he summed up the debut of the so-called Azimuth Coordinator. "Our ideas," Mason admitted, "were far more advanced than our musical capabilities."

At least three audience recordings of Pink Floyd in its Syd Barrett–led lineup do exist; while the audio quality on these is less than optimal—the vocals are all but inaudible—they do provide a sonic window into the band's onstage musical character. "We've had problems with our equipment and we can't get the P.A. to work because we play extremely loudly," Waters told Chris Welch of *Melody Maker* in an August 1967 interview. "It's a pity because Syd writes great lyrics and nobody ever hears them."

The 2016 box set, *The Early Years*, features a recording of a Stockholm, Sweden, concert, the second show in a five-night Scandinavian tour. Alongside four tunes from *Piper* (which had been released a month earlier), the set includes an unreleased song, "Scream Thy Last Scream." The live arrangement is quite close to the studio recording (the latter of which wouldn't see official release for some forty-nine years) but focuses more on a hard, insistent rhythmic groove that underpins an exploratory guitar solo from Barrett.

A highlight of that Stockholm show is a seven-minute track the compilers of *The Early Years* call "Reaction in G." The title's provenance says a lot about Pink Floyd's attitude toward live performance; reportedly frustrated at repeated calls from the audience to play their popular singles, the band launched into a free-form improvisation in the key of G major. Remarking in a 1970 *Georgia Straight* interview about the fact that some people came to Pink Floyd gigs to dance, Roger Waters quipped to the interviewer, "We cleared more ballrooms than you've had hot dinners."

Eventually, "Reaction in G" became a featured part of the band's live set, though—save for a very brief snippet on a BBC session, "Reaction in G" would not be attempted in the studio. Confusingly, two other audience tapes from the era feature an opening tune labeled "Reaction in G," but while those sound somewhat like each other, they bear no resemblance to the so-called "Reaction" on *The Early Years*.

Yet perhaps the most notable song from the Stockholm performance is a Roger Waters composition, the spooky, minor-key "Set the Controls for the Heart of the Sun." An example of Pink Floyd road-testing a song before committing it to tape, the Stockholm recording shows that the hypnotic, increasingly malevolent arrangement was fully developed before the group entered the studio to record it in October 1967. Built around two chords—E minor and A—"Set the Controls for the Heart of the Sun" features near-whispered vocals from Waters, mallet and tom-tom work by drummer Mason, and celestial organ runs from Richard Wright. Barrett's guitar is limited to some subtle strumming. Notably, the version of the song as eventually released on the band's second LP, 1968's *A Saucerful of Secrets*, would not feature Syd Barrett (or if it did, his contribution is subtle to the point of inaudibility). His rapid mental decline resulted in greatly diminished participation in the *Saucerful* sessions; in the end, he'd only appear on two tracks.

One other show from the Scandinavian mini-tour was captured on tape by a fan; the third of a three-night run at Copenhagen, Denmark's Starclub featured a similar set list, but does contain one rarity: the only known (or at least only recorded) version of a song known as "One in a Million." Yet another Waters lead vocal, its presence suggests that the band was already making adjustments to compensate for Barrett's growing onstage unreliability. Built upon a repetitive bass line, "One in a Million" has little in common with the Barrett-penned *Piper* material; its doom-laden demeanor is much more of a piece with the band's post–Syd Barrett output, and presages the "tribal psych" of twenty-first-century psychedelic revival groups such as Austin, Texas's Black Angels.

Another unreleased fan recording of the era was made at the Hippy Happy Fair in Rotterdam, the Netherlands, in mid-November 1967; Pink Floyd appeared on the third night of a four-day festival that also featured the Jimi Hendrix Experience, Soft Machine, and Tomorrow. The most notable performance from the Rotterdam tape is a more than eleven-minute reading of "Pow R. Toc H." In a 1970 interview conducted while Pink Floyd was on tour in New York City, Nick Mason recalled the genesis of the tune. "One geezer went up to the microphone and started [vocalizing], and then everyone picked up on it and put the other things in it. And then the drums picked up and . . . that was more or less that, wasn't it?"

At nearly three times the length of its studio counterpart, the live "Pow R. Toc H." enters free-form musical territory, and previews the kinds of sounds the group would explore in greater detail on *A Saucerful of Secrets*. Sessions for that album were already well under way by the time of the Rotterdam show.

After the Hippy Happy Fair, the remainder of Pink Floyd's 1967 concert engagements consisted of twice-nightly performances. With Barrett's deteriorating mental state and a demanding schedule—two brief sets sandwiched among other acts on a bill topped by the Jimi Hendrix Experience—the band had little opportunity to engage in the long-form musical excursions they clearly favored.

Melody Maker's Chris Welch may have been intentionally provocative when he wrote in August 1967 that Pink Floyd's live set was "thunderous, incomprehensible, screaming, sonic torture." In that same piece, Waters responded that "the sort of thing we are trying to do doesn't fit into the sort of environment we are playing in." The supporting bands on the bill, he explained, often played covers of Wilson Pickett's "In the Midnight Hour," making for an incongruent musical experience at best.

The exact date remains a matter of contention, but contemporary reports suggest that Barrett missed a December 2 show in Brighton, England, and that guitarist (and Syd's childhood friend) David Gilmour—late of moderately successful Cambridge band Jokers Wild— filled in for him on that date. At least one other performance from that period featured guitarist David O'List of the Nice filling in for the absent-without-leave Barrett.

Along with several other acts, the Nice and Pink Floyd were both part of the late 1967 Jimi Hendrix tour of England; each band had a very brief time onstage. "We had seventeen minutes for a show," recalls manager Peter Jenner, "and we had to do it twice nightly." O'List was already a fan of Pink Floyd, and he says that on the tour he used to go out into the audience every night after his band's set and watch Pink Floyd play. "That's how I learned their stuff," he says. "I was very interested in their sounds, and with what Syd was doing with echo."

O'List says that there was little rivalry between the bands on the Hendrix tour. "Remember, this was 1967," he says. "Everybody was handing each other flowers." Even though they weren't close friends, O'List saw enough of Barrett on the tour to know something wasn't quite right. "I did think he was a bit distant," O'List recalls. "He used to get on the coach; everyone else would be saying 'hi' and smiling. He'd look quite serious and walk to the back of the bus. So I thought there was *something* going on."

On November 18, mere moments before taking the stage, Pink Floyd found itself without its guitarist. O'List recalls the scene. He bumped into three members of Pink Floyd in the dressing room backstage. One of the band asked aloud, "Is that Syd walking off?" When they realized he was gone, they turned to O'List and asked him to step in. "I was pretty flabbergasted," he recalls. He was concerned that fans would recognize him and be disappointed—or worse—that Barrett wasn't fronting the group. "Don't worry about that," he recalls being told by one of the band members. "You just wear Syd's hat, and they'll think you're him." So he donned Barrett's big black hat.

"They knew what I could do, and I knew their music," O'List says. The guitarist joined Waters, Wright, and Mason onstage, and when it came time for a guitar solo, O'List felt he was in his element. "We did twenty minutes of 'Interstellar Overdrive,'" he recalls. "And I did a ten-minute guitar solo." O'List says that his approach was different from that of Syd Barrett. "Their music suddenly changed with me," he says, "because I did a proper lead guitar solo, which Syd didn't quite do; he did more noises and sounds."

Another group, Tomorrow, shared management with Pink Floyd, and on one occasion the band's guitarist got a call of his own to fill in for Barrett. "One night we were playing somewhere else, says Steve Howe. "I was rushed to London to stand in for Syd. I was delighted; I love playing with people I hadn't played with before." But once he arrived, he was met by Steve O'Rourke of Pink Floyd's management team Blackhill Enterprises, who told him, "Well, thanks a lot, but actually Syd's just about going to make it."

Though his guitar style was far more sophisticated than Barrett's, Howe remains convinced that he would have fit in seamlessly. He concedes that Tomorrow "had songs, but they weren't the main thing we had. We had this explosive instrumental interpretation-improvisation going on onstage." Like Pink Floyd, the live and studio music of Tomorrow had little in common with each other. "When Syd got on stage, I think he ad-libbed a lot more across the music," Howe says. "And I imagine that's what I would do. 'Okay, we're in C? Well, I could do something here.' 'Oh, nobody's singing? Okay. I'll open up.' 'Somebody's singing? I won't open up.' So I would have just bluffed my way through it, and enjoyed it because of that." Though the bands crossed paths often in those days—Howe believes Tomorrow and Pink Floyd were on the same bill more than a dozen times—he didn't have a clear sense of just how unstable Barrett had become. "A lot of stories were exchanged . . . gossip of knowing that Syd was a bit on the edge," he says. "Maybe he dropped too many tabs [of LSD] and he was all going a bit shaky at times. So you kind of accepted that."

Between Barrett's often incapacitated onstage demeanor and his band mates' increased ambitions, something clearly had to give. Waters voiced his frustrations concerning the latter in August 1967 when he spoke to *Melody Maker*'s Chris Welch. "We can't go on doing clubs and ballrooms. We want a brand new environment . . . we'll have a huge screen 120 feet wide and 40 feet high inside and project films and slides." While there was little precedent for that kind of performance in 1967, Waters's vision for the future sounds very much like the live shows Pink Floyd would mount in the years after Syd Barrett's departure.

In one of his increasingly rare lucid moments, Syd Barrett expressed much the same sentiments when speaking to *Melody Maker* in December 1967, mere weeks before his exit from Pink Floyd. "We feel that in the future, groups are going to have to offer much more than just a pop show. They'll have to offer a well-presented theatre show."

Peter Jenner notes that for Pink Floyd circa 1967, "there was always the strain between whether they were an art group or whether they were making hit records. The market and the record company were saying, 'Make hit records,' but in some other senses, there was also a strong sense of the art thing. And that was perhaps why Syd became . . ." his voice trails off for a moment, "why it started breaking up in time."

By January 12, 1968, Gilmour had been added to the group, ostensibly as a "second" guitarist. The five-piece lineup played no more than five—likely only four—live dates. En route to a January 26 concert at Southampton University, a group decision was made not to collect Barrett. For all practical purposes, Pink Floyd with Syd Barrett ceased to exist on that date.

5

BBC ONE

In 1967, as the band got off the ground both creatively and commercially, Pink Floyd could be seen to have something of a split personality: though the band did play some of its studio songs in concert, and did incorporate its exploratory side into some studio tracks, the contrast between live and studio Pink Floyd was striking.

Yet in significant ways, a reconciliation of those two distinctive characteristics would be found in the band's performances for broadcast on the British Broadcasting Company. Through 1967, Pink Floyd appeared on BBC radio on no fewer than three occasions, showcasing material that drew from the band's recorded catalog (*The Piper at the Gates of Dawn* and a handful of singles and B-sides) as well as hinting at the sound the band created live onstage. Though some of those performances are lost forever, two sessions have survived and received their first official release as part of the Pink Floyd box set *The Early Years*.

When the opportunity came to perform on the BBC, Pink Floyd stood apart from most of the band's contemporaries: the band never performed covers. This stood in stark contrast to groups such as the Beatles, who used their many BBC appearances to showcase material from their massive set list, songs they had been performing since the late 1950s.

Pink Floyd's earliest surviving BBC session dates from September 25, 1967; the four musicians arrived at Piccadilly Studios in London, where they cut six songs, ostensibly live, for broadcast on the popular *Top Gear* radio program. In practice, the BBC did allow some primitive overdubbing—usually vocals—and the presence of what sounds like double-tracking (multiple unison vocals by one singer) strongly suggests that Pink Floyd was offered and took full advantage of such an opportunity. The October 1 broadcast of that performance was notable for the first appearance of guest host John Peel; Peel would soon become one of Pink Floyd's most enthusiastic supporters, and gave the band's music prominent focus on his radio shows through the next several years.

The BBC performance of *The Piper at the Gates of Dawn*'s "Flaming" is quite close to the album version, but does feature a much more prominent and muscular drum part from Nick Mason. While the LP version finds Mason carrying the beat with little more than taps on the bell of one of his cymbals, the BBC performance of "Flaming" has forceful, full-kit drumming that moves the tune away from the slightly twee arrangement toward something more rocking. The BBC version also features less in the way of backing vocal harmonies. It's likely that the few onstage performances of "Flaming" would have lacked backing vocals as well: "monitors" (speakers that would allow the band members to hear their vocals among the loud instruments) would not become part of Pink Floyd's onstage gear until the 1970s.

Pink Floyd's BBC version of "The Scarecrow" isn't appreciably different from its album counterpart; the radio performance does serve to illustrate the band's ability to play a tricky song with odd musical phrasing in a more or less live context. This is all the more remarkable in light of Barrett's worsening mental state; by all evidence he was having an especially good day in this late September session. More troublesome days were to come.

Musically, "The Gnome" is among the less challenging numbers on *The Piper at the Gates of Dawn*, so it's little surprise that the band played it well on its first BBC date. For the radio recording, Waters's uncharacteristically bouncy bass line is a bit more forward in the sound mix. "The Gnome" is as close as Pink Floyd would ever come to a campfire-style singalong, with the possible exception of "Seamus" on 1971's *Meddle*.

Keyboardist Richard Wright takes his turn on lead vocal for the *Top Gear* broadcast of "Matilda Mother." The radio version features less refined vocal harmony work, but otherwise it's a near copy of the recording on *Piper*. The primary difference is Wright's use of his Farfisa organ ("Compact" both in nature and model name), a much more practical instrument to bring to a radio session than the much larger and heavier Hammond organ used on the album. Wright's keyboard is also run through a wah-wah pedal, alternating the amount of bass and treble signal coming from the instrument.

A very brief snippet of one of Pink Floyd's live numbers—thirty seconds of "Reaction in G"—could have been the most tantalizing moment on the *Top Gear* session; sadly, Peel and co-host Pete Drummond speak over the recording, making jokes. What remains is barely enough to identify it as the free-form tune that appeared often in the band's live set around this time.

Radio listeners on that October afternoon were treated to one completely new track, Roger Waters's "Set the Controls for the Heart of the Sun." Studio sessions for the new composition had only begun in mid-August, and other than a pair for performances at UFO and four other London-area dates in September, there were no opportunities for British fans to have heard the tune. "Set the Controls" wouldn't be released until the following summer, by which time Syd Barrett had been gone for several months. Though few—including the band—would have known at the time, the *Top Gear* broadcast of the song was effectively a preview of Pink Floyd's future direction. "Set the Controls for the Heart of the Sun" would remain a fixture of the band's live set into the new decade. The version for BBC is slightly less developed than the studio recording; other than its decidedly hypnotic sound, the most notable quality of the recording is Richard Wright's Farfisa organ solo, variations upon the three-note motif around which the song is based.

Pink Floyd would return for a second *Top Gear* session—the group's last with Barrett—on the morning of December 20, 1967. In contrast to the band's previous BBC appearance, this session would feature mostly new and previously unheard material. In fact, studio versions of two of the four songs recorded that day for the BBC would remain unreleased until 2016.

"Scream Thy Last Scream" would remain drummer Nick Mason's sole lead vocal on a Pink Floyd recording, save for his heavily treated spoken part on *Meddle*'s "One of These Days." At the time of this broadcast, promoting the song made sense, as the band hoped "Scream" would be the next Pink Floyd single, following "See Emily Play." But its strange, borderline-nonsensical lyrics about an old woman with a casket led EMI to veto its release. The song as performed on *Top Gear* features many Barrett sonic trademarks: odd musical phrasing, descending melodic lines, and outré subject matter. A double-speed voice (Barrett) in unison with Mason's vocals would be part of the studio version, but is not part of the radio broadcast recording, presumably due to technical limitations of the BBC's recording studio.

Even less commercially minded is the next song from the December *Top Gear* session. "Vegetable Man" has long been a part of the Pink Floyd legend as one of the last tracks to feature Syd Barrett. "Vegetable Man" is an oblique autobiographical account of Barrett's mental decline. Its arrangement is in some ways pure *Piper*-era Barrett, but the song stands one of his songwriting conventions on its head. Abandoning the oft-used descending melodic line, "Vegetable Man" instead creeps upward on the scale, in half-steps. Its insistent arrangement yields little in the way of catchy melody, and there's a sinister air about the band's overall sonic attack. While the studio version fades out on a blues-based chord structure, the version recorded for *Top Gear* reveals that a good part of "Vegetable Man" is closely related to Neal Hefti's "Batman Theme," with its title lyrics replacing "Batman."

At least a few enterprising fans taped that performance off the radio, and—especially as Barrett faded from the scene—its very existence became legendary. Bootleg copies of the studio version wouldn't appear for many years, so the *Top Gear* recording was the one shared among the most dedicated fans. One of those fans was Robyn Hitchcock, then leading the Cambridge-based neo-psychedelic group The Soft Boys. "I heard it on a cassette," he recalls. "Quite primitive, with kind of a hum in the background." During the band's sessions for the 1980 album *Underwater Moonlight*, The Soft Boys cut a faithful cover of "Vegetable Man." Other hip bands of that first psychedelic-revival era covered the previously obscure tune as well, including the Jesus and Mary Chain.

A reading of "Pow R. Toc H." takes Pink Floyd back in time a few months to when Barrett's psychological state was much more stable. The *Top Gear* performance isn't remarkably different from the studio version on *The Piper at the Gates of Dawn*, though Barrett's guitar playing feels a bit more inspired and/or manic, with a guitar tone closer to that found on the 1965 demos than anything in Pink Floyd's more recent catalog. Also, Roger Waters's screams on this BBC recording are a notch more terrifying than those on *Piper*.

"Jugband Blues" would appear in studio form on Pink Floyd's second album, *A Saucerful of Secrets*. By the time of the December *Top Gear* performance, the studio version was complete, and the BBC performance is quite different from its studio counterpart. Barrett's tune shifts time signatures, and a favorite technique of his—shoehorning lyrics into phrases where they wouldn't normally fit—is a defining feature of the song. The Salvation Army band accompaniment—prominent on the studio version—is wholly absent here, but a mid-song freakout has more in common with "Astronomy Dominé" and "Pow R. Toc H." than the ditties on *Piper*.

With the BBC sessions completed, never again would Pink Floyd concern itself with songs about unicorns, scarecrows, and gnomes. A new chapter—notably, not one the band had anticipated nor sought—was about to dawn.

6

SPEAK

In happier and more organized times during 1967, Pink Floyd embarked on a musical sideline that would eventually become a defining part of the band's character. Though the group's initial efforts were tentative and perhaps not taken very seriously, Pink Floyd produced works for use in film. Because the band's onstage presentation had always incorporated visuals, the combining of sound and image was not an alien concept to Barrett and his band mates.

In fact, the first piece recorded for use in a film was one of the band's showcase numbers, "Interstellar Overdrive." In January 1967, Pink Floyd assembled at London's Sound Techniques Studio to record for Peter Whitehead's loosely documentary-style film *Tonite Let's All Make Love in London*. The film aimed to chronicle the then-current music and fashion scene of "Swinging London," and Whitehead wanted appropriate music for its soundtrack. Some of the artists featured on the original soundtrack album released in 1968 were relatively well known: the Small Faces and Chris Farlowe had both scored several hits in the UK by the time of the soundtrack's release. Others like Vashti Bunyan were closer to the underground scene from which Pink Floyd arose.

Joe Boyd produced Pink Floyd's two-day session at Sound Techniques, which consisted of a nearly seven-minute version of "Interstellar Overdrive" and a track that would remain unreleased for some time, "Nick's Boogie."

The version of "Interstellar Overdrive" on *Tonite* is harder-edged than the recording Pink Floyd would make two months later for its debut album, *The Piper at the Gates of Dawn*. Boyd's production style is somewhat more immediate and up-close than that of EMI's Norman Smith, and the *Tonite* version has more of a live feel. After stating its "head," "Interstellar Overdrive" dissolves into its abstract and exploratory style. Wright's haunted house organ runs brush up against Mason's manic drumming, while Roger Waters's bass and Syd Barrett's guitar are largely consigned to providing atmosphere. Barrett's guitar stabs, in particular, dispense with conventional ideas concerning meter and melody. For use on the soundtrack, the "Interstellar Overdrive" recording was broken into smaller sections. This January 1967 recording is often cited as one of the earliest examples of psychedelic improvisation captured on recording tape. Arguably superior to its *Piper* counterpart— and owing to the quick-get-it-done, audio verité manner in which it was recorded by Boyd—the *Tonite* version of "Interstellar Overdrive" is perhaps the best high-fidelity example of how the song would have sounded at one of Pink Floyd's live shows of the era.

"Nick's Boogie" is curiously named: there's absolutely nothing boogie-related about the twelve-minute instrumental named after Pink Floyd's drummer. In sound and style, "Nick's Boogie" lies halfway between "Interstellar Overdrive" and the later Roger Waters composition "Set the Controls for the Heart of the Sun." Less "rock" in style and altogether more atmospheric, the track provides evidence for why the label "space rock" would often be applied to Pink Floyd's music. With its hypnotic mallet drumming, keyboard lines that suggest the twirling of a radio knob late at night, and abstract, effects-laden guitar splashes, "Nick's Boogie" sounds like none of the tunes on the soon-to-be-recorded *The Piper at the Gates of Dawn*, yet very much like the sound and style Pink Floyd would adopt once Syd Barrett was gone.

Regardless of the degree to which working for film might have interested the group, Pink Floyd would soon have other matters on its collective mind; less than three weeks after completing work on their part of the *Tonite Let's All Make Love in London* soundtrack, the four members of Pink Floyd signed a recording contract with EMI.

In October 1967, by which time the earliest sessions for Pink Floyd's second album, *A Saucerful of Secrets*, had already begun, Pink Floyd traveled to the BBC Radiophonic Workshops in London, with a goal of composing soundtrack music for a proposed television program. While nothing came of this effort, mere days later the band cut a series of abstract pieces collectively known as "John Latham." A conceptual artist, Latham was a classmate of Roger Waters and Nick Mason at London's Regent Street Polytechnic (now part of University of Westminster). Latham had produced a 16mm film in 1962 titled *Speak*; Pink Floyd had projected the proto-psychedelic film at some of its live performances, and eventually set out to create a studio soundtrack to accompany the film. The idea was abandoned, and the nine takes of "John Latham" remained unreleased. The tracks also remained outside the reach of enterprising bootleg collectors; until the release of the 2016 box set, *The Early Years*, "John Latham" had been heard by few if any outside the band's immediate orbit.

Ranging in length from two and a half to over five minutes, the nine takes of "John Latham" reprise some of the sonic ideas employed in the more abstract sections of "Interstellar Overdrive" and "Pow R. Toc H." All takes are seemingly improvised; there's little to suggest that the musical exploration within the recordings was planned in advance. "John Latham" almost completely dispenses with melody, and to many listeners the tracks will seem closer to a collection of sound effects than what most would consider music. There's a strong sense of leaving events to chance; an approach not wholly dissimilar to the one employed by American West Coast psychedelic group the Grateful Dead. In fact, aside from its prominent featuring of Richard Wright's celestial Farfisa organ, much of what Pink Floyd called "John Latham" sounds like what the Dead would call "Space" or "Drums."

As 1967 ended, *Tonite Let's All Make Love in London* had yet to be released; the BBC Radiophonic Workshop idea had come to nothing, and the experimental tracks made to accompany John Latham's *Speak* went onto the shelf. But Pink Floyd's interest in the potential of music created to accompany moving images was piqued. In time, the group would create entire works for film, and elements of multimedia production would become an integral part of the group's on- and offstage persona. Yet all of these future endeavors would take place without the group's original leader and founder, Syd Barrett.

Part II

Point Me at the Sky (1967–1968)

7

SCREAM THY LAST SCREAM

Sessions for what would become *A Saucerful of Secrets* had commenced a mere three days after the UK release of *The Piper at the Gates of Dawn*. As Barrett's behavior became increasingly erratic, the sessions yielded little of use from among his contributions. Between early August 1967 and late January 1968, Pink Floyd and producer Norman Smith booked more than two dozen days' worth of studio time in three different London studios. Those sessions were largely abortive. Other than the non-album single "Apples and Oranges," for many decades the only officially released fruit of the sessions would be songs written by Roger Waters or Rick Wright.

The band did complete two songs—and made significant progress on a third—though all would remain officially unreleased until their inclusion on 2016's *The Early Years* box set. But dedicated collectors have long had access to copies: "I have to admit I released those 'Syd-o-files' into [circulation] years ago," admits Peter Jenner. "I always was rather cross that they wouldn't let those things go out, because although they weren't flattering to Syd, I think they were brilliantly wonderful pieces of work." Jenner characterizes the tracks as special "in a sort of psychotic way; they're a bit like those Van Gogh paintings of the birds over the fields, and the sky against it. There's something about [those songs] that told you about his mental condition."

On its surface, "Scream Thy Last Scream" is a continuation of Syd Barrett's musical approach—descending chord lines, disjointed phrasing—and his penchant for unusual lyrical subjects. But with its mention of an old woman and a casket, the tune reveals a darker mindset than its composer had displayed on the songs from *The Piper at the Gates of Dawn*. "Scream" also betrays a certain lyrical laziness: whereas before Barrett's use of seemingly unrelated words and phrases felt childlike, here it feels as if Barrett is losing interest.

"Vegetable Man" is quite close to its BBC broadcast counterpart; the primary difference here is that the sound fidelity on the studio version is far superior, and the song's ending section is truncated. But where Barrett may have been phoning it in for "Scream Thy Last Scream," "Vegetable Man" is a tight—if characteristically baffling—piece of songwriting. While very few of the song's lines rhyme in the traditional sense, as Barrett fan Robyn Hitchcock points out, "Barrett had quite a lot of internal rhymes." Darkly autobiographical lyrics like "In my paisley shirt I look a jerk" fit thematically, but don't rhyme with previous or subsequent lines of the song. And while the tune lacks a discernible chorus (other than perhaps the query, "Vegetable Man, where are you?"), it does feature a piling-up of words as the song reaches its musical climax. "One of Syd's first trademarks was just putting in as many words as he wanted to," Hitchcock notes. "And there was a lot of assonance."

Barrett wrote "Vegetable Man" while in the front room of manager Peter Jenner's home. "It was a description of him at the time," Jenner says. When he looked at himself it was like, 'Oh, fucking hell!'" Jenner characterizes both "Scream Thy Last Scream" and "Vegetable Man" as "great music [full of] great sorrow."

Another song recorded in late 1967 remained unreleased in any form until 2016, and—although its existence had been documented many years ago—it escaped falling into circulation among trader-collectors of unreleased Pink Floyd material. "In the Beechwoods" would surface on *The Early Years*, where listeners could enjoy the rare treat of a previously unheard Barrett-era track. Though it lacks vocals—and there are no known written lyrics—as an instrumental work, it sounds close to complete.

"In the Beechwoods" features a remarkably straightforward and catchy melody. Opening with some trademark organ swells from Richard Wright and hypnotic mallet work from Nick Mason, the song works into a sprightly, uptempo chord progression that sounds little like anything Syd Barrett had written for *The Piper at the Gates of Dawn*. The chorus—as the melody clearly is designed to support a vocal line—features a call-and-response between guitar/bass and drums. Nearly two minutes in, the song's "bridge" is musically less interesting than the rest of the tune; listeners are left to speculate if lyrics might have been intended as the primary focus of the section. Some quick glissandi from bassist Roger Waters leads the song back into its main structure. Nearly the final two minutes of "In the Beechwoods" are given over to repeated voicing of the song's chorus. The instruments fade out, not in the customary manner of the recording engineer pulling all of the volume faders toward zero, but by the four musicians gradually reducing the complexity and volume of their playing. Though he would appear on one or two tracks destined for *A Saucerful of Secrets*, Syd Barrett's contribution to "In the Beechwoods" would serve as his effective studio swan song with Pink Floyd.

A sense of gallows humor seems to have pervaded what is generally accepted to have been the final Pink Floyd recording session with Syd Barrett present as a member of the group. Session notes for a pair of dates at EMI's Abbey Road Studios in late January suggest the band knew that ideas were in short supply: the piece being worked on was given the provisional title "The Most Boring Song I've Ever Heard Bar 2."

By these early 1968 sessions, it was clear to all parties—except Barrett—that Pink Floyd could not continue as it had done. "We'd spent the previous two, three, four months trying to keep them together with Syd," Jenner recalls, "to keep Syd in the band and working and making records, and it became increasingly difficult." Jenner explains that circumstances reached the point at which "the band couldn't know where Syd was, and then when he *was* onstage, they didn't know what song he would play."

Waters, Wright, and Mason (and to a lesser extent because he was a new member, Gilmour) made the decision to forge ahead without Syd Barrett, and informed managers King and Jenner and booking agent Bryan Morrison. Jenner recalls what happened next. "Bryan said, 'Hey: *you're* the Pink Floyd. But no one knows who the Pink Floyd are, so you can just keep going.'"

The group had first thought it could continue with Barrett as a non-performing member who remained as songwriter. Jenner calls the idea "doing a Brian Wilson," referencing the Beach Boys leader's mid-1960s retirement from live performance. "But Syd *didn't* go on writing the songs," Jenner says. The decision was made to break up Blackhill Enterprises (Pink Floyd plus the management team of Andrew King and Peter Jenner). King and Jenner duo chose to remain with Syd.

While there would never be a publicly announced formal diagnosis of Barrett's condition, from his point of view, Jenner saw drug use as—at the very least—a contributing factor to his mental condition. He suggests that Pink Floyd's 1967 tour of America may have provided the pivotal set of circumstances. "At the time there was a lot of 'theological' acid taking," he says. "It was a sort of, 'this is not just getting stoned; this is expanding your horizon, growing your sense of awareness. This is a new religion.' I suspect Syd had a lot of acid either deliberately or accidentally or both, and so he was never the same by the time he came back."

Once guitarist David Gilmour was brought on board as a member—initially as a backup, but quickly becoming a "replacement" for Barrett—Pink Floyd would have taken stock of its situation. Syd Barrett had written most everything the band performed or recorded. Waters had composed a song or two, as had the most musically accomplished of the lot, keyboardist Rick Wright. Drummer Mason never made claims to being a songwriter. Newcomer David Gilmour had nearly no song-writing experience (his Jokers Wild band mate Willie Wilson recalls a Paris session in which a Gilmour original was recorded, but demurs from elaborating. "And Dave won't thank me if I do otherwise," he says. "He wouldn't have wanted you to hear it."). Still—experienced song-writers or not—EMI expected Pink Floyd to come up with an album to follow its debut.

There's an old saw in the pop music world that goes something like this: "An artist has his entire life to write songs for his debut album, and a few weeks at best to compose songs for the follow-up." There's a kind of universal truth in that assertion, as evidenced in countless examples of what critics refer to as the "sophomore slump." Tasked with creating material on par with their first batch of songs, some songwriters come up short. Having exhausted their backlog of songs for the first album, the second record sometimes takes the form of discarded tracks, leftovers, and songs that for one reason or another didn't make the cut for the debut.

For Pink Floyd in January 1968, this problem would have been more serious, as the man who had written most of the band's material was gone, and he had left little behind. Neither "Vegetable Man" nor "Scream Thy Last Scream" was seriously considered for inclusion on the band's second LP. Pink Floyd would have to start fresh, mustering up whatever creativity it could to create material for a new album.

Sessions resumed in earnest, sandwiched between live dates scheduled in England, Wales, and the continent. Pink Floyd would work on material destined for *A Saucerful of Secrets* until May 28, with the album appearing on UK record store shelves exactly one month later. But because of pressure from EMI for a single—ostensibly to sustain the band's commercial momentum—by late February 1968 attention turned at least briefly to the task of cutting an A- and B-side of a planned 45-rpm release. Like another pair of tunes the band would cut for a second 1968 single, the defining characteristic of these tunes is their similarity to the kind of songs Syd Barrett might have written. Or at least that was the plan; neither "It Would Be So Nice" nor "Julia Dream" ranks among the most distinguished entries in the Pink Floyd catalog.

"It Would Be So Nice" does get off to a promising start: the repeated chorus is delivered in exuberant fashion, with the band providing dramatic instrumental support. But the tone shifts jarringly into the verses, which owe more to the English music hall tradition, a style at which the Kinks' songwriter Ray Davies excelled. Songwriter Rick Wright is clearly doing his best to conjure up a Syd Barrett–style tune, and while "It Would Be So Nice" has period charms, this piece of musical fluff doesn't portray Pink Floyd in a positive light.

The single's flip side, "Julia Dream," marked David Gilmour's first appearance as lead vocalist on a Pink Floyd song. Here it's Roger Waters attempting to write a Barrett-flavored tune, and he fares slightly better than does Wright. The gentle arrangement presages a style the group would explore more fully on the soundtrack for the film *More*. Admittedly a slight—if inoffensive—ditty, "Julia Dream" is notable as one of only a handful of Pink Floyd songs in which Rick Wright makes use of the Mellotron, an early tape-based sample playback keyboard. The tune stands out in one other, small way: "Julia Dream" is but one of only a handful of songs in the Pink Floyd catalog that could be considered a love song.

As the first release from the post–Syd Barrett lineup, Pink Floyd's "It Would Be So Nice" backed with "Julia Dream" failed to set the charts alight. Though "Julia Dream" would be performed for a BBC session, neither song is known to have made it into the band's regular live set list.

8

SOMETHING ELSE

A Saucerful of Secrets would be released in the UK at the end of June 1968. The band had not gone out of its way to publicize Syd Barrett's exit, though an early March press release had made his departure official. His most significant contributions to the band's second album, however limited, would be positioned at the end of the second side of the LP.

With David Gilmour still settling into the band and working toward defining his role as something more than a Barrett stand-in, it would fall to bassist Roger Waters to provide most of the songs for *Saucerful*. In a 2003 retrospective interview—not one of his more diplomatic moments—Waters reflected on the situation the band faced as 1968 began. "After Syd went crazy, and Dave joined in '68, we were all of us searching, fumbling around, looking for 'Where do we go now?'" he said. "Because here was the guy who started producing all these songs and was sort of the heartbeat of the band." But speaking with the benefit of hindsight, he also noted, "You have to work to your strengths. And it's a very good thing that we couldn't write singles. We might not have done some of the interesting work that we did."

"Let There Be More Light" opens the LP with a pulsing and insistent bass line, soon joined by subtle drum work from Nick Mason and one-chord keyboard textures from Wright. As the instrumental introduction approaches the one-minute mark, the overall musical intensity and complexity builds. Everything then dissolves in a wash, giving way to a slow, deliberate melody built on a Waters bass line doubled an octave higher by Wright's organ. Wright also provides the hushed, gentle vocals of the verse while Waters whispers along. That approach is contrasted by the chorus where the band plays forcefully, and Gilmour takes over on vocals. Three more verses and choruses—the song has no traditional lyric chorus; each refrain has its own set of lyrics—ratchet up the intensity, and the lyrics briefly namecheck the Beatles' "Lucy in the Sky With Diamonds." An extended instrumental run provides the remainder of "Let There Be More Light," giving David Gilmour an opportunity to display his lead guitar skills.

Richard Wright's "Remember a Day" follows. A gentle yet somewhat ominous introduction features slide guitar glissandi—allegedly from Syd Barrett—and some gently played, high-register piano chords. When the song-proper kicks in, the tempo increases significantly, with the drum figure (featuring not Mason but instead producer Norman Smith) using mallets on tom toms. Wright plays right-hand chords, jumping up by octaves, and more slide guitar is featured. Waters holds things together with a simple bass figure. As each verse comes to an end, the slow, gentle arrangement returns. The song's bridge accentuates the song's dreamy feel, and subsequent verses follow the earlier pattern of cutting the tempo toward the end of each.

Next comes the song that—along with the record's title track—would provide a template for Pink Floyd's future musical direction. "Set the Controls for the Heart of the Sun" is built around little more than two chords, and the entire band plays in the most subtle manner possible. Mason performs most of his work using mallets, with occasional quiet taps on a large cymbal or gong. Wright overdubs multiple instruments: his oscillating Farfisa organ and vibraphone play separate yet complementary melodic lines that dance around the single-note center. The guitar—played either by Barrett or Gilmour; likely a combination of the two—provides effects that sound uncannily like humpback whale vocalization, an idea that would find more extensive use on 1971's epic work "Echoes." Vocalist Roger Waters never raises his voice above a whisper, but the combined effect of his vocals and the low-key instrumental work is seething with tension; "Set the Controls" feels more foreboding than calm and comforting.

"Corporal Clegg" opens with a stomping bass line, with Gilmour repeatedly hitting a dominant seventh sharp ninth chord (sometimes called the "Hendrix chord"). The song's lyrics are Roger Waters's decidedly less whimsical take on Syd Barrett's storytelling style. In Waters's tune, the title character loses a limb in the war; his wife drinks too much, and people laugh at him. The song's bridge approaches proto–heavy metal in its intensity, creating an overall ambience that wouldn't seem out of place to Pink Floyd fans familiar only with 1979's *The Wall*.

The song's midsection—in which Mrs. Clegg is addressed—moves in a more melodic direction, with high-pitched harmony vocals and some wah-wah guitar deep in the mix, providing some worthwhile musical contrast and variety. But rather than leave well enough alone, Waters—or someone—decided to add an instrumental break, complete with multiple kazoos, thus sounding like a children's parade. In the process, the song's entire mood is shattered. The entire pattern in repeated, and while the second kazoo-led refrain is joined by war sound effects (explosions, air raid sirens), the damage is done. What could have been a solid track to end the first side of the *A Saucerful of Secrets* LP is instead reduced to the level of a novelty tune. Still, "Corporal Clegg" deserves recognition as the first in a long series of obliquely autobiographical lyrics from the pen of Roger Waters. The bassist's father was killed in the battle of Anzio in 1944, the same year that the fictional Clegg lost his leg.

The second side of Pink Floyd's second album opens with its extended title track. Credited to all four post-Barrett band members, "A Saucerful of Secrets" is perhaps the first studio release from Pink Floyd that bears some of the stylistic flourishes that would come to be most associated with the group. Broken into four "movements," the track opens with "Something Else," featuring malleted cymbal from Nick Mason, and some spacey, somewhat amelodic keyboard lines from Rick Wright. Listeners and critics who wish to apply the "space rock" tag to Pink Floyd could easily turn to the opening moments of "A Saucerful of Secrets" to bolster their argument.

Two minutes in, a curious sound stabs into the mix: it's the sound of an acoustic piano's strings being strummed like a guitar. Keith Emerson would later use the same technique on Emerson Lake and Palmer's self-titled debut, but whereas Emerson would employ the technique in a "musical" fashion, here Richard Wright uses it more as an effect. David Gilmour's heavily reverberating guitar produces a sound that suggests the brass section of an orchestra, something Pink Floyd would actually use in 1970 on the album *Atom Heart Mother*. Just short of the four-minute mark, the movement ends abruptly.

The track's second movement, "Syncopated Pandemonium," is constructed out of a section of audio tape containing a Nick Mason drum figure played across multiple floor drums. The tape has been looped to create a repetitive percussive track. Wright adds some low register, seemingly random attacks upon a piano. A few cymbal crashes—played in reverse—introduce a swirling, heady squall of electric guitar from David Gilmour. The various sounds collide with one another to nightmarish, cataclysmic effect. More involved guitar work from Gilmour mimics the sounds of screeching missiles, and occasional piano note clusters from Wright sound as if he is playing the piano with a closed fist. The cacophony continues to unfold, with an overall air of violence and mayhem. Just past the seven-minute mark, the scene fades out, replaced by a long rumble that suggests the aftermath of a great explosion. Exemplifying Pink Floyd's occasional lazy attitude toward naming works in progress, in its earliest form, "Syncopated Pandemonium" was provisionally titled "Nick's Boogie." But other than featuring some hypnotic drumming, the second movement of "A Saucerful of Secrets" bears little if any sonic resemblance to the "Nick's Boogie" that Pink Floyd recorded for Peter Whitehead's film *Tonite Let's All Make Love in London*.

As "Storm Signal" begins, Richard Wright's organ arises out of the aural smoke and ash, playing a slow and spooky figure that's almost a parody of church music. The movement seems designed to elicit mental images of the wake of a savage battle; on its surface somewhat serene, but just below the surface, filled with unspeakable horrors.

At the eight-and-a-half-minute mark, the rumble subsides, and for the first time in "A Saucerful of Secrets," a conventional melody—the movement "Celestial Voices"—is revealed. Wright plays a forlorn sequence of chords on a Hammond organ, making effective use of the organ's bass pedals. At the ten-minute mark, a wordless choir joins Wright's organ; the "chorus" is actually a Mellotron keyboard. With bits of guitar squall subtly added low in the mix along with Mellotron strings, Gilmour and Wright add some subtle vocalizing of their own as "A Saucerful of Secrets" draws to a majestic close.

Though it lacks lyrics, "Saucerful" can be seen as a musical statement on the horrors of war. Great Britain's military deaths exceeded

380,000; untold numbers among those were fathers, sons, or brothers. Though World War II had formally ended in Great Britain with the May 8, 1945, declaration of V-E Day, bombed-out buildings, rubble, and unexploded bombs would be a feature of the London landscape well into the 1960s. Widespread rationing of food and consumer goods persisted until the mid-1950s. Thus, even a generation born in Great Britain during or shortly after the war would have suffered the direct effects of the conflict in a way that many of their North American Allied counterparts would not. In its particular Englishness, "A Saucerful of Secrets" may have had a resonance with British listeners, one lost upon American ears.

After a moment of silence that follows "A Saucerful of Secrets," Rick Wright's waltzing and melancholy "See-Saw" begins. While the earliest attempts at recording the song—then waggishly called "The Most Boring Song I've Ever Heard Bar 2"—were done at a session in which Syd Barrett was nominally present, he does not appear on the finished track in any form. The song itself doesn't rank among Wright's most memorable compositions, but the use of instruments in "See-Saw" is creative. Of particular note is Wright's Mellotron, playing a string sound remarkably similar—and likely identical, as there were not many sound options on a Mellotron in 1968—to the ones used extensively on the Moody Blues' second album, *In Search of the Lost Chord*. As it happened, the Moody Blues were recording their album at almost the same time as Pink Floyd was working on *A Saucerful of Secrets*. Wright employed numerous instruments—piano, Farfisa organ, Hammond organ, xylophone—in the recording of "See-Saw," and the contributions of the other band members are subtle at best. Only Gilmour's occasional guitar figures pierce the keyboard-heavy arrangement.

When Pink Floyd decided upon the song sequence for *A Saucerful of Secrets*, the sole number written for the album by Syd Barrett was chosen for the last track. Coming as it does after the sonic explorations of "Set the Controls for the Heart of the Sun" and the title track, "Jugband Blues" sounds like a song by some other group, accidentally appended to the album. Syd Barrett sings a song about being lost, strumming on an acoustic guitar. The jagged, halting melody of "Jugband Blues" serves as a link between the fully formed (if at times unconventional) songs Barrett had written for *The Piper at the Gates of Dawn* a mere year earlier, and the song fragments he would later bring to the sessions that yielded his two solo albums, *The Madcap Laughs* and *Barrett*, both released in 1970.

Most everything about "Jugband Blues" is disjointed. Barrett's final composition for Pink Floyd shifts between three time signatures, and features two separate brass sections. The first of these finds musicians from the local Salvation Army Band playing a pre-planned melody; the second is a totally spontaneous and free-form performance that bears no musical connection to what has come before. Whether or not such conjectures have any basis in reality, countless observers have pointed to Barrett's cracked "Jugband Blues" lyrics as a farewell from the songwriter. Syd Barrett may or may not be ruminating on the lyrical nature of his fantasy-focused and/or playful body of work when in the final lines of "Jugband Blues" he asks, "And what exactly is a dream? And what exactly is a joke?"

By the time *A Saucerful of Secrets* was released in the United Kingdom—June 29, 1968—it was clear that if Roger Waters, Richard Wright, Nick Mason, and new guitarist David Gilmour were interested in answering those rhetorical questions, they would be doing so without the man who had written all of Pink Floyd's best-known material.

Critical reaction to *Saucerful* was mixed; some critics seemed unable to decide if they loved or hated the record. In his review for *IT*, Miles described various tracks on the album as "unimaginative . . . too long . . . too boring . . . uninventive." He singled out the title track for praise and concluded with, "A record well worth buying!" A writer for *Melody Maker* encouraged its readers to "Give the Floyd a listen . . . it isn't really so painful."

Rolling Stone's Jim Miller displayed far less enthusiasm in his review, calling the title track "eleven minutes of psychedelic muzak" and impugned the songwriting and musician skills of each of the band's four members. "Unfortunately," Miller wrote, "a music of effects is a weak base for a rock group to rest its reputation on—but this is what the Pink Floyd have done."

Without question, Pink Floyd lost some of their fan base once Syd Barrett's departure became known. Whether one liked the band's musical direction post-Barrett, there was no denying that it was different. "I could straight away feel that there was something [different]," says Robyn Hitchcock, who was living in London when he turned fifteen in 1968. "There was a lack of power; there was a lack of intensity in what they'd become." He characterizes the band's work from 1968 onward as "a slightly more manageable version of what they'd been doing with Barrett," but acknowledges that the new approach "was the beginning of their real success." Hitchcock points out an additional factor that aided in Pink Floyd's eventual fame: "David Gilmour was a virtuoso, which Barrett wasn't."

With the release of *A Saucerful of Secrets*, Pink Floyd was well on its way to becoming an "album band," focusing on the long-playing record as the primary medium of putting its music across to listeners. Just prior to making a collective decision to not release singles in the UK—a resolution to which they would adhere for several years—the band would take one last stab at the singles market.

Co-written by Roger Waters and David Gilmour, "Point Me at the Sky" is a self-conscious attempt to write a hit single. Betraying hints of the rarely displayed sardonic humor that informed later songs like "Free Four" on 1972's *Obscured by Clouds*, "Point Me at the Sky" weighs in on issues of overpopulation, insanity, and game-playing. Pink Floyd's concern with "big" ideas such as these would find its most effective expression with *The Dark Side of the Moon*, but even within the confines of a three-and-a-half-minute single, "Point Me at the Sky" does a creditable job of moving past moon-june love songs. Considering the long shadow Barrett would cast upon Pink Floyd's subsequent work, it's not unreasonable to suggest that the closing repeated lyrics of "Point Me at the Sky" might have been written and sung with him in mind: "All we've got to say to you is goodbye!"

The tune's arrangement features an effective contrast between the waltzing verses with Gilmour's lilting vocals and the stomping chorus featuring a notably insistent bass line from Roger Waters. Because the track was specifically intended as a non-album single, "Point Me at the Sky" was mixed to monaural, not stereo. "It was pretty awful," says friend of the band (and drummer) Willie Wilson, who was present during the session. "I hope that [the band] would agree with me."

The flip side of the single released in December 1968 would go on to become a signature Pink Floyd song and a durable part of the band's live set for several years. "Careful With That Axe, Eugene" starts out with an arrangement and feel quite close to "Set the Controls for the Heart of the Sun"—right down to Roger Waters's whispered vocals—but unlike that album track, "Eugene" builds in intensity to a manic crescendo in which Waters lets loose with a bloodcurdling scream. Nick Mason's drumming explodes on cue with Waters's scream, and the effect is cinematic. (Fittingly enough, "Eugene" would later find use in various forms as the audio component of some motion pictures.)

Pink Floyd had long ago discovered the creative advantages of extending its songs beyond the confines of traditional single length, and the music business was beginning to catch up with that thinking. At nearly six minutes, "Careful With That Axe, Eugene" would be uncharacteristically long for a single—much less a B-side—but arguably the Beatles had paved the way for lengthy singles four months earlier with the release of the single "Hey Jude," running in excess of seven minutes.

Two other studio recordings of note were made by Pink Floyd in 1968, though neither would see release until included in the 2016 box set, *The Early Years*. Until that time, the existence of "Song 1" and "Roger's Boogie" had gone unnoticed by collectors of Pink Floyd's unreleased material; even the 2010 edition of Glenn Povey's exhaustive *Echoes: The Complete History of Pink Floyd* makes no mention of the August 1968 recording sessions at Capitol Studios in Los Angeles.

That one-day recording session in Hollywood was Pink Floyd's first without producer Norman Smith; the group would handle production duties without supervision. Neither recording was finished, but both explored the musical direction Pink Floyd would pursue on its next album project, the soundtrack for Barbet Schroeder's *More*.

"Song 1" begins with a gently strummed E minor chord; the tune quickly settles into a stuttering meter. There's a breezy, largely contemplative and pastoral feel to the song for most of its three-plus minutes. But toward the end, David Gilmour unleashes unexpected bursts of feedback guitar, making liberal use of the tremolo ("whammy") bar on his electric guitar.

"Song 2" (also known as "Roger's Boogie," though like "Nick's Boogie" before it, the tune is anything but a fast blues number) is an eerie, vocal-led tune. Progressive in its structure and use of different meters, "Song 2" suggests the influence of some of the West Coast psychedelic bands with which Pink Floyd might have come into contact on their American trip. Lead guitar is downplayed on the track in favor of some effective, almost jangling rhythm playing. A brief organ solo from Rick Wright takes the song briefly in another direction, while Mason's drumming remains understated throughout.

Days after the Los Angeles sessions, Pink Floyd was back across the Atlantic, continuing a rather frenetic schedule of concert and festival appearances; between Syd Barrett's departure and the end of 1968, the group racked up no fewer than 125 live performances in England, the United States, Benelux, and France. All of these would be sandwiched between recording sessions, appearances on BBC radio, and work on the soundtrack for *The Committee*, an avant-garde motion picture.

9

BY COMMITTEE

"As long as the dialogue goes on," suggests the main character in Peter Sykes's 1968 film *The Committee*, "there's a chance at rationality." Inadvertently summing up critical response to the movie, another character responds, "Not everyone would agree with that."

The Committee has not worn well. The hour-long, black-and-white film has been variously described as avant-garde, film noir, and experimental. At its heart, *The Committee* is a black comedy, an attempt at biting satire. A kind of poor man's existentialist film essay, *The Committee* tells—after a fashion—the story of an unnamed man (played by Paul Jones, lead singer of Manfred Mann) who hitches a car ride, murders his driver, revives him, and at some point in the future takes part in a committee that seems to function as a kind of focus group. It's never made clear what the goals of the titular committee might be, but the unnamed main character begins to suspect that the whole thing is a kind of ruse seeking to bring him to justice for his crime. That never happens, and the film ends with him driving away with a woman he met at the focus group. Apropos of absolutely nothing, she asks him, "Do you play bridge?" The credits roll.

The Committee does feature some interesting music, and nearly all of that music was created expressly for the film by Pink Floyd. Peter Jenner recalls the informal approach surrounding the entire project. He says that producer Max Steuer "was someone I knew from the London School of Economics. We were on the scene, so various film people would say, 'produce the music for it,' and we'd go and do some music for them. We didn't really know about stage licenses and contracts and things like that, so if one artist wanted you to do some music, you did some music." He notes that with Syd Barrett more or less out of the picture, the band faced a challenge. "It became very hard to deliver anything coherent, because there was no one [else] who could really write songs. But the Floyd did sort of pick up quickly and start; they realized that they *had* to write."

In early April 1968, Pink Floyd assembled at the London home of two actors in the film; *The Committee* was projected onto a screen, and the band largely improvised along to the moving images. Save for a pair of songs from The Crazy World of Arthur Brown (who, unlike Pink Floyd, appears onscreen during *The Committee*'s most engaging and memorable few moments), the remaining music is largely instrumental. Two tracks—best described as the film's theme music—are built around a pop-leaning progression of seven chords, led mostly by Rick Wright's organ and subdued guitar from Gilmour. Nick Mason plays an atypically "straight" drum part with fills in between phrases, and Roger Waters's bass part largely confines itself to the root notes of the chords. The reprise of the theme features a keyboard lead melody played over the chord progression.

Another of the tracks features much more significant contributions from David Gilmour; screeching guitar figures showcase the "whale" effect he would use extensively on *Meddle*'s "Echoes." One track features Rick Wright's organ as a central instrument, with bits of piano, suggesting either that the sessions involved overdubbing or that one of the other musicians played the piano. A longer track features a throbbing, deliberate, one-note Roger Waters bass line that suggests the "heartbeat" sound Nick Mason would create for *The Dark Side of the Moon*.

Though it's not credited as such, a single-length (2:38) version of "Careful With That Axe, Eugene" forms part of *The Committee*'s soundtrack. While the track features a bit of quiet, wordless warbling, it ends without segueing into the studio version's musically explosive section.

Approximately fifteen minutes of audio from that session was used in the film, spread throughout, but used primarily during *The Committee*'s laborious second half, during which Jones's character is engaged in mock-philosophical conversation that's meant to "sound" deep yet reveals itself as bereft of content and meaning. At one point, the central figure says, "I know that sounds awful; I probably don't even mean it." That sentence sums up the "plot" and dialogue of *The Committee* quite tidily. Yet as a sonic backdrop for the extended interchanges between the two characters, Pink Floyd's untitled instrumentals are effective; if nothing else, they convey the arty end of the hip, swinging London scene of 1968.

The film's soundtrack does contain a mysterious anomaly. The first thirty-second snippet of music used is played backward in the film. It features a most unusual mix of sounds: drums sound like Indian tabla, guitars sound like sitars (or electric sitars), and the keyboard sounds seem to be coming from an early modular synthesizer. It's worth noting that none of these instruments had made an appearance on a Pink Floyd recording previously, and none—save synthesizer—would in the near future. Since there is no official soundtrack album from *The Committee*, there is good reason to suspect that this first bit of music may be some other (uncredited) group of musicians. Had Pink Floyd made use of sitar and tabla, it stands to reason that those instruments—still relatively exotic in the pop landscape of 1968—would have made at least a fleeting appearance in the sessions for *A Saucerful of Secrets*, already in progress. In any event, this untitled piece of music (which plays over the film's opening credits) doesn't sound very different played backward as opposed to forward.

The provenance of this piece of music is hinted at in Julian Palacios's book, *Syd Barrett & Pink Floyd: Dark Globe*. As Palacios points out, when producer Max Steuer contracted with Pink Floyd to provide the film's soundtrack, Syd Barrett was still in the group. And more than two months before Pink Floyd began their session for the film soundtrack, Syd Barrett reported for duty. Apparently Barrett showed up at Sound Techniques studio on the appointed day, January 30, 1968, without a guitar or band. As Steuer had booked session time in advance, phone calls were made, and an ad hoc band was assembled. That group may have included Steve Peregrin Took (later of T. Rex) and Brian "Blinky" Davidson, Davy O'List's band mate in the Nice. Though Palacios does not suggest that the single track they recorded was actually used in the film, he asserts that Barrett insisted the twenty-minute recording be played backward once it was completed. The untitled number has never received official release, but does circulate among collectors.

While not a landmark project within the context of Pink Floyd's body of work, the band's soundtrack music for *The Committee* nonetheless represents a progression. The group's earliest forays into creating music for film were executed with little regard for the specific images that would be displayed simultaneously with that music. Simply put, in those cases—*Tonite Let's All Make Love in London* and the other film projects from 1967—Pink Floyd recorded some music from its repertoire and handed it over to the filmmakers. In contrast, the music made for *The Committee*—however formless that music might be—was created with the express purpose of enhancing the viewer's experience of watching the film. That aesthetic would be built upon as Pink Floyd embarked on its next major studio project/film soundtrack, 1969's *More*.

Long unavailable in any legitimate form, *The Committee* was included (on DVD and Blu-ray) as part of the 2016 Pink Floyd box set, *The Early Years 1965–1972*. Two audio tracks—the ones described above as themes—are featured on a CD included in Volume 7 of *The Early Years*, the only part of that massive set not to receive subsequent break-out release as a standalone volume.

10

BBC TWO

Pink Floyd appeared on BBC radio programs several times in 1968. The band's selection of songs extended in wildly diverging directions: while the first sessions (two separate performances of the same four-song set, broadcast later on two different days) focused on music from the impending release of *A Saucerful of Secrets*, another radio session late in the year featured a tune never to be released (at least until the 2016 box set, *The Early Years*). And Pink Floyd's final sessions for broadcast in 1968 on BBC radio featured a live performance of the band's last single release for many years, a completely new song, and—in one last look backward—a reading of one tune from the band's days with Syd Barrett.

Around May 1968—and as captured on a widely circulating bootleg recording of an Amsterdam concert—Pink Floyd debuted a new work-in-progress called "Keep Smiling People." By late June, the band had played a dozen more concerts, and the piece had tightened up enough for performance on BBC Radio 1's *Top Gear*. A performance of that tune would be introduced by deejay John Peel as "'The Murderotic Woman' or 'Careful With That Axe, Eugene.'"

Perhaps the sound crew at BBC's Piccadilly Studios wouldn't allow it—lest it damage their equipment—or maybe it had yet to be incorporated as part of the arrangement of "Careful With That Axe, Eugene," but the broadcast version of the song does not contain Roger Waters's trademark scream. As it is, the one-chord song conveys a fair degree of malevolence in this purely instrumental reading.

It's worth considering just how far pop music had come in a short time in Great Britain; in response to pressures from "pirate" radio stations, the staid British Broadcasting Company had launched Radio 1 in September 1967. Less than a year later, listeners tuning in at 3 p.m. on a Sunday in August would have been treated to nine-plus minutes of the decidedly abstract tune soon to be known as "A Saucerful of Secrets." Even a half century later, "Saucerful" is no one's idea of commercial, radio-friendly programming.

"The Massed Gadgets of Hercules" was an early, working title for the title track of Pink Floyd's second album. The *Top Gear* version of "A Saucerful of Secrets" follows its eventual studio counterpart's four-movement structure, but the first movement ("Something Else") is cut in half; presumably it was decided that radio listeners might not bear four minutes of atonal music. The second movement, "Syncopated Pandemonium," is slightly shorter than the album version but otherwise follows its form.

The brief "Storm Signal" movement features a Richard Wright organ solo that's initially quite different melodically from the version released on the album. All of the section shortening allows for the full performance of the fourth and final movement, "Celestial Voices." As performed on the BBC, it's nearly a Rick Wright solo piece, with band members' voices taking the place of the "choir" Mellotron. "Now, that is the sort of music they ought to have coming out of churches; it's incredible," enthuses *Top Gear* host John Peel once the piece concludes.

Other than Nick Mason coming in with the drum beat a fraction of a second late, Pink Floyd's BBC version of "Let There Be More Light" is nearly identical to its counterpart on *A Saucerful of Secrets*. David Gilmour struggles greatly on some of the song's higher vocal lines; double-tracking inadvertently emphasizes the difficulty he experiences. Gilmour's guitar solo enters late, and is more bluesy than on the studio take. The *Top Gear* performance is a full minute shorter than the album version.

Roger Waters's "Julia Dream" gets an intimate reading for the BBC. A more sparse arrangement showcases the song's virtues. David Gilmour's loose-limbed acoustic guitar work suits the song's feel, and a slight retard at the song's end emphasizes the "live" nature of the performance.

Pink Floyd would remain exceedingly busy throughout most of the second half of 1968, but with the Christmas holidays looming, the band's schedule let up a bit. In between the group's still-packed list of appointments, more BBC spots were put on the band's calendar.

The first December appearance for the band was recorded on the second broadcast, on December 15. The band previews its upcoming single, "Point Me at the Sky," and turns in a performance of the Barrett-era (but still popular) "Interstellar Overdrive." The set also features a new tune, "Embryo." Along with a clutch of other new compositions, "Embryo" would eventually form the core of a suite of extended set-pieces in Pink Floyd's live performances. But for its initial BBC performance, "Embryo" runs just a shade over three minutes.

The other song played at that session—and as of 2017, the only recording from the session to have received commercial release—would be a new instrumental, then titled "Baby Blue Shuffle in D Major." A David Gilmour solo performance on acoustic guitar, "Baby Blue" displays a heretofore unheard side of the band, one that draws on the instrumental prowess of its guitarist. The piece would eventually be incorporated as the first section of a larger, twelve-minute, three-part work titled "The Narrow Way." That studio track would fill half of an LP side on Pink Floyd's 1969 double album, *Ummagumma*.

A second performance would be recorded that same day, for broadcast the following January. It features nearly the same set list, but without Gilmour's solo piece. "Point Me at the Sky" in particular benefits from the more straightforward (some would say primitive) recording facilities of the BBC; the performance for *Top Gear* has an energy and immediacy that the studio version would lack.

"Embryo" is a Roger Waters composition, sung by David Gilmour. In this, its earliest form, "Embryo" points the way toward the largely acoustic textures Pink Floyd would explore on its next studio album, *More*. "Embryo" displays a greater attention to melody, moving decisively away from the experimental approach of much of the group's other material from the period. Roger Waters's bass line is a melody in and of itself, and Rick Wright's organ work provides a pleasing counter-melody while Gilmour sings in a hushed, lilting voice.

After its premiere on *Top Gear*, "Embryo" would remain unheard for nearly a year. The song would resurface in greatly extended form as part of Pink Floyd's live set beginning in early 1970.

The centerpiece of Pink Floyd's December 1968 BBC spots, however, would be "Interstellar Overdrive." While the song itself had been part of the group's set since before signing with EMI, the arrangement of the tune had changed a great deal from the manner in which it was played by the Syd Barrett–era lineup. Here, "Interstellar Overdrive" is taken at a slower, more deliberate pace, one that dials back the frenetic tone of Barrett's guitar work in favor of something altogether more dreamlike. Rick Wright's organ becomes a more central melodic element, and while the reading contains its fair share of improvisation, there's a greater musicality to the instrumental work.

Gilmour elicits all manner of otherworldly squeals from his guitar, while Waters turns in a hypnotic bass line that displays the progress he has made as a player. A new, stomping two-chord interlude has been introduced into the song, set against a section in which Gilmour plays more atonal figures on guitar; the call-and-response between the two sections serves both to heighten tension and root the more abstract parts of "Interstellar Overdrive" in a more conventional musical foundation.

Guitarist Eric Clapton had seen Pink Floyd live onstage several times during this period, and counted himself as a fan. Trying to describe them to a *Rolling Stone* reporter, he said, "I can't even think of a group you can relate them to," adding, "They do things like play an hour set that's just one number."

The countless hours spent playing in front of audiences in England and the continent (and, briefly, the United States) were now paying dividends in the form of a tighter, greatly improved instrumental ensemble. All that would be needed now were some suitable songs.

Part III

The Narrow Way (1969)

11

QUICKSILVER

As 1969 began, decisive changes were under way for Pink Floyd. After making two albums and a number of singles with Norman Smith in the control room, Pink Floyd began to move toward self-producing. And having had successful experiences, at least from a creative standpoint, working on film soundtracks, the band decided to plunge ahead and provide all of the music for a major motion picture.

While some recording sessions for the album that would become *Ummagumma* had begun in January 1969 at EMI's Abbey Road studios with producer Norman Smith, when Pink Floyd began work on the soundtrack for Barbet Schroeder's *More*, the band booked studio time at Pye Recording Studios in London's Marble Arch district.

In 1969, Barbet Schroeder had already made a name for himself with his production company, creating edgy, well-received films. A dramatic motion picture chronicling the downward spiral of a young man who succumbs to heroin addiction, *More* would be the directorial debut for the Swiss-born Schroeder.

For the soundtrack of this decidedly downbeat film, Schroeder chose Pink Floyd. Barry Miles quoted the director explaining his choice. "Pink Floyd were making the music that was best adapted to the movie at that time—spacey and very in tune with nature." As used in the film, the songs the band wrote and recorded are subtle additions; often as not, the songs flit in and out of the soundtrack in the form of sounds coming from a radio. Because a variety of styles would be needed to evoke certain specific moods, Pink Floyd was called upon to create a suitably diverse collection of music. Over a period spanning all of February through May of 1969, the band worked on songs for *More* in between its now-customary schedule of concerts. For a variety of reasons—owing at least in part to difficulty obtaining overseas work permits—Pink Floyd largely remained in Great Britain during this period, playing at numerous festivals, benefit concerts, and other dates that often included several other acts.

The band had a rather short deadline for the *More* film score, but the movie itself was mostly complete when Pink Floyd set about creating music to accompany the moving images. Nick Mason recalled in his book *Inside Out: A Personal History of Pink Floyd* that the band "went into a viewing theatre [and] timed the sequences carefully" using a stopwatch. David Gilmour was quoted about the sessions in Miles's *Pink Floyd: The Early Years.* "It was eight days to do everything from writing, recording, editing . . . but everything we did was accepted by the director. He never asked us to redo anything."

Record-buying fans who had been following along with Pink Floyd's progress may have been nonplussed as the needle dropped on side one of *More*. The pastoral opening of "Cirrus Minor" features birds chirping in the trees for a full minute before the first strains of music begin. As he gently strums an acoustic guitar, David Gilmour sings of churchyards, rivers, and lying in the grass. Rick Wright's Farfisa organ has its vibrato setting on full, causing his block chords to wobble in the background. Intentionally or not, the folky "Cirrus Minor" has surface similarities to some of Syd Barrett's songwriting: the song has no chorus, and it is built on a foundation of descending chords. The vocal section of "Cirrus Minor" ends after a minute and a half; the remaining nearly three minutes of the song feature a stately Hammond organ melody from Richard Wright. Additional organ overdubs toward the tune's end take on a woozy, otherworldly quality.

"The Nile Song" is a true oddity in the Pink Floyd catalog. With a crushing sequence of guitar chords, the heavily distorted tune—with a heavy arrangement to match—has more to do with the kind of acid rock being churned out by such bands as Blue Cheer on its 1968 LP, *Vincebus Eruptum.* Perhaps Schroeder specifically asked for a heavy rock song to accompany that particular scene in the film, and the band willingly obliged. But the song's forced, cliché lyrics (a character spreads her wings to fly) coupled with an unsubtle AAA rhyme scheme—eventually scaled back simply to AA—suggest that composer Roger Waters may have been having a laugh. Nearly half a century after its recording, "The Nile Song" sounds like nothing so much as a parody of heavy metal. Keyboardist Richard Wright doesn't even play on the track.

As a song, "Crying Song" is a slight piece of work, but as a hint of directions Pink Floyd would pursue, it's instructive. David Gilmour turns in a distinctive, unforced lead vocal while Rick Wright adds some melodic vibraphone. Overdubbed vocal harmonies—again from Gilmour—preview what would soon become one of Pink Floyd's chief musical assets. Gilmour's electric slide guitar, too, would take its place in the group's sonic arsenal, but the solo on "Crying Song" seems offhand, as if it were laid down in a single take so that the band could move on to another track. And songwriter Waters—who doesn't take a lead vocal at all on any of the *More* songs—clearly still has a thing or two to learn about David Gilmour's vocal range; the lead vocal line pushes the bass-note limits of Gilmour's ability.

"Up the Khyber"—the title an example of Cockney rhyming slang (in this case for "up the arse")—is equal parts Nick Mason drum solo and Richard Wright playing some very exploratory, jazz-flavored chordal runs on an acoustic piano. The song may have grown out of a similar-sounding section in the band's "Interstellar Overdrive," and would appear again under a different title as part of Pink Floyd's 1969 live set piece, "The Man and the Journey." A dizzying bit of tape manipulation ends the song.

The next two songs on *More* would provide Pink Floyd with some of its most compelling live material, in greatly expanded and extended versions. But for Schroeder's film soundtrack, both "Green is the Colour" and "Cymbaline" would be presented in acoustic-based, relatively brief readings. Another folk-flavored tune with a sprightly tin whistle, "Green is the Colour" is built around Gilmour's acoustic guitar and high-pitched vocals. The rest of the band enters the arrangement gradually, with Wright turning in a country-and-western-flavored piano melody that begins simply and develops as the song winds out, eventually evolving into a Floyd Cramer–styled solo.

The moody minor key melody of "Cymbaline" provides a suitable backdrop for David Gilmour's heavily reverberated lead vocal. "Cymbaline" sports one of the strongest melodic lines on *More*, and, for that matter, in the post-Barrett Pink Floyd catalog to this point. By 1969,

Roger Waters was putting more care and effort into his lyric writing, and "Cymbaline" reflects this. The song makes a reference to Marvel Comics character Doctor Strange, and trades in some compelling lyrical imagery (likening the feeling of apprehension to a tube train creeping up one's spine). And humor makes a fleeting appearance as Gilmour sings lyrics that ask if the song's final couplet will rhyme. It doesn't.

A very brief instrumental, the unimaginatively named "Party Sequence" features Nick Mason on several overdubbed bongo drums, with wife Lindy trilling along on penny whistle.

Side Two of the original *More* album opens in grand fashion with "Main Theme." The gong would become an integral component of Pink Floyd's live set as well as its studio recordings, and the gong that opens "Main Theme" provides a dramatic introduction to the number. Richard Wright plays a series of dissonant chords and melodic lines on his Farfisa; it is only with this song that the experimental side of Pink Floyd—so thoroughly explored just months earlier on *A Saucerful of Secrets*—is displayed on the *More* soundtrack. But here that experimentalism is couched in a format that effectively reconciles Pink Floyd's ambitious ideas with conventional songcraft. Built mostly around a single chord, the impressionistic "Main Theme" is more song-like than many other Pink Floyd instrumentals of the era. It shows the band channeling its energies into music that could be considered more accessible.

The opening chords of "Ibiza Bar" are nearly identical to "The Nile Song," but as the song unfolds, it shows a greater emphasis on melody, and a lead guitar solo from David Gilmour is placed up front in the tune. Even as the vocals come in—buried deep in the mix here—Gilmour's lead playing continues, and remains the song's most distinctive feature. For once, Waters's lyrics may have a connection with the film; his lyrics speak of an epilogue that reads like a sad song.

The self-explanatory "More Blues" is a very brief and airy twelve-bar blues instrumental. And while Pink Floyd was never most people's idea of a blues band, twelve-bar instrumentals would become a regular part of the band's live set in the early 1970s. Curiously, Mason's drums are mixed significantly louder than David Gilmour's guitar. Waters's bass and Richard Wright's organ are subtle almost to the point of inaudibility.

Musique concrète is a kind of experimental music making with beginnings in the 1920s; modern-day listeners might describe it as "soundscapes" or even sound effects. Whether or not the band's use of it was predicated on familiarity with earlier experiments by composers like Stravinsky, Stockhausen, and Varèse, there are commonalities between the work of those serious composers and Pink Floyd tracks like "Quicksilver." Like "A Saucerful of Secrets" before it, this lengthy and atmospheric piece from the *More* soundtrack is composed of seemingly random effects amid more conventional musical sounds from organ, vibraphone, and percussion.

The final two tracks on the *More* soundtrack are examples of writing to specification. Even the titles make that clear: "A Spanish Piece" and "Dramatic Theme." The former is an exceedingly brief Flamenco piece with Gilmour playing nylon string guitar while whispering Spanish phrases. The *More* soundtrack ends with a spare tune based on the film's "Main Theme," and prominently features David Gilmour's slide guitar with layers of reverb and echo.

Pink Floyd would write and record additional songs for Barbet Schroeder's *More* film soundtrack, though none would appear on the album. Four of these are included in the 2016 box set, *The Early Years*. The verse sections of the short instrumental track "Hollywood" are a two-chord vamp based on the opening chords of "Cymbaline," and the chorus—a few bars—provides enough variety to qualify "Hollywood" as a separate song. David Gilmour plays a simple, appealing melody on his guitar through a wah-wah pedal. At its core, "Hollywood" displays the bare bones of what could have been developed into a proper song.

A "beat version" of the *More* theme wasn't used in the film or on its soundtrack, but does showcase Pink Floyd's ability—largely untapped—to make relatively conventional pop music when the inclination or need arises. Many of the group's signature sonic qualities—a simple, throbbing bass line, driving yet straightforward drumming, lengthy and exploratory organ runs, chugging electric rhythm guitar, and shifting musical dynamics—are all present in the "beat" version, and are corralled into a catchy tune.

The Early Years includes an alternate take of *More*'s "More Blues." Unlike the take used on the soundtrack, the alternate version is mixed so that all four instruments—guitar, bass, drums, and organ—are audible. Still, it's relatively undistinguished and is notable primarily as an anomaly in the Pink Floyd catalog. "Seabirds" did find its way into the film, but was left off of the soundtrack album. Rather than having a drum beat, "Seabirds" uses the resonating sound of a gong as its percussive device. Wright plays Farfisa organ lines and some subtle vibraphone; eventually David Gilmour adds some slide guitar, used here more for texture than as a vehicle for any sort of melody. Near the track's end, the gong is struck again, more forcefully, and allowed to ring out completely as the organ lines fade into oblivion.

Looking back on the *More* album, Nick Mason said, "It wasn't a Pink Floyd album, but a group of songs." The band came away from the experience with generally positive feelings about soundtrack work; Pink Floyd would assist Schroeder again on another film (*Obscured by Clouds/La Valée*), and would team up—albeit less successfully—with another popular filmmaker for a project in 1970.

The *More* experience had one important benefit for Pink Floyd: it helped break the band in Europe. "The Continent has just exploded for us now—particularly France," Waters told *Georgia Straight*'s Mike Quigley. "What really made it for us in France was the film *More*."

The *Rolling Stone Record Guide* awarded *More* merely one star, but in his accompanying review, Bart Testa characterized the record's music collectively as "suggestive of impressionist sketches" and "far more sentimental than the film." Long hard to find on home video, in 2016, Barbet Schroeder's *More* received release on DVD and Blu-ray in Pink Floyd's *The Early Years* box set.

12

SYSYPHUS

As 1969 began, the four men of Pink Floyd found themselves short of creative ideas. The band had recently completed and released the soundtrack for Barbet Schroeder's film *More*, but that record's mix of pastoral, near folk-rock tunes and pastiches of hard rock didn't accurately represent the breadth of the group's collective musical nature. Pink Floyd's concert dates of the era would include only a handful of *More* tunes, and save two, none would remain in the band's set list for long. A typical Pink Floyd concert in early 1969 included two or three songs from the Barrett era (usually "Astronomy Dominé," "Pow R. Toc H.," and "Interstellar Overdrive"), perhaps an instrumental improvisation, and three from June 1968's *A Saucerful of Secrets*. The only new material in the group's set was "Careful With That Axe, Eugene."

But EMI expected another album, and so sessions began in April for what would become *Ummagumma*. Like *More* before it, *Ummagumma* was perhaps not what fans might have expected: rather than a collection of new material that would form the basis of Pink Floyd's live concerts, it would be a double album. The first disc features live tracks: concert versions of songs from the group's still rather slim catalog, recorded in England during early 1969. And the second disc dispenses with the group concept completely, featuring instead solo works from each of the band's four members.

Though by April the band had put together a stage show that combined old and new material into a loosely defined thematic work (a pair of suites called "The Man" and "The Journey"), a decision was made to record at least three concerts around England in hope of capturing material for a live album. The shows at which the mobile recording setup was used did not feature the new set, but instead fell back on older tunes.

The first show to be recorded live was an April 26 set at Bromley Technical College, billed as "Light & Sound Concert." In the end, none of the recordings from this date would be used for *Ummagumma*, none has surfaced on the collectors' circuit, and none appeared on the 2016 box set, *The Early Years*. The following night, Pink Floyd had a club date scheduled at Mothers in Birmingham. The popular club had opened the previous August above a furniture store on Birmingham's High Street, and would host hundreds of rock, blues, and jazz acts, including the Who, Fairport Convention, Peter Green's Fleetwood Mac, Elton John, and King Crimson, during its two-and-a-half-year run. Birmingham's own Traffic (featuring former Spencer Davis Group vocalist/multi-instrumentalist Steve Winwood) made its debut live appearance at Mothers.

Pink Floyd's five-number set would be recorded, and two of those tracks would be featured on *Ummagumma*. "Astronomy Dominé" had changed a great deal in performance since the departure of Syd Barrett; in some ways the band's live readings of the song would bear greater similarity to the studio version on *The Piper at the Gates of Dawn* than earlier live performances. David Gilmour and Richard Wright provide the dual lead vocal lines, and Gilmour's more accomplished guitar work lends the song a greater musicality than it had with Barrett. Gilmour also makes judicious and effective use of a wah-wah pedal as he spins out leads on his guitar. For his part, Roger Waters displays great facility on bass guitar; undoubtedly, the band's heavy live performance schedule had served to improve his instrumental skills.

The midsection of "Astronomy Dominé" as recorded at Mothers shows the band's mastery of nuance and dynamics; at one point, the song's arrangement is brought down to near-silence; seconds later, the band is firing on all cylinders, playing loudly and aggressively while Nick Mason pounds his drum kit furiously. And moments later, the band plays quietly again. When Gilmour and Wright reach Barrett's "Pow! Pow!" lyrics, the foursome explodes once again, only to drop into a relatively quiet approach for the song's end. The *Ummagumma* performance of the song would be the most successful example of Pink

Floyd recasting songs from its Syd Barrett days into a framework that reflected the band's new musical personality.

So successful was the *Ummagumma* version of "Astronomy Dominé" that when Harvest/EMI repackaged Pink Floyd's first two albums (*The Piper at the Gates of Dawn* and *A Saucerful of Secrets*) as a 1973 double LP for American release, that album—playfully titled *A Nice Pair*—dropped the original studio version of "Astronomy Dominé," replacing it instead with the live *Ummagumma* recording. "Astronomy Dominé" would remain in Pink Floyd's live set into 1971, and many years later it would be featured as a concert opener on the Gilmour-led Pink Floyd 1994 world tour. As recently as 2016, Gilmour still sometimes included the song in his concert set lists.

In contrast to Barrett's "Astonomy Dominé," Roger Waters's "Set the Controls for the Heart of the Sun" displays the post-Syd band's nascent ability to create a song/soundscape that showcases its evolving musical aesthetic. The band's rhythm section provides a deeply hypnotic musical bed for the song—Waters's repetitive bass line joined by Nick Mason's pseudo-tribal mallet work on the drums—as Waters delivers his vocals in a near whisper. Initially, Richard Wright lays down a simple and straightforward melodic line on his Farfisa organ, doubling the vocal melody. But as the song unfolds, Wright ventures into some exploratory keyboard work. David Gilmour provides occasional stabs of electric guitar chording, and peppers the song with ambient tones from his guitar as well. Like "Astronomy Dominé," the live reading of "Controls" showcases Pink Floyd's now finely honed skill at employing dynamics—chiefly volume and intensity—to create the desired ambience.

"Set the Controls for the Heart of the Sun" would remain in the band's set list up until tours for *The Dark Side of the Moon* in 1973. It would become a staple of Roger Waters's post–Pink Floyd live set for many years to come as well.

Five days after the Sunday show in Birmingham, Pink Floyd ventured ninety miles north on the M6 motorway for a gig at the College of Commerce in Manchester. The night's set list would be identical to that at Mothers, and the night's recordings would yield two tracks that would see release on *Ummagumma*.

Yet another example of Pink Floyd's shade-and-light approach to musical dynamics, the version of "Careful With That Axe, Eugene" on *Ummagumma* hews closely to the studio recording. Opening with some subtle, rhythmic cymbal tapping by Nick Mason and a two-note (octaves apart) Roger Waters bass line, the rhythm section lays the groundwork upon which Rick Wright enters on Farfisa. With Gilmour adding near-ambient shading on guitar, it's Wright who provides the melodic elements of the first few moments of "Eugene." After more than a minute of instrumental introduction, David Gilmour provides some far-away-sounding scat vocals in a yearning, melancholy fashion. By this point, Mason has settled into a simple rhythmic pattern, mostly on snare, with occasional subtle flourishes on cymbals.

Waters begins to increase the volume and intensity of his two-note bass figure, while he and Mason hasten the song's tempo almost imperceptibly. Waters leans into the vocals to loudly whisper the song's title lyrics—the song's only words—and the music swells. Just after the three-minute mark, Roger Waters lets loose with a terrifying series of screams that sustains for almost a full minute; the band follows suit instrumentally, playing with ferocious intensity while holding fast to the song's still-deliberate pace. Gilmour scat-vocalizes over his guitar, and as the six-minute mark approaches, the foursome settles back into a groove that slowly reduces the musical intensity. Mason punctuates the arrangement with some aggressive drum fills. Near the seven-minute mark, "Careful With That Axe, Eugene" has returned to the spare, quiet ambience of its opening section, with Wright's organ once again dominating the melody. The band plays more and more quietly, taking more than a full minute to approach silence at the song's end, nearly nine minutes after it began.

The group-composed "Careful With That Axe, Eugene" would, in various forms, become a staple of many Pink Floyd projects of the late 1960s and early 1970s. "Eugene" would remain in Pink Floyd's live set through 1973, and another live version is featured in the *Live at Pompeii* concert film; the soundtrack to that 1972 film would receive belated official release as part of the 2016 box set, *The Early Years*.

The last song recorded for *Ummagumma*'s live disc would be the title track from *A Saucerful of Secrets*. Lasting nearly thirteen minutes, the Manchester recording of "Saucerful" demonstrates just how much tighter Pink Floyd has become instrumentally. While all of the work's free-form characteristics remain, there is a sense of purpose that permeates the *Ummagumma* version. The playing remains abstract in places, but there is a palpable sense that the four musicians know where they are going musically; as such, this reading of "Saucerful" feels substantially less improvisational, more deliberate, and thus more effective and conventionally accessible.

"A Saucerful of Secrets" would be performed at various Pink Floyd concerts until it was retired from the band's set list in 1972.

▲

For the second disc of *Ummagumma*, the band decided to allot one half of each album side to each of the four musicians. This highly experimental outing would feature some music that had become part of Pink Floyd's new live set piece, "The Man and the Journey," but none of the works from *Ummagumma*'s second disc would become a long-standing part of the band's live set beyond that.

Presumably inspired by the ancient Greek myth of Sisyphus—the god banished to an eternity of rolling a large stone up a hill only to see it roll back down again—Richard Wright's "Sysyphus" is a four-part work performed almost solely by its composer on keyboard instruments.

Despite its popularity among the more innovative groups of the era (the Beatles, the Zombies, the Moody Blues, King Crimson), the Mellotron would not figure prominently in Richard Wright's keyboard work for Pink Floyd. Each of the organ-style keys on the device triggers playback of magnetic tape; each tape features a recording of musicians playing the relevant note, and available sounds included flute, choir, classical strings, and the like. "Sysyphus, Pt. 1" is a notable exception for Wright, as it features the Mellotron as its central instrument. With a portentous tympani accompaniment, Wright layers multiple Mellotron parts to create a doom-laden introduction to his four-part suite.

As the suite gives way to "Sysyphus, Pt. 2," the tympani and Mellotron fade away, replaced by a piano solo. While the melody of "Sysyphus, Pt. 2" is not especially memorable, it does feature some beautiful piano work from Wright that displays his classical inclinations. Around the halfway mark of the three-plus-minute piece, Wright's piano playing becomes more abstract and atonal; by the two-minute mark, he mixes jazzy, fleet-fingered right-hand work with fist-pounding in the piano's lower register. A few abrasive scrapes of the piano's internal strings and heavy doses of reverberation wrap up the track.

"Sysyphus, Pt. 3" moves completely into abstract territory. Seemingly random stabs on the piano's lower keys, occasional plucks at the instrument's strings, and odd-time-signature percussion are the hall-marks of the track. Some odd sounds redolent of David Gilmour's "humpback whale" guitar effect appear, but all available evidence suggests that Wright worked alone on the track. The cacophony builds to a noisy crescendo, and ends suddenly.

Wright's Mellotron returns for "Sysyphus, Pt. 4," and features a minor-key melody similar to the sounds found on King Crimson's *In the Court of the Crimson King*, recorded two months after Pink Floyd's *Ummagumma*. As the lengthy (near eight-minute) track unfolds, Wright adds vibraphone and organ. Just past the three-minute mark, a loud and violent stab of Mellotron punctures the listener's reverie; rolling drums and crashing cymbals add to the musical maelstrom.

Seconds later, another atonally played collection of instruments begins its work. Here Wright's arrangement sounds quite like the more abstract sections of "A Saucerful of Secrets." Most every instrument that has appeared earlier in the track returns once again, with little sense of order or structure. As the six-minute mark approaches, Wright reprises the low-register theme melody on Mellotron, again supported by tympani. The melody retards and ends with a dramatic flourish, aided by a strike upon a gong.

Roger Waters's solo contributions to *Ummagumma*'s studio disc touch upon both ends of the accessibility spectrum. "Grantchester Meadows" is a pastoral outing that would have fit seamlessly onto the *More* soundtrack. A recording of a chirping skylark extends across the entire length of the song, while Waters sings and plays gently picked acoustic guitar. His contemplative lyrics bear little of the acerbic social commentary that would become the defining characteristic of his later songwriting. An ode to the joys of an idyllic day outdoors, "Grantchester Meadows" represents a musical style that Waters would continue to explore on subsequent Pink Floyd albums (as well as on his outside project, the soundtrack to *The Body*). And the song's guitar style would be echoed strongly on "Goodbye Blue Sky," a track off Pink Floyd's 1979 double album, *The Wall*, though in the latter case the guitar would be played by David Gilmour, not Waters. In 1969 "Grantchester Meadows" would be incorporated into Pink Floyd's "The Man and the Journey" live performances.

"Several Species of Small Furry Animals Gathered Together in a Cave and Grooving with a Pict" represents Roger Waters at his most bizarre and self-indulgent. Not a song in any traditional sense, "Several Species" is merely five minutes of strange sound effects, most created by hand percussion and vocalizing. It's very much a piece with the kind of tracks Waters collaborator Ron Geesin would create for *The Body* soundtrack. Here, Waters taps on a microphone, imitates various animals, wheezes and hums in exceedingly odd fashion, and eventually affects a faux Scottish burr spouting gibberish. When a reporter for the University of Regina *Carillon* in Saskatchewan, Canada, asked Waters about the track in a 1970 interview, he suggested the tune was an attempt to get inside the listener's head. Waters agreed. "And," Waters added, "just push him about a bit, nothing deliberate, not a deliberate blow on the nose, just to sort of mess him around a bit."

David Gilmour would provide the most musically accessible moments on *Ummagumma*'s studio record. His contribution to the album is a three-part track called "The Narrow Way." A corkscrew-like tape-effect electric guitar opens the track, and then shifts quickly into a picked acoustic guitar melody. The track's first section is a variation on the instrumental "Baby Blue Shuffle in D Major," a track performed on the BBC in 1968. Gilmour's multiple guitar overdubs—at least two acoustic guitars and one electric slide—create a sound reminiscent of a twelve-string guitar. Slide guitar would become a defining characteristic of Gilmour's playing for the remainder of his career.

The corkscrew effect returns in the later part of the song's first section, joined by some additional effects-laden sounds. A final guitar figure that suggests a spring uncoiling signals the end of the first part of "The Narrow Way."

The second of three parts of "The Narrow Way" is built around a heavily distorted electric guitar figure, accompanied by hand percussion. As the hypnotic figure is played repeatedly, Gilmour layers more heavily processed guitar sounds atop it. Eventually, the distorted melody fades deep into the aural background, leaving abstract, atonal guitar sounds in its place.

The third and final part of "The Narrow Way" provides the only part of *Ummagumma*'s studio disc that resembles that which most listeners think of as the Pink Floyd "sound." A conventional song—one with lyrics, melody, verses, and chorus—"The Narrow Way, Pt. 3" presents a memorable song that switches between a minor key in its verses and a major key for its chorus. Stately, melancholy, and suitably mysterious and foreboding, "The Narrow Way, Pt. 3" showcases David Gilmour in one-man-band mode; he plays guitar, bass, piano, drums, and sings all of the tune's vocal parts. Gilmour does an especially impressive job of mimicking Nick Mason's drumming style, right down to his trademark tom-tom fills found on countless Pink Floyd tracks.

Nick Mason provides a three-part instrumental work to close *Umma-gumma*. "The Grand Vizier's Garden Party" is, for most of its run time, a drum solo. But the brief first "movement" in the piece—subtitled "Entrance"—features a lovely flute solo played by his wife Lindy. The lengthy middle section ("Entertainment") features odd bits of tuned percussion, gong, brief snippets of conventional drum kit work, and xylophone. A ghostly variation of Lindy Mason's opening figure is re-created on a Mellotron, buried deep in the sonic mix. Were it not for the track's mostly percussive nature, it could be considered ambient. Toward the end of the second part, the track conforms more to a conventional rock drum solo.

Mason began his experiments with tape manipulation when creating "The Grand Vizier's Garden Party," and the experience he gained working on the track would serve him and the group well on future Pink Floyd projects, most notably *The Dark Side of the Moon*.

Released on EMI's new Harvest subsidiary—home to more experi-mental-leaning rock acts—the double LP *Ummagumma* was budget priced to encourage buyers to pick it up. The album reached #5 on the UK album charts, doing equally well in the Netherlands. In the United States, *Ummagumma* made it only as high as #74 on the *Billboard* 200. Its experimental character may have made it ideal for airplay on FM radio stations, but the idea of releasing a single off *Ummagumma* was not even considered by EMI. Writing a decade later in the *Rolling Stone Record Guide*, Bart Testa described *Ummagumma* as "a failed but fascinating experiment in the construction of avant-garde rock." In the pages of *Inside Out*, Nick Mason sums up the *Ummagumma* experience succinctly. "I don't think we were that taken with it," he writes, "but it was fun to make." He goes on to note that the studio disc's individual sections provided evidence that "the parts were not as great as the sum."

Quoted in *Beat Instrumental* in a 1970 interview, Rick Wright gave a quick summary of his thoughts on *Ummagumma*. "It was an experiment," he said. "I don't really know if it worked or not . . . but I like it."

While writing from a jazz-centric point of view (and for a jazz audience), Joachim Berendt wrote briefly about *Ummagumma* in the first English-language edition of his seminal work, *The Jazz Book*. Though less impressed with the group's later work, Berendt—unlike many other music critics of his era—championed the importance of Pink Floyd's 1969 double album. *Ummagumma*, Berendt wrote, "laid the foundations for a cosmic outer-space sound—that, in rock, had a similar function as Sun Ra and His Solar Arkestra in jazz." He went on to note (with some prescience) that the group's work in that era would have "an immense influence on German rock groups," and, adding a further bit of editorializing, "not always for the best."

While Pink Floyd was making *Ummagumma*, the band finally created a quasi-conceptual work for live performance. Constructed largely from existing material—and never seriously considered for release as an album because much of its material had or would soon appear in other forms—"The Man and the Journey" would be the band's first attempt at linking multiple pieces of musical material into a cohesive, thematic work. Though record buyers would never hear "The Man and the Journey" in its original form until 2016, the extended work nonetheless pointed the way forward for Pink Floyd as the 1960s came to a close. And as it would happen, in the twenty-first century, one of those aforementioned German groups would release its own version of the work, calling it Pink Floyd's "lost album."

13

THE MAN AND THE JOURNEY

In late March 1969, Pink Floyd debuted two new suites of music; no recordings exist of that performance, and the next scheduled concert was canceled. But the third planned show—April 14 at London's Royal Festival Hall—would be recorded by an audience member. Most of the music performed on this Monday night wasn't actually new; what *was* new was the manner in which it would be presented.

Wanting to push the boundaries of stage performance in the direction of a show that was at once more structured yet still highlighting the group's experimental tendencies, Pink Floyd went through its existing material and crafted two sets of music based around unified thematic elements. The concert debut of Pink Floyd's "The Man and the Journey" has not been released officially, though film excerpts are included on DVD and Blu-ray in *The Early Years* box set, and audio of the entire performance circulates officially among collectors. But a later performance of "The Man and the Journey" is included in near entirety on *The Early Years*, allowing fans to experience a seminal work on Pink Floyd's creative path toward *The Dark Side of the Moon*.

The term *multimedia* was coined in 1966 by American visual artist and musician Bob Goldstein, and although the word had not yet entered into widespread use by 1970, in retrospect it succinctly describes the presentation that was "The Man and the Journey." Rather than compose a clutch of new material, Pink Floyd set about arranging selected pieces into a form that took on a narrative of sorts.

Much of the material that forms the two suites is instrumental, and audience members would not be provided with anything like a libretto to guide them through the putative narrative. And outside of an occasional "good evening," "thank you," or song announcement, neither Roger Waters nor his band mates directly address the audience between songs. So it is left to the music and onstage activity to convey the ideas the band hopes to put across.

The first part of the live presentation, "The Man," is a sort of distant cousin to the Beatles' 1967 track "A Day in the Life." Pink Floyd's suite aims to portray an everyman's typical day. The Roger Waters tune "Grantchester Meadows"—released on the studio disc of *Ummagumma*—serves as the opening. Retitled, as would be most of the material used for "The Man and the Journey," for the purposes of the performance as "Daybreak," the live performance begins with tape playback of skylark birdsongs. Roger Waters's acoustic guitar forms the basis of the tune. The primary difference between the studio "Grantchester Meadows" and the live "Daybreak" is the latter's more prominent featuring of David Gilmour on acoustic guitar and harmony vocals. Richard Wright reprises his Farfisa solo from the studio version. In all likelihood, although no film exists to verify this, Nick Mason remains offstage for the suite's opening number.

The gentle pastoral reverie of "Daybreak" is rudely punctured by the jarring sound of a whistle, summoning laborers to the start of their day jobs. This performance piece—one of a select few not based on existing material—is titled appropriately enough as "Work." While Nick Mason lays down an insistent and forceful beat—one heavy on bass drum and hand-muted cymbal—Richard Wright plays all manner of clattering percussion, including vibraphone. Waters and Gilmour have put down their musical instruments, and instead have picked up various hand tools, including saws and hammers; rhythmic interplay and faux day labor ensues, with Gilmour and Waters assembling a table. On the Amsterdam tape, "Work" continues for four minutes; at the Royal Festival Hall five months earlier, the piece had extended over eight minutes; it's likely that the group noticed audience attention flagging and shortened the "Work" period.

Though it is not documented on the officially released Amsterdam concert tapes (nor on any of the tour tapes circulating among collectors), in the British tradition, "Teatime" follows "Work." As part of "The

Man and the Journey," "Teatime" consists of Waters, Wright, Gilmour, and Mason taking seats onstage and being served tea by the band's roadies. It's quite possible that "Teatime" took place simultaneously to the second half of "Work."

"Afternoon" comes next. Though the studio recording of this song—eventually known as "Biding My Time"—would not be released until its inclusion on the 1971 compilation LP *Relics*, it was recorded in July 1969, just after the *Ummagumma* sessions were completed. Along with "San Tropez" and "Seamus" (both on *Meddle*), "Biding My Time" is one of the most anomalous songs in the Pink Floyd canon. Closer to cocktail jazz with a blues foundation than to anything in the rock idiom, "Biding My Time" is a lighthearted, wistful piece in which David Gilmour's facility at playing so-called jazz chords is showcased. If Waters's "Biding My Time" (or "Afternoon") is a pastiche of non-rock styles, it's a loving one, full of understanding with regard to what makes such an arrangement work.

Both live onstage as part of "The Man" and on its studio release, the track builds in energy with each repeated verse (there is no chorus as such). And in a move that must have caught early audiences by surprise, "Afternoon" features Richard Wright on trombone. Gilmour turns up the blues feel of the song on later instrumental verses; by its conclusion, the song has shed all of its jazz feel, reverting to midtempo blues rock. But its playful nature remains intact.

After the solid rhythm of "Afternoon," a song that is (uncharacteristically for Pink Floyd) suitable for dancing, "Doing It" comes next. An instrumental, largely percussive work, "Doing It" is likely based upon Nick Mason's "The Grand Vizier's Garden Party (Part 2: Entertainment)" from *Ummagumma*. Roger Waters adds percussion of his own, and David Gilmour provides occasional splashes of effects-laden guitar. Occasional, unintelligible pre-recorded voices are heard. Mason would employ similar techniques—a drum foundation with assorted sound effects and non-musical elements—for "Speak to Me," the opening track on 1973's *The Dark Side of the Moon*.

The opening strains of "Sleeping" may sound familiar to listeners acquainted with *The Dark Side of the Moon*. The recorded sounds of a ticking clock and heavy breathing provide the introduction to the tune. Eventually, Richard Wright's vibraphone enters the sonic landscape, joined by David Gilmour's eerie guitar lines. "Sleeping" represents the first point in Pink Floyd's "The Man and the Journey" in which the band sounds much at all like its early improvisational works "Astronomy Dominé" and "Interstellar Overdrive." Gilmour employs a guitar effect redolent of birds. Especially in its later moments, "Sleeping" bears some surface similarities to "Quicksilver" from Pink Floyd's *More* soundtrack.

Live onstage, "Sleeping" segues seamlessly into "Nightmare." For only the third time in "The Man," a song with lyrics is used to move the narrative along. "Nightmare" is an extended "Cymbaline" (also originally from the *More* soundtrack album), rearranged and extended. In sharp contrast to the quiet and understated acoustic studio version, the onstage "Nightmare" adopts a soaring, electric arrangement that provides David Gilmour the opportunity to showcase not one but two of his trademark expressive lead guitar solos. Richard Wright's Farfisa solos—he takes two as well—have more in common with the studio recording, displaying a character that is both contemplative and exploratory. Nick Mason's drumming is deeply expressive, and helps to guide the arrangement through its various parts that are in turn moody and exuberant. Even after "The Man and the Journey" set piece would be retired, "Cymbaline" would remain a central component of Pink Floyd's live set for some time.

An alarm clock rings, waking the piece's putative central character from his dreams. The ticking of a clock is once again heard, signaling the beginning of yet another day for the Man. "The Man" thus ends with this short piece, titled "Labyrinth."

Official and unofficial recordings from "The Man and the Journey" tour show that Pink Floyd did not take a break—or even pause for more than a few seconds—between the end of "The Man" and the start of "The Journey," the second suite of songs performed live. Whereas "The Man" is conceptually based in the workaday life of a character meant to represent everyone, "The Journey" is a more abstract work, a musical representation of a mystical (some might say psychedelic) odyssey through an otherworldly landscape. Once again, the conceptual work is built around already existing material, including one number that dates back to Pink Floyd's *The Piper at the Gates of Dawn* era.

Fittingly enough, "The Journey" suite begins with "The Beginning," otherwise known as "Green is the Colour" from the *More* soundtrack (fertile ground indeed for sourcing "The Man and the Journey" material). David Gilmour plays electric guitar instead of acoustic, and Richard Wright plays piano. With greater musical force and energy overall, the live reading leans more in a rock direction than its studio counterpart. Gilmour provides some "do do do" scat vocalizing that more or less doubles his lead guitar lines.

As "The Beginning" reaches a crescendo, the mood changes suddenly; Pink Floyd is now playing the wordless "Beset by Creatures of the Deep," otherwise known as "Careful With That Axe, Eugene." Roger Waters stays silent when he would customarily whisper "careful . . ." but still screams at the song's halfway point. Gilmour contributes some additional scat vocals, once again using his lead guitar melody as a guide. The song fades out to the whooshing sound of wind.

David Gilmour's "The Narrow Way, Part 3" is notable as the only track in "The Man and the Journey" that never went by an alternate title. The live version is quite similar to the *Ummagumma* studio recording, save that here the entire band plays. Most existing live recordings of the song demonstrate that Gilmour—still a relatively new lyricist—may have written a vocal melody that pushed the limits of his voice; he strains badly to reach many of the high notes in the song's chorus. Though some songs from the tour would remain in Pink Floyd's repertoire well into the future, once the run of "The Man and the Journey" dates concluded in June 1969, "The Narrow Way, Part 3" would be retired from Pink Floyd's live set.

Pink Floyd may have called the next song "The Pink Jungle," but to most listeners' ears, it's a faithful reading of "Pow R. Toc H.," one of the few 1967 Pink Floyd tracks not composed solely by Syd Barrett (it's credited to Barrett, Waters, Wright, and Mason). While the live performance of "Pow R. Toc H." maintains all of the original's mayhem, it does display Pink Floyd's substantially more assured and controlled instrumental work.

The recorded sound of someone—or something—careening earthward from the sky and into what sounds like a roiling cauldron leads the listener into "The Labyrinths of Auximines." Similar to the instrumental midsection of *A Saucerful of Secrets'* "Let There Be More Light," the track features a hypnotic Roger Waters bass line and Nick Mason's deliberate mallet work. Richard Wright conjures celestial tones from his organ, and Gilmour brings forth malevolent sonics using a slide on his heavily effected electric guitar.

Three minutes of what is noted as "Footsteps/Doors" follows. By manipulating the joystick control of his Azimuth Coordinator, Rick Wright is able to control sound distribution through four speaker clusters situated about the concert hall. With the Azimuth Coordinator, Wright creates the "quadrophonic" audio illusion of someone walking down a hall, up stairs, closer, and farther away from the audience. Even once "The Man and the Journey" tour came to an end, Pink Floyd would continue to make use of these three-dimensional sound effects as part of their live shows.

"Behold the Temple of Light" is an instrumental piece largely based upon previously unheard material. The opening strains of the tune are similar to the very beginning of "The Narrow Way, Part 3," but the remainder of the tune is closer to the feel of the band's *More* soundtrack material, albeit played here in a much more forceful and electric manner. Mason serves up multiple flourishes on cymbal and gong; Wright plays an organ solo that climbs and descends; Gilmour plays long, sustaining chords that serve more as rhythmic accompaniment than a solo. Eventually the song dissolves into near silence.

"The Man and the Journey" ends in dramatic style with "The End of the Beginning," otherwise known as the elegiac "A Saucerful of Secrets, Pt. IV: Celestial Voices." Richard Wright's majestic Hammond organ provides the foundation of the piece. As the song unfolds, Wright's band mates join in one at a time, adding texture, increasing the volume and intensity of the performance. Roger Waters's bass guitar leads the way, followed by Nick Mason (first on tympani, then on full drum kit), with David Gilmour's electric guitar completing the instrumental scene. After an assured Nick Mason drum fill, Gilmour adds wordless vocals, Wright solos under the vocal line, and Pink Floyd plays "The End of the Beginning" to its conclusion.

By the time "The Man and the Journey" tour wrapped, Pink Floyd had performed the work nearly thirty times, on stages in England, Northern Ireland, and West Germany. On a few occasions, the band would—after a brief thank-you—return to the stage to play an encore, a practice that had not generally been part of the group's onstage set. Those rare encores generally featured older material such as "Set the Controls for the Heart of the Sun" (from 1968's *A Saucerful of Secrets*) or "Interstellar Overdrive" from Pink Floyd's 1967 debut LP.

Those who witnessed "The Man and the Journey" tour, or subsequent dates that featured parts of the work, were often impressed by its ambitious and somewhat unconventional nature, as well as its combining of visuals, extra-musical audio elements, improvisation, and paced structure. Bassist Lee Jackson of the Nice tried to describe the scene to *NME*'s Richard Green in January 1970. Referring to "Work" and "Teatime," he said, "They had an amazing percussion thing with tea cups, nails, hammers and saws and things."

Lon Goddard—by this time a music journalist—saw Pink Floyd at the National Jazz & Blues Festival at Plumpton Racetrack in 1969, a show at which the band performed "The Journey" section of its live production. Having first seen the group with Syd Barrett at London's Middle Earth in 1966, he could not help but marvel at the change in the band's sound. "They were doing lots of stuff that was very patterned," he says, "which to me was a vast improvement."

Reviewing the Royal Albert Hall date, Chris Welch described the scene this way in *Melody Maker*: "A silent, attentive crowd, joss sticks waving, a huge gong booming, and the Pink Floyd looning." Praising the group's gentle sense of humor, he noted, "The Floyd don't claim to be great individual technicians, but between their collective playing and writing ability, and the secrets of the Azimuth Coordinator stereo sound effects system, they can create an unforgettable musical experience."

As a concert event, "The Man and the Journey" was an experiment that did indeed work. But when considered as a source of material and inspiration for a new studio album, it was found lacking. Nick Mason admitted as much when discussing the project forty-seven years later. "I think it was a bit too advanced, even for us," he told the French-language *Rock & Folk*. "It worked onstage, but there was not enough stuff for people to buy it on disc."

Though "The Man and the Journey" would remain among Pink Floyd's least-known works, its underground influence would persist. German rock group RPWL formed in 1997 initially as a Pink Floyd tribute group playing the latter's most well-known songs to appreciative audiences across Europe. By 2000, RPWL had transitioned into playing its own original music, but the influence of Pink Floyd pervaded those songs. As a side project between release of its eleventh and twelfth albums, RPWL scheduled live dates in Germany and the Netherlands, setting aside the original material in favor of something quite different: a start-to-finish performance of "The Man and the Journey." "I'm still impressed about how Pink Floyd began, and the roots of this music," says Yogi Lang, the band's keyboardist, vocalist, and, with guitarist Kalle Wallner, founding member. The band wanted to respond to its fans' repeated call to cover Pink Floyd live in concert, but wished to do it in a different way. Lang decided, "let's do it really as a historic thing, and bring the people what they may not know."

More than forty years after its premiere, "The Man and the Journey" had lost none of its edge. As presented by RPWL, the work would confuse, entertain, and fascinate concert audiences. Lang laughs as he recalls reaction to "Teatime." "Everyone there said, 'What the hell are they doing? They're doing a break! They're doing a tea break on stage!'" RPWL's choice of concert venues—theaters, much like the rooms in which the original work was presented—offered the intimate vibe necessary for "The Man and the Journey." Lang contrasts that audience–band connection with Pink Floyd's 1979–1980 tour for *The Wall*. "In '69 there was a connection; you felt that they were playing for the audience, and the audience [was] reacting."

RPWL added some of its own character to the performances, most notably during the non-musical numbers like "Work." Lang says that the musical textures the band brought forth were designed to complement the onstage visuals of him and his band mates with saws and hammers. "We thought of what the Floyd did: to make noises that combine this music with this work thing that isn't nice," he says. "The sound of work doesn't sound 'nice,' this was a mixture of that."

The concerts were successful, and on October 28, 2016—two weeks before Pink Floyd released *The Early Years* with its own live recording of the show—the German group released *RPWL Plays Pink Floyd's "The Man and the Journey"* on CD and DVD. Lang views the original 1969 concerts as a pivotal point in Pink Floyd's development. "It's the beginning of the new Floyd," he says, "not only of the songs but also of thinking about how music should be and how music should be presented to people." He sees a direct line between the conceptual presentation of "The Man and the Journey" and later works, specifically *The*

Dark Side of the Moon and *The Wall*. And he notes that flow and structure became even more important for the band, even when a concept wasn't central, noting that when one listens to the work, "you have this feeling that the first song is the first song, and the last song was the last song."

Ummagumma would be released four months after the final "The Man and the Journey" show at London's Royal Albert Hall; the two-suite presentation would never again figure in the band's live show, but much was learned through the experience of developing and playing "The Man and the Journey." Its ideas about thematic linking, however tenuous, would inform many of Pink Floyd's projects to come, culminating in 1973's seamlessly unified work, *The Dark Side of the Moon*.

Part IV

Crumbling Land (1970)

14

LOVE SCENES

With "The Man and the Journey" and *Ummagumma* behind them, the four members of Pink Floyd could begin their next project, the soundtrack for Michelangelo Antonioni's *Zabriskie Point*. But the group had taken part in another soundtrack project of sorts mere days after wrapping "The Man and the Journey" tour. Invited by the British Broadcasting Corporation to play along to film footage of the United States' *Apollo 11* moon landing, the group traveled to BBC TV Centre's Studio 5 in London. An hour-long episode of the program *Omnibus* titled "So What if It's Just Green Cheese?" was broadcast at 10 p.m. on Sunday, July 20, 1969, minutes after the NASA lunar module *Eagle* touched down on the moon's Sea of Tranquility.

For the broadcast, Pink Floyd would improvise five minutes' worth of music, likely using some musical ideas that the group had been kicking around as potential song ideas. The improvisation—known among collectors as "Moonhead" and released officially in 2016 (as part of the Pink Floyd box set *The Early Years 1965–1972*) with that same title— has as its central motif a funky, minor-key Roger Waters bass line and melody. In revised and expanded form, the work would show up again two and a half years later as one of the band's signature tunes, *The Dark Side of the Moon*'s "Money."

David Gilmour recalled the experience in a short 2009 essay for *The Guardian*. "There was a panel of scientists on one side of the studio, with us on the other," Gilmour wrote. "I was 23." Good-naturedly dismissing the piece as "a nice, atmospheric, spacey, 12-bar blues"—and ignoring its embryonic "Money" bass line—he wrote that Pink Floyd "didn't make any songs out of the jam session," and that the improvisation "didn't have a significant impact on our later work."

In that same essay, Gilmour did recognize that in its own way "Moonhead" may have signaled the end of one Pink Floyd era and the beginning of another. He wrote that lyricist Roger Waters "was looking more into going inwards, going into the inner space of the human mind and condition. And I think ['Moonhead'] was sort of the end of our exploration into outer space."

In late fall 1969, Pink Floyd set aside studio time—both in London's EMI Studios and, for the first time, in Italy—for just over a month. The goal would be to create music for *Zabriskie Point*, a film by multiple-award-winning Italian film director Michelangelo Antonioni. And like "Moonhead," the *Zabriskie Point* soundtrack sessions would yield a landmark piece of music. This time, it would come from the band's dark horse—keyboardist Richard Wright—and would find new life as part of another major tune in the band's body of work, "Us and Them" from *The Dark Side of the Moon*.

By the time Waters, Gilmour, Mason, and Wright arrived in Italy, they were old hands at the task of making music for films. Through their experiences with *The Committee* and *More*, the band had learned a great deal about the process of crafting music-to-order to fit the demands of a director. But Antonioni employed a more hands-on approach than did Peter Sykes or Barbet Schroeder. As Nick Mason recalled in *Inside Out*, "The problem was that Michelangelo wanted total control, and since he couldn't make the music himself he exercised control by selection." Thus began an arduous and ultimately frustrating back-and-forth between band and director; Pink Floyd would end up recording multiple versions of several tracks in hope of delivering whatever it was that the director wanted.

The band went so far as to create multi-channel mixes of several songs, allowing Antonioni the ability to manipulate the channel faders in the studio control room, adding or subtracting instrumental parts that changed each song's character to his liking. But even after going to such lengths, the director was not satisfied. In his biography of Pink Floyd, Nicholas Schaffner amusingly cites Roger Waters's recollection of presenting tracks for the director's approval. "Eet's very beautiful," he quoted Antonioni as saying, "but eet's too sad." Or, "Eet's too stroong." Waters summed up the experience as "sheer hell."

In the end, only three Pink Floyd songs would be used in the film. Instead, Antonioni selected an odd, seemingly random assortment of already existing tracks by artists including Patti Page (the 1950 hit single "Tennessee Waltz") and "I Wish I Was a Single Girl Again" by high-lonesome folk singer Roscoe Holcomb.

Adding insult to injury—though Pink Floyd did get its travel expenses covered—when the *Zabriskie Point* soundtrack LP appeared on MGM Records, the band was third-billed behind the Grateful Dead and Kaleidoscope. Notoriously unhip MGM Records president Mike Curb ended his LP liner note essay with a prescriptive message: "The film and the music are not really meant to be understood, but to be lived."

The three Pink Floyd tracks that did appear in the *Zabriskie Point* film and soundtrack LP are nonetheless worthy of note. "Heart Beat, Pig Meat" is based upon a hypnotic, cymbal-less drum beat from Nick Mason. Atop that repetitive, almost looped-sounding percussion, Richard Wright adds simple yet melodic single-note runs on his Farfisa organ. Neither Roger Waters's bass nor David Gilmour's guitar is audible on the track; additional interest is provided by flown-in bits of sound effects and dialogue—and even brief snippets of orchestra music—from the film. The version that appears onscreen is mixed in mono and runs slightly longer than its LP counterpart; some of the found sounds are different between the two versions, as well.

"Crumbing Land" is one of the tracks for which Pink Floyd would create multiple versions and/or mixes. As released in the *Zabriskie Point* film, the song has a West Coast folk rock vibe, with instrumental hints of the Grateful Dead, and massed high vocal harmonies—mostly courtesy of David Gilmour—that strongly recall Crosby, Stills & Nash. "Crumbling Land" would not have been out of place on the soundtrack for Barbet Schroeder's *More*. The recording included on the soundtrack LP brings Roger Waters's bouncy, insistent bass line forward in the mix, with Nick Mason tapping along, mostly on hi-hat. That version's midsection has a dreamy interlude much more in keeping with the customary Pink Floyd sound; a gong signals a return to the main melody.

Multiple versions of "Crumbling Land" exist, both released (including one on *The Early Years*) and unreleased (on bootlegs). Some run as long as nearly six minutes; perhaps the most interesting outtake is an unreleased version featuring a rock (electric, full-band) introduction; it's essentially a different song, albeit one very much in the style of Buffalo Springfield, with Gilmour playing in a more "twangy" manner than is his usual style, and thunderous tom-tom runs from Nick Mason. After about a minute, the rock arrangement segues into the familiar folky section.

The third and last Pink Floyd track in *Zabriskie Point* would be used for the film's climactic and explosive final scene. Yet unlike "Crumbling Land" and "Heart Beat, Pig Meat," "Come In, Number 51, Your Time Is Up" is not truly a new work. Instead, it's yet another permutation of "Careful With That Axe, Eugene." For the film, Waters leaves out the title phrase (as he did when the tune was called "Beset By Creatures of the Deep" and part of "The Man and the Journey" set piece), and the band plays in a different key than on the original. Here, Roger Waters's whispering is more prominent, as is David Gilmour's wordless, high-register vocalizing. Waters's bloodcurdling scream—and the accompanying musical mayhem—is used in the film to coincide with the highly stylized, slow-motion depiction of an explosion, and—even against the backdrop of so little of the band's music being used in the finished movie—represents one of the most effective uses of Pink Floyd's music on the silver screen.

It's pointless nearly half a century after the fact to relitigate Michelangelo Antonioni's decision to use so little of what he had hired Pink Floyd to create for *Zabriskie Point*, but fans of the band's work have for years compiled and shared all available unused tracks and alternate versions. Nearly thirty minutes' worth of these appeared in 2016 as part of the massive Pink Floyd box set, *The Early Years*. While some of the recordings had circulated among collectors, others could be heard for the first time.

The first *Zabriskie Point* outtake on *The Early Years* is the brief "On the Highway." It's nothing more than a retitled snippet of "Crumbling Land" that seems to end prematurely. "Auto Scene Version 2" is an instrumental featuring Richard Wright playing a pretty, chord-based melody on a harpsichord; a version including Nick Mason's count-in and a brief announcement from the studio control room circulated among collectors for years under the speculative title "Country Song." As the bootleg track ends, someone in the control booth can be heard telling Wright, "Okay, come hear it."

Despite its title, "Auto Scene Version 3" is a very different tune. Much simpler and more straightforward than most Pink Floyd compositions, it's a boogie rock number that features a prominent and driving Waters bass line and a slightly jazzy organ part from Rick Wright that is redolent of Brian Auger's Trinity.

Long known among collectors—since its appearance on the 1972 bootleg LP *Omayyad*—by the (again speculative) title "Fingal's Cave," "Aeroplane" opens with the slowly unfolding sound of a gong, possibly tape-reversed. The whole band enters, with David Gilmour's winding, heavily distorted guitar as the sonic centerpiece. Richard Wright's over-dubbed organ and harpsichord are low in the mix (another still-unreleased alternate mix seems to have some Mellotron keyboard sounds as well). "Aeroplane" is easily the hardest-rocking track from the *Zabriskie Point* sessions, and the uncharacteristically metallic number can be thought of in that sense as a musical cousin to "The Nile Song" from the *More* soundtrack.

"Explosion" is still another version of "Careful With That Axe, Eugene," complete with David Gilmour's high-register moaning serving as a counterpoint to his initially subtle lead guitar lines. Roger Waters plays two notes an octave apart, and Nick Mason lays down a solid beat. Richard Wright's organ provides an interesting melodic line in the song's first half; after the crescendo, David Gilmour plays some lead guitar lines that are more conventionally rock-oriented compared to other versions of the tune.

"The Riot Scene" is easily the most noteworthy previously unreleased track from the *Zabriskie Point* sessions. Known among collectors as "The Violent Sequence," the short track is a stately piano melody from Richard Wright. Much unlike anything that had come before in the Pink Floyd catalog, "The Riot Scene" features only Wright on piano with a bit of sympathetic bass guitar by Roger Waters. The instrumental is unmistakably the basis—both in its verse and chorus sections—for "Us and Them," a track that would appear (with lyrics by Roger Waters) on 1973's *The Dark Side of the Moon*. As Nick Mason wrote of the

Zabriskie Point sessions in *Inside Out*, "We quietly gathered up all our out-takes. There was sure to be some opportunity to use them in the future."

At just under two minutes, "Looking at Map" is a country-flavored piano melody with band accompaniment, a tune that once again hearkens back to Pink Floyd's *More* sessions. David Gilmour provides some soothing do-do-do vocalizing; his electric guitar and Wright's piano engage in sympathetic—if simple—melodic runs.

Pink Floyd would record at least seven different tunes titled "Love Scene." While none were included in the finished film, two versions ("Version 4" and "Version 6") appear on Rhino Entertainment's 1997 expanded CD reissue of the film soundtrack. More musical sketches or improvisations than actual songs, some of these—like "Version 7"— sound a great deal like parts of "The Narrow Way, Part 3" from *Ummagumma*. "Love Scene Version 7" features David Gilmour on at least two acoustic guitars, and possibly as many electric guitars. There is neither bass nor drums on the track, and percussion is minimal, featuring only a brushed snare.

The melancholy "Love Scene Version 1" is built around a sustained series of organ notes from Richard Wright. Gilmour adds some ghostly, high-pitched electric guitar, applying echo effects to the signal.

"Love Scene Version 2" is remarkably similar to "Version 1" save for the subtle addition of more guitar, vibraphone, and percussion. Confusingly, the melody of both "Love Scene (Take 1)" and "Love Scene (Take 2)" circulated for decades among collectors, among whom it was known as "Love Scene #4." It's a vaguely jazzy mood piece featuring Richard Wright's piano and vibraphone.

The hard-rocking "Take Off" is a one-minute, one-chord jam featuring Nick Mason's pummeling drums, an exploratory Farfisa run by Richard Wright, a two-note bass line from Waters, and screaming guitar from David Gilmour. "Take Off Version 2" is a straightforward rock tune; it doesn't rock as hard as "Auto Scene Version 3," but it's otherwise similar in its approach.

"Unknown Song (Take 1)" circulated on the traders' circuit for years under the speculative title "Rain in the Country." Another multiple-guitar instrumental, it is very much of a piece with David Gilmour's solo section on *Ummagumma*. But as it unfolds, the song provides additional interest in the form of Gilmour's band mates joining him. The melody doesn't go anywhere, but as a folk-leaning tune in the *More* tradition, it's effective at setting a mood, and perhaps with Roger Waters adding lyrics, could have developed into a fully formed song.

The Early Years' "Crumbling Land (Take 1)" is similar to the unreleased "rock" version of the song discussed previously, albeit without the rock introduction. It's also taken at a quicker pace.

Still unreleased—even after the exhaustive *The Early Years* project—are two takes of one of the most unusual recordings from Pink Floyd's *Zabriskie Point* sessions. At nearly eight minutes, "Love Scene #2" and "Love Scene #3" are also the lengthiest recordings from the Rome sessions. The tracks, likely different mixes of a single recording, both feature Wright's organ and vibraphone creating a static, sonic landscape; the net effect is not unlike the opening moments of "Shine On You Crazy Diamond" from Pink Floyd's 1975 LP, *Wish You Were Here*. The track anticipates Brian Eno's ambient musical excursions of the 1970s as well as the synthesizer-based tone poems of German group Tangerine Dream. David Gilmour provides muted guitar textures, and Nick Mason supplies dramatic swells of gong. "Love Scene #2" (not to be confused with the now-released "Love Scene [Take 2]" discussed above) features wordless moaning and gasping—from Roger Waters and David Gilmour—explicitly simulating the sex act. At one point, just before some ecstatic screams, one of the musicians gasps, "Penetration!" The track ends with uncontrollable laughing as Waters comments on the session, "Fucking long three minutes . . . and I *do* mean fucking!"

Though Michelangelo Antonioni was a darling of the film community around this time—thanks in large part to the success of his 1966 film, *Blow-Up*—*Zabriskie Point* was both a commercial and critical disappointment. The film's overall personality sat between two styles: the art-house film that its director had hoped to make, and the American International Pictures–style youth-exploitation movies for which the Curb-led MGM often provided soundtracks. Still, some reviewers did take note of the effective use of Pink Floyd's music in the film. Reviewing *Zabriskie Point* for Atlanta-based underground paper *Great Speckled Bird*, Steve Wise wrote of the "awesome, pounding, soaring music which accompanied that symbolic instantaneous blow-up of the bourgeoisie," describing its sheer emotional impact and calling it "rock music at its best."

For its part, when Pink Floyd decamped Rome, Italy's Technicolor Sound Services in late November 1969, the band believed its music would form the core of *Zabriskie Point*'s soundtrack. Some additional sessions took place back in London at EMI's Abbey Road studios in mid-December, after which the band considered the project complete. Speaking the following month to a writer for *Beat Instrumental*, Waters said, "We've done the complete score with the exception of a few bits of canned music." *Zabriskie Point*, he said, "seems to be an excellent film." In the same story, Richard Wright said, "*Zabriskie Point* should attract more offers, because working with Antonioni is starting at the top for us."

Once the film was released, Pink Floyd's disappointment with the project was manifest. Speaking with a Pasadena, California, disc jockey in 1971, Nick Mason said, "it was a huge disappointment to us. There were things that we might have did which we really thought were better than what eventually went on." Richard Wright chimed in: "I don't know really what's going on with that movie."

After putting its creative energies into making music to someone else's specifications—and finding that work-product unused—it was once again time for Pink Floyd to begin work on an album of its own. But no new material was yet at hand. *Ummagumma* had been half live performance of older material and half experiments, and *Zabriskie Point* was a work for hire. And however effective it might have been in live concert, "The Man and the Journey" was a stitched-together suite of existing material. It had been several months since the band had added a new piece of music to its live show.

With EMI/Harvest ready for another album, something had to give. In the end, Pink Floyd would do something it had never done previously (and for that matter, would never again do). The band would rely upon an outside composer for fresh ideas. But before embarking on that project, the members of Pink Floyd would put their energies into additional outside projects.

15

NO GOOD TRYING

In early 1968, mere months after Syd Barrett left (or was dismissed from) Pink Floyd, his management team of Peter Jenner and Andrew King encouraged him to begin work on a solo album. Upon Barrett's exit from Pink Floyd, Jenner and King had cast their lot with Barrett, believing that the prime architect of Pink Floyd—and its primary song-writer—had the better potential for ongoing creative and commercial success. In a 1996 interview, Rick Wright recalled that the band's managers "thought Syd and I were the musical brains of the group, and that we should form a breakaway band, to try and hold Syd together." Barrett's managers thought that his unschooled approach would combine effectively with Wright's more traditional musical foundation. "I doubt if Syd could read music," Jenner says. He had observed Wright's strengths within the context of Pink Floyd. "Rick could read music; he knew what chords were. He was always the one who set the harmonies and things in the studio," Jenner recalls. "If we said, 'let's have some backing vocals,' he would be the one who would get the notes together for them."

That January, Wright and Barrett were sharing a flat in southwest London. "Believe me," Wright told interviewer Mark Blake, "I would have left with him like a shot if I had thought Syd could do it." But by most accounts, Barrett could not.

Jenner had seen potential in the few songs Syd had written near the end of his time with Pink Floyd, though he was fully aware that the material was not of an especially commercial nature. "As his songwriting became more interesting, it also became more sort of weird and psychotic," Jenner says. "It wasn't what the record company wanted." An attempt was made to get Syd—now a solo artist—into the studio. But early recording sessions with Jenner producing yielded little suitable for release; the producer would later admit that he had underestimated the difficulty of working with Barrett in his current state. Today, Jenner says that working with Syd reminded him of the electric trolleys he encountered as a child in postwar London.

"You'd stand there in the fog and you couldn't see anything," Jenner says. "Trolley buses were silent; they were electric, so this light would come toward you out of the fog, and then it would disappear away again into the fog. And I always thought that that's what had happened to Syd in the studio. Something would emerge from what he was doing, and we'd say, 'Oh, that's good! Can we get more of that, please? Can you do that again?' And then he would go back into the fog. And then the next time he came out of the fog, it was something different." Shortly after those abortive May 1968 sessions, Barrett returned to Cambridge and went under psychiatric care.

By the end of the year, Syd seemed well enough to return to work on recording his debut album. The project was handed off to Malcolm Jones, the head of Harvest Records, EMI's progressive subsidiary label. Sessions with Jones producing took place in April 1969, focusing on both new recordings and overdubs and edits to the 1968 tapes. Barrett enlisted the help of friend Willie Wilson from Jokers Wild, David Gilmour's old band.

"I knew Syd from when I lived in Cambridge," Wilson recalls, noting that Barrett sometimes sat in with Jokers Wild. Once David Gilmour joined Pink Floyd, he, Wilson, and Syd all lived in close proximity to one another. "Syd just said to me one day, 'I'm going into Abbey Road in a few days' time; will you come and play drums on a couple of tracks?'"

The handful of recordings in which Wilson took part would initially feature only him and Barrett at EMI's Abbey Road. "It was a huge, cavernous studio. I had my drums, and Syd had his Telecaster." Wilson's friend Jerry Shirley—drummer for Humble Pie—was at Abbey Road as well. "I was a chauffeur," Shirley says with a laugh. "You couldn't rely on Syd to get himself there. They needed somebody reliable to make sure Syd got to Abbey Road. I had a car, and Willie had a license."

"After we recorded the tracks, it was then decided that bass was needed," Wilson says, "So Jerry got the job." "They needed a bass player and there wasn't one," Shirley recalls. "But there was a bass. So I picked it up and played it."

"But because of Syd's erratic chord changes—and Jerry not being an actual bass player—he found it really hard," Wilson says. He describes Shirley's bass on those tracks as "a bit of hit and miss as far as the particular note he should be hitting." Shirley recalls adding "percussion bits and pieces" for several tracks on *The Madcap Laughs* as well.

Even though *The Madcap Laughs* sessions represented the first time Wilson had been in a recording studio, Syd's loose style of playing didn't present a challenge for the drummer. "Not having to follow a chord sequence, it didn't really make a lot of difference to me," he says. "Syd was fine rhythmically." Comparing Barrett's approach to meter with that of old blues men, Wilson says, "if it sounds right in your head, then you do it that way." Shirley concurs. "That was Syd all over. He was obviously listening to a lot of blues when he was younger."

Barrett didn't offer much in the way of direction for Wilson, leaving him free to sort out his own drum parts on the Jones-produced sessions. "I don't seem to remember too much of anybody saying, 'This is what you should do,' or, 'That's what you should do.' So I just played as I played at the time."

Later sessions involved overdubs to Barrett solo recordings; those featured three members of Soft Machine: bassist Hugh Hopper, keyboardist Mike Ratledge and drummer Robert Wyatt. These sessions, too, were fraught, as Barrett's idiosyncratic approach to songwriting, coupled with his mental instability, made communication and progress difficult. Though they would yield recordings for use on the final album, in general those sessions with Malcolm Jones producing didn't go well, and by the end of May 1969, Jones had given up. Wilson says that Jones "found it a bit hard going; he couldn't quite keep up with Syd, the way that Syd was. So Dave and Roger took over production on that."

Barrett had approached his old friend David Gilmour—then on holiday in Ibiza, Spain, the setting for the Barbet Schroeder film *More*— and asked him and Roger Waters to produce. They agreed, and scheduled overdub and recording sessions on spare days between live performances and post-production work on Pink Floyd's *Ummagumma*.

On its January 1970 release, *The Madcap Laughs* would feature thirteen original Syd Barrett songs; the finished product was an attempt to organize the hodgepodge of recordings Barrett made over the previous year and a half. Five of the finished tracks bear a Gilmour–Waters production credit; two others are listed as Barrett–Gilmour productions. Most of the remainder is sourced from the Malcolm Jones sessions of April 1969, with one track ("Late Night") featuring a Jones-overdubbed take of a recording from the earliest sessions produced by Peter Jenner.

Though neither Gilmour nor Waters had any official production credits prior to 1969, the band's work on the *More* soundtrack at Pye Studios had given the pair a good deal of hands-on experience behind the recording console. Jerry Shirley says that by this time Gilmour "had already grasped what it took to be an excellent engineer and then producer. He was learning as he went. I'm sure that whole experience was a huge learning curve for him."

Unlike the Jones-produced sessions, most of the songs overseen by Gilmour and Waters would be solo performances featuring only Syd Barrett's voice and acoustic guitar. Production duties, then, would have less to do with technical matters and more to do with marshaling a suitable performance from Barrett. Syd's unwillingness to conform to conventional rules of song structure and meter meant that no two takes of a song were the same, so the idea of post-production editing-together of acceptable sections from multiple takes could not even be considered; Gilmour and Waters would instead have to coax several takes out of their charge, and select from among those.

The haunting "Dark Globe" employs Barrett's signature unconventional compositional approach, and the solo performance would appear unadorned on the record. "Long Gone" features Barrett's overdubbed vocal harmonies and a sympathetic organ part supporting his acoustic guitar melody; it features one of Barrett's strongest lyrics and an unusually disciplined musical approach.

The very brief "She Took a Long Cold Look" finds Barrett wedding a simple folk-style acoustic guitar part to his typically stream-of-consciousness lyrics; the take threatens to break down at the halfway point, but Barrett catches himself and continues. The song ends suddenly, to the sound of Barrett flipping the pages of a notebook. After a message from the control room ("'Feel,' take one"), Barrett delivers a disjointed tune featuring oblique lyrics and seemingly random chord sequences. "If It's in You" is even less disciplined; it's barely a song, and sports an odd vocal melody; the recording includes a snippet of Barrett speaking, expressing frustration at the manner in which the session is progressing.

The pair of tracks noted as Barrett–Gilmour productions ("Octopus" and "Golden Hair") are the product of a more conventionally fruitful session several weeks earlier, in mid-June 1969. Though additional "Golden Hair" musicians aren't listed on the album sleeve, it's possible that an uncredited Rick Wright provides a vibraphone accompaniment that doubles the song's melodic line. Otherwise the recording features only Barrett. On "Octopus," Barrett plays both acoustic and electric guitars, and the song is closer in style and structure to the songs he had written for Pink Floyd's *The Piper at the Gates of Dawn* two years earlier. David Gilmour adds basic drum and bass guitar parts, likely overdubbed after the guitar and vocals were cut, in reversal of the customary studio overdub procedure. Barrett's meter is erratic as ever; Gilmour would have faced a challenge following it, but the experience may have helped prepare him for his next album project with Barrett.

Syd Barrett spoke to *Melody Maker*'s Chris Welch about the album in January 1970, days after its release. Welch prefaced his printed interview with a disclaimer of sorts: "It was not always so easy to understand his erratic train of thought," he wrote, adding, that in his estimation, Syd was "only as confused as he wanted to be."

Referring to "Octopus," a song chosen off *The Madcap Laughs* for release as a single, Barrett said, "I like to have really exciting, colorful songs. I can't really sing. But I enjoy it and I enjoy writing from experiences. Some are so powerful they are ridiculous." Perhaps responding to the solo acoustic nature of the Gilmour–Waters-produced tracks on the LP, he noted, "When I was with the Floyd . . . the volume [they] used inclined to push me a little."

Likely owing at least in part to the romanticizing of Syd Barrett's legend in the years to come, *The Madcap Laughs*—which had received mixed reviews on its original issue—would be lauded in some quarters as a cracked classic, even a work of genius. A more measured perspective could be found in Allan Orski's brief Syd Barrett entry in the weighty tome *MusicHound Rock: The Essential Album Guide*. Characterizing a 1994 compilation that collected all officially available Syd Barrett solo recordings, the reviewer described *The Madcap Laughs* as "a harrowing set of rough sonic quality, full of false starts and half-finished compositions that harshly illuminate the muse of a bright talent." Other modern-day reviewers were wholly unmoved. In a 1994 review in *MOJO* Tom Hibbert described the song "No Good Trying" as "a song less than pleasant to listen to," and suggested that its title "seemed to sum the whole matter up."

In a 2003 interview with *Record Collector*'s Daryl Easlea, Gilmour recalled the sessions for *The Madcap Laughs* as "pretty tortuous and very rushed." Describing Barrett as "very difficult," Gilmour found himself quite frustrated. Barrett, on the other hand, seemed unfazed and blissfully unaware of any problems with the sessions. "I want to record my next LP before I go on to anything else," he told a *Beat Instrumental* reporter in March 1970. "And I'm writing for that at the moment."

And despite the challenges of *The Madcap Laughs* sessions, Gilmour would return to help Barrett a few months later—this time in a more hands-on manner—as both producer and sideman for Syd's second solo album, *Barrett*.

16

BIRTH TO A SMILE

In January 1970, Roger Waters would embark on a brief project that was equal parts new and familiar. The songwriter would begin work on another film soundtrack, but this time he would work with someone outside the band. And in that way characteristic of Pink Floyd projects, there would be a direct conceptual line from *Music from The Body* to not one but two subsequent album projects.

Documentary film director Roy Battersby produced a 1970 motion picture called *The Body*. Narrated by actors Frank Finlay and Vanessa Redgrave, *The Body* explored human biology. Battersby decided his idiosyncratic ninety-three-minute film required a musical soundtrack, so he asked producer Tony Garnett for advice. Garnett in turn asked radio deejay John Peel for ideas; Peel recommended avant-garde Scottish composer-musician Ron Geesin.

At this stage, Geesin had one album to his credit, 1967's *A Raise of Eyebrows*. That record is a characteristically odd—and wholly uncommercial—collection of spoken word, vocalizing, avant-garde banjo instrumentals, trad-jazz (known in the US as Dixieland), and audio experiments. Its title track was likely an influence upon Roger Waters's "Several Species of Small Furry Animals Gathered Together in a Cave and Grooving with a Pict" on 1969's *Ummagumma*. Geesin's brand of music—often made without the use of conventional instruments—was just strange enough for *The Body*.

But it was felt that the film needed actual songs as well. "I recommended Roger because he did songs and I did not," Geesin recalls.

"That's not to say I couldn't do a song," he hastens to add, "but I just didn't think I was going to." For the most part, Geesin and Waters worked separately on their respective compositions for the film. Their approach for creating music to accompany the onscreen images was nearly as primitive as the 1968 Pink Floyd sessions for *The Committee*. As Geesin recalls, the filmmakers would make a "reduction copy" of *The Body* for Waters and Geesin. But he says that he doesn't think Waters had access to the required 16mm film projector, "so it may be that he just worked the timings," using a stopwatch as a guide to crafting music to fit a specific length of time. "We'd go through it about the right length," he says. "And if we needed to adjust the length, we'd do it either a bit slower or a bit faster."

Geesin says that Waters "wrote the songs and then recorded them in his little studio in the area of Islington in London. And all the other stuff—the funny, organized noisy sounds and music sequences and twitterings and body sounds and all that—I did in my studio across the west side of London in the Notting Hill Gate area." Ron Geesin's works would receive suitably odd, descriptive titles such as "More Than Seven Dwarves in Penis-Land" and "Dance of the Red Corpuscles."

Toward the end of the project, Geesin worked directly in the motion picture editing suite, adding sounds to the final dub. Meanwhile, he says that Waters finished his own compositions quite quickly, as Pink Floyd had a steady schedule of live dates both in England and on the Continent during this time. "And he wasn't the greatest of singers," says Geesin, "so [the songs] were pretty rough by modern-day standards. But they worked all right on the film."

Months after work had finished on the actual film music, Waters would return to Island Studios in London, where he would record new versions of much of his tracks for the soundtrack album *Music from The Body*; this time he took more time and created more finished-sounding tunes. Geesin says that the differences between the original and later recordings are significant. Waters "re-made them all with better instrumentation and more in-tune singing," Geesin explains.

And at the very end of the project, Waters and Geesin would finally collaborate directly. "We made new pieces that were nothing to do with the film, far more to do with the body," he says. In addition to the re-recorded versions of Waters's tunes, the pair recorded two songs that—

while thematically relevant to the film's subject matter—were not part of the film itself.

"Our Song" features Geesin on tape-editing and piano. "All that Roger contributed to that was some teeth grinding and armpits squeaking, and a couple of moans," Geesin says with a chuckle. He describes the other track, "Body Transport," as "us with two microphones doing a mini drama of moving a body from one room to another. It's a proper joke," he explains.

Roger Waters's "Sea Shell and Stone" features a beach sound effect that leads into a plaintive solo piece with voice, picked acoustic guitar, and a quiet bass guitar overdub. Its breezy lyrics initially center upon of sunrise and breezes, but near its end—accompanied by the sound of massed cellos—the lyrics speak of loneliness and isolation, a favorite Waters theme. Later on the record, "Sea Shell and Soft Stone" presents a reprise of Roger Waters's earlier tune, with a more fully developed cello melody composed by Ron Geesin.

"Chain of Life" finds Waters singing of "holidays and happy days" along to a gently picked melody; he would use a similar instrumental approach—applied to far more melancholy lyrics—on "If," a song that would feature on Pink Floyd's next album, *Atom Heart Mother*. Many years later, *The Wall*'s "Mother" would be based upon a similar acoustic guitar ambience. Credited to Geesin and Waters, "The Womb Bit" is an atmospheric bit of audio that—except for its chirping sounds—would have fit neatly into *A Saucerful of Secrets*. Waters plays a short lick high on the neck of his acoustic guitar.

"Breathe" uses the same melody as "Sea Shell and Stone," but presents different lyrics. Its opening phrase, "Breathe in the air," remained in Waters's mind; he would use those same words as the opening lyrics on another song called "Breathe," the first vocal number on 1973's monumental release, *The Dark Side of the Moon*.

For "Give Birth to a Smile," Waters and Geesin work together as well, enlisting the musical talents of David Gilmour, Richard Wright, and Nick Mason. Once again using the simple melody that serves as the basis for "Sea Shell and Stone" and two other tracks on *Music from The Body*, this tune features upbeat, hopeful lyrics. The closing moments of *The Body* feature Pink Floyd—plus Geesin on piano—playing and singing the song's title phrase, but in a clear foreshadowing of *The Dark Side of the Moon*, Waters's remake for the LP employs a soulful (albeit uncredited) chorus of female vocalists. For the first—but certainly not the last—time on record, Waters would enlist the talents of outside singers to help deliver his lyrics in the most effective manner possible.

Geesin says that he and Waters could have gone on to do more projects as a duo. "We were great friends and we were getting on great," he says, noting that they could have developed further musical ideas together. "But there was no need or desire for [Roger] to continue that. The Floyd were becoming a total entity, and from that period up to and beyond *The Dark Side of the Moon*, I think he used the Floyd to speak many of his ideas."

Yet at the time of its recording, both Waters and Geesin enjoyed the experience of making a soundtrack for *The Body*; that project laid the groundwork for a much more consequential and high-profile collaboration. Geesin's involvement with Pink Floyd's *Atom Heart Mother* would commence even before *Music from The Body* was completed.

17

PLEASE KEEP ON THE TRACK

Amid a busy schedule of concert dates and Pink Floyd recording commitments—sessions for *Atom Heart Mother* would begin at EMI's Abbey Road Studios on March 1, 1970—David Gilmour began producing a follow-up to Syd Barrett's *The Madcap Laughs*. Simply titled *Barrett*, the second album from Syd would enjoy a far more disciplined approach than did its predecessor. Taking a page from Pink Floyd's own highly organized and methodical working methods, Gilmour and coproducer Richard Wright scheduled sessions that they hoped would provide the structure Syd Barrett needed to complete a cohesive album of songs.

"Dave always had a flair for the production and engineering side of a studio," says Jerry Shirley. "After all, 90 percent of a great production is how the record's engineered. Then the rest of it is just how you place the condiments on top, so to speak. And Dave was brilliant at that from as long as I can remember."

In addition to producing *Barrett*, Gilmour and Wright played on nearly all of its twelve songs, joined on various tracks by two veterans of *The Madcap Laughs* sessions, drummers Jerry Shirley and John "Willie" Wilson. The combination of a consistent lineup of musicians, a single production team, and that team's eye toward discipline would result in *Barrett* emerging as a more cohesive album than its predecessor. Moreover, the material recorded included songs that—by Syd Barrett's standards, in any event—were more conventional and fully formed than the songs that appeared on *The Madcap Laughs*. Of course, no one involved could have known that the sessions for *Barrett* would be the final studio efforts of consequence for Syd, who was only twenty-four years old when recording was completed.

Two days before recording for the album began, Syd Barrett made a rare radio appearance, performing four songs on John Peel's *Top Gear* radio program. The band—Barrett on guitar and vocals, David Gilmour on bass guitar, and Jerry Shirley on percussion—played "Terrapin" from *The Madcap Laughs* as well as an unreleased Rick Wright tune called "Two of a Kind" ("Syd . . . thought it was *his*," Gilmour told Barrett biographers Mike Watkinson and Pete Anderson). They also performed three new originals. All three would be recorded for *Barrett*.

Only a few tracks from the *Barrett* sessions would be recorded with all the musicians playing together in real time. Jerry Shirley recalls those session vividly. "That was myself on drums, Dave Gilmour on bass, Rick Wright on keyboards, and Syd Barrett on guitar." Though "Gigolo Aunt" came out quite well, Shirley says that the session was "pretty shambolic, because you never knew which way Syd was turning."

As with Willie Wilson on *The Madcap Laughs*, Barrett didn't provide much musical direction for Shirley on the tracks recorded together live in the studio. "The guidance I remember from Syd were things like, 'It sounds a bit cold,' or, 'I'd like it a little windy,' or, 'Maybe it could be kind of shiny over here and purple over there,'" Shirley says. "He talked in abstracts, in comparisons that weren't musical."

"Gigolo Aunt" is one of the album's most effective tracks, capturing the essence of Syd Barrett's songwriting and delivery within the full-band context for what would be the last time. For the remaining songs, it was clear that another approach would be necessary.

Gilmour realized that the best—and perhaps only—method to capture Barrett's mercurial presence on magnetic tape would be to reverse a traditional studio method. While countless recordings have been made via overdubbing or layering, the customary procedure is first to record a "basic track." This often includes bass, drums, some guitar, and a "scratch" vocal for reference. Once the basic track is complete, musicians generally replace the guitar part, add additional instrumentation as needed, and record a more refined vocal track.

Such an approach was largely impractical for a producer working with Syd Barrett in 1970. Instead, Gilmour rolled tape while Syd played and sang multiple takes of a dozen or so songs, later reviewing the recordings and selecting the most usable versions.

Shirley says that approach yielded some quality material. Citing "Effervescing Elephant" as an example, he says, "That was one of the several songs that Syd wrote as a schoolboy. They all used to sit around and idolize him before he was famous, because he had this knack of writing songs that nobody else had. 'Effervescing Elephant' was one of those that Dave reminded him of and, sure enough, he went right to it, reverted to type, and just played it."

At his best—as on the nearly minute-long introduction to "Baby Lemonade"—Barrett seems in nearly complete control of his faculties, peeling off an impressive blues guitar solo. But such moments would be rare during the *Barrett* sessions.

For most of the songs, Gilmour, Wright, and Shirley would undertake the arduous task of playing along with Barrett's previously recorded guitar and voice, doing their best to match his often wavering tempo and always unconventional musical phrasing. Richard Wright's part in this was perhaps the easiest: mostly playing organ, Wright simply holds down a chord corresponding to whatever Barrett had played, following the changes regardless of meter. For the rhythm section of Gilmour and Shirley or Wilson, the work was far more daunting: the musicians had to apply a consistent beat to material that often resisted any such regimented approach.

"Syd was all over the place," says Shirley. "So Dave sort of charted it and remembered all the rhythmic foibles—where Syd would speed up, where he'd slow down, where he would do something different that you couldn't possibly follow—and he conducted me. We got through it."

Shirley believes that David Gilmour deserves a great deal of credit for the cohesiveness of the *Barrett* album. He recalls that Gilmour instituted a set of "rules" for the sessions, and that structure helped give the sessions a shape they would otherwise have lacked. "Dave insisted that Syd had to play *all* the guitars: rhythm and lead. Dave would *not* pick up the guitar. He made sure that Syd did it all."

As he had done on his own "The Narrow Way" on Pink Floyd's *Ummagumma*, Gilmour would play drums on Barrett's "Dominoes." Shirley recalls, "They got this beautiful, ethereal backing track with Dave overdubbing some lovely drums, and it just sounded great. But Syd could not get a good guitar solo going over it." But then Gilmour had a moment of Syd-style inspiration. "Out of nowhere, Dave says, 'Turn the tape backwards. Play it to him backwards,'" Shirley says, marveling at the memory. "And then Syd played to it, so that when you turn it back around, the guitar is backward. And he did it perfectly, first take. That was Syd for you."

▲

Jerry Shirley played live with Syd Barrett once during the period surrounding the making of *The Madcap Laughs* and *Barrett*. "Having actually played a live gig with him, I can attest to his ability to not stick to a structure. It worked in songs some of the time, and it didn't work live on that one disastrous gig that Dave and I did with him." He's referring to a set—Barrett's first-ever post–Pink Floyd solo concert performance—at the Music and Fashion Festival at London's Kensington Olympia on June 6, 1970, in between *Barrett* sessions.

"It was me on drums, Dave on bass, and Syd," Shirley says, noting that a bootleg audio document of the abortive set circulates among collectors and online. "To be fair to everybody, including Syd, we didn't exactly rehearse for weeks. It was a real 'fly by the seat of your pants' thing; I had probably heard about the fact that we were doing it that afternoon!"

The set gets off to a reasonably solid start, though problems with the PA system would make Barrett's vocal hard to hear. "In the middle of the third or fourth song, Syd just took his guitar off and walked off," Shirley recalls. "Dave and I just stood there." Shirley gamely attempts to cover Barrett's exit with a drum flourish, but clearly the gig is over.

The Madcap Laughs drummer Willie Wilson had returned for some of the *Barrett* sessions to add bits of percussion overdubs. Those sessions were by no means the last time Willie Wilson would work with David Gilmour; the Pink Floyd guitarist produced releases by Wilson's later band Sutherland Brothers & Quiver. Wilson played drums on Gilmour's self-titled 1978 solo LP debut, and was an onstage Nick Mason doppelganger as part of the "surrogate band" for live dates in support of 1979's double album *The Wall*. Wilson would also play on Gilmour solo releases well into the twenty-first century.

Jerry Shirley had helped out on the pair of Barrett solo albums in spare moments between his commitments with massively successful supergroup Humble Pie; he would remain with that band until its very end, drumming on all eleven studio albums, plus more than a half dozen live sets (most notably the 1971 hit *Performance: Rockin' the Fillmore*). He also worked on other artists' album sessions, took part in the group Natural Gas with former Badfinger guitarist Joey Molland, and worked as a radio deejay. Shirley published his lively memoir, *Best Seat in the House*, in 2011.

The end product released as *Barrett* can in many ways be heard as the proper follow-up to the songs and recordings Syd Barrett had made with Pink Floyd three years earlier for *The Piper at the Gates of Dawn*. Had he been working with a less sympathetic team than his ex-band mates and close friends, it is quite likely that Syd Barrett would never have been in a position to release a record as relatively finished and conventional as *Barrett*. In any event, save for *Opel*—a 1988 compilation of outtakes from 1968 and 1970—*Barrett* would be Syd's final recorded work. But the artist himself seemed more than open to the possibility of further musical endeavors. In 1971, he told *Beat Instrumental*'s Steve Turner that he was thinking about assembling a new group and recording new material. "It'd be a groove, wouldn't it?" he said. "I'm still in love with being a pop star, really."

And despite his reputation for being difficult at best, there would be no shortage of high-profile names who would, in the years to come, express keen interest in bringing Syd Barrett back into the studio to create new recordings. Writing for *New Musical Express* in 1974, Nick Kent cited a list of interested parties that included Jimmy Page of Led Zeppelin, former Soft Machine guitarist Kevin Ayers, and Roxy Music's Brian Eno. He also mentioned David Bowie, who had just released an all-covers album, *Pin-Ups*, featuring the Syd Barrett–era Pink Floyd song "See Emily Play." None of that interest came to fruition, however, and Bowie told Kent, "I think Dave [Gilmour] is the only one who could pull it off. There seems to be a relationship there."

In that *Beat Instrumental* interview, Barrett was cogent and articulate. Addressing the stark contrast between his solo work and the kind of sounds emanating from his former group—*Atom Heart Mother* had been released a few months earlier—Barrett explained, "I think that people miss the fact that [*The Madcap Laughs* is] obviously a gentler thing because it's clever and it's into that more than content. The message," he suggested with a flash of self-awareness, "might be a bit lost because people find it hard to grasp."

In a statement issued after Barrett's death in July 2006, David Gilmour sought to sum up that which made Pink Floyd's founding guitarist a special artist. "Do find time today to play some of Syd's songs and to remember him as the madcap genius who made us all smile with his wonderfully eccentric songs about bikes, gnomes, and scarecrows. His career was painfully short, yet he touched more people than he could ever know."

With their production work on *Barrett* completed in July (the album would be released in November 1970), David Gilmour and Rick Wright turned their attention fully to completion of Pink Floyd's album-in-progress, *Atom Heart Mother*.

Part V

Remergence (1970)

18

EPIC

Whether it was true—as Pink Floyd biographer Nicholas Schaffner would claim in hindsight—that "the turn of the decade found Pink Floyd floundering for direction," or whether it was merely a case of the band's having been so focused for an extended period on work for others (*Zabriskie Point*, *The Body*, *The Madcap Laughs*, and *Barrett* all required time and energy that could have instead been applied to creating new Pink Floyd music), as 1970 began, the group found itself without a bounty of new ideas for its fifth album.

In September 1969, Richard Wright told *Top Pops & Music Now* of the band's plans: "We're still recording in December; the idea for the album will probably come out of our new concert tours." But things didn't work out that way: Pink Floyd's only studio sessions in December 1969 included work on material planned—but ultimately not used—for Antonioni's *Zabriskie Point* film. And from there, the four members of Pink Floyd turned their attention to various extracurricular musical projects.

Amid that flurry of activity, Pink Floyd kept up a steady schedule of live performances through 1970. The band's set lists in January were built mostly around older material, but did include two newer works, "Embryo" and an extended work initially titled "The Amazing Pudding." The latter had developed out of a particularly inventive chord sequence written by David Gilmour; in its earliest form, he informally called that sequence "Theme for an Imaginary Western." Apparently, Gilmour was unaware that former Cream bassist Jack Bruce had already written a tune with that very title, released on his 1969 LP, *Songs for a Tailor* (American hard rock group Mountain played "Theme" onstage at Woodstock, and released its cover version in 1970).

Once the song made its way to the stage—debuting at a Hull University concert in mid-January—it was introduced as "The Amazing Pudding." Gilmour's sophisticated sequence of chords became the central theme of the long piece, joined by more abstract and improvisational sections. Building upon the concept of multiple-movement works begun with "A Saucerful of Secrets" and carried forward with "The Man and the Journey," the wordless "The Amazing Pudding" focused on melody and texture rather than lyrics.

As "The Amazing Pudding" developed onstage, various ideas were created, tested, incorporated, and sometimes discarded. While specific recording dates have not been revealed, an early studio take of this extended piece, one that would become known as "Atom Heart Mother," is featured in the Pink Floyd box set *The Early Years*. This undated recording, likely from early to mid-1970, finds the track already running nearly twenty minutes. Nick Mason's insistent snare introduction—a feature of early live performances—would soon be dropped from the arrangement, but Gilmour's basic theme was already the centerpiece of the work. A grand and dramatic melody featuring Richard Wright's organ gives way to a second, dreamier section highlighted by Gilmour's fluid slide guitar. Each repeating of the phrase features added emphasis, generally in the form of more overdubbed lead guitar from Gilmour. Even though his bass playing centers primarily on the root note of each chord, the unusual, shifting chords result in one of Roger Waters's most interesting and memorable bass guitar parts.

Four and half minutes in, the song enters its third "movement." A simple, hypnotic Hammond organ line is joined occasionally by judicious strikes upon Nick Mason's tubular bells. After a minute of this, Wright adds a bridging chord sequence, joined by Waters and Mason, both playing with restraint and subtlety. As with Gilmour's earlier sections, this part of the early version of "Atom Heart Mother" is lacking in a top-line melody, yet in its first several minutes, the tune does not sound particularly unfinished. As Wright continues to play this basic progression, Mason liberally adds his trademark fills.

As that section gives way to another, a bluesy, three-chord jam foundation provides the opportunity for David Gilmour to peel off a lengthy, highly melodic electric guitar solo. The guitarist adds interest by occasionally inserting some major chords into what is primarily a minor-chord workout. The section that follows finds Gilmour receding into the sonic background, giving space for Wright to add some jazzy chord fills while Roger Waters provides the melody.

At thirteen-plus minutes, a grandiose bridging section brings the song back to its theme, delivered now—most notably by Nick Mason—with greater gusto and complexity. A drum roll fades out, and then—after a few seconds of silence—back in, giving way once again to the "second" theme, played through several more times with increasing emphasis. The piece ends with Gilmour's original "first" theme, also played multiple times.

It seems clear from this early version that Mason's lengthy drum rolls throughout the work were meant to serve as placeholders. But while even in its early form "Atom Heart Mother" had quite a few signature melodies, the band seemed at a loss as to what they might add into the unfinished sections. And as dramatic as this early "Atom Heart Mother" could be—especially onstage—there is no denying its repetitive nature. Something more would be needed.

Feeling that they had hit a creative wall with the piece, the other band members were receptive to a suggestion from Roger Waters that they call upon Ron Geesin for help. The composer's avant-garde credentials were next to none; perhaps he could give "The Amazing Pudding"—or whatever the band's latest epic would eventually be called—what was needed to bring it into shape for release.

"When we did *Atom Heart Mother*, they were at their lowest point of creativity," says Geesin. Acknowledging how busy the members of Pink Floyd had been with outside projects, he says, "they were pretty exhausted, and they didn't really know where to go. It just happened that I was on the spot around that time."

In some ways, Geesin was an odd choice. For one, Pink Floyd had never worked with an outside composer or used session musicians (save Norman Smith's drumming on *A Saucerful of Secrets'* "Remember a Day"). And by 1970, the group had largely taken control of its studio work: on release of *Atom Heart Mother* in October, Smith would be listed as "executive producer." More significantly, perhaps, was the fact

that Ron Geesin wasn't even a fan of the band's work. "I wasn't interested much in their music," he says. "I'm still not. It doesn't do anything
for me." Speaking about progressive rock—a term often applied to Pink
Floyd's music—Geesin sniffs, "it doesn't matter how progressive it
thinks it is; it's not actually very progressive at all." Even though Geesin
had shared billing with Pink Floyd as far back as 1967, he contrasts his
music with the sounds they made. "I would just do my thing, which is a
sort of an absurdist eruption," he says, describing it as "a nice contrast
to what was going to come on next."

Still, owing to his friendship with Roger Waters and the positive
experience of collaborating on the soundtrack for *The Body*, Geesin
agreed to help. In early April 1970, the band provided Geesin with
work-tapes of the early version of "Atom Heart Mother" and then got
on a plane to New York City, where they would begin a North
American tour that would run through late May.

From Geesin's perspective, the material he had been given was rather basic and lacking in melody. He characterizes Pink Floyd's musical
approach this way: "If it wasn't a defined song, then they would be
making what was equivalent of a background wash to which the public
supplied its ethereal melody in its own [collective] head." But for "Atom
Heart Mother," it was—among other things—Geesin's job to create an
actual melody. "With 'Atom Heart Mother,' I supplied the melody to
their background, literally," he says.

When it comes to popular music—be it rock, country, or many other
styles—the concept of repetition is a feature, not a bug. But for the
avant-garde-minded Geesin, the repetitive nature of the Pink Floyd
track he was working on was a bridge too far. Upon hearing the main
theme reprising for what to him seemed like the umpteenth time, he
recalls exclaiming, "Oh God, not again!" So he decided to change it.
"The last two choruses—if you want to call the sequence a chorus,
which is the same chord sequence as the first theme—I just changed it
to a whole completely new melody," Geesin says. "Which really works:
you've got the repetition underneath but you've got the top doing
[something] different."

With "Atom Heart Mother," Geesin sought to transform Pink
Floyd's piece—noted on early session documents as "Untitled Epic"—
into something a bit more musically weighty and serious. One way in
which he pursued that goal was to compose parts for a brass ensemble

and choir. While choir-like vocals had cropped up toward the end of "A Saucerful of Secrets," Syd Barrett had brought in a Salvation Army band for his final Pink Floyd session, and Rick Wright had performed a trombone solo on "Biding My Time," Geesin's plans would represent exploration of new territory for the band.

"When we got in the studio, they had no bloody clue what was going to happen with those brass players," Geesin says. The members of Pink Floyd had not yet heard a note of Geesin's score, he says, "because I couldn't play those ten brass parts on the piano to them." But once the ensemble did record Geesin's written parts on top of a basic track cut by Waters and Mason, everyone seemed satisfied. "They'd run the tape with my new stuff, and it seemed to sound right," Geesin says.

The vocal choir that appears toward the middle of "Atom Heart Mother" splits its time between somewhat conventional—if wordless—vocalizing and some truly weird recitations ("Suck! Suck!" in the section subtitled "Funky Dung") that are unlike anything in the Pink Floyd catalog before or since.

The part of "Atom Heart Mother" known as "Mind Your Throats Please" is closer in spirit to Pink Floyd's own outré musical excursions, such as "A Saucerful of Secrets," but Geesin's contributions are faded in and out of the mix as well on the final version. And in keeping with the band's penchant for including found sounds into its works, toward the final moments of "Atom Heart Mother," two snippets of studio chatter ("Here is a loud announcement!" and "Silence in the studio!") are woven into the sonic mix.

Geesin would experience great frustration during the sessions for "Atom Heart Mother." Owing to EMI's prohibition on tape splicing, the basic track laid down earlier by Waters on bass and Mason on drums had to be performed as a single performance rather than a spliced-together collection of shorter tracks. In practice, that meant that the tempo wavered throughout; that, in turn, made it quite difficult for classically trained brass and choral musicians to follow along when overdubbing their parts. "The tempo goes up and down," Nick Mason told *MOJO* in 1994. "We just staggered through it." Furthermore, once the orchestral parts were added, it was realized that the entire score was off from Pink Floyd's basic track by one beat; there was no way to correct the error.

Despite the great amount of time and attention put into the track eventually known as "Atom Heart Mother Suite," it represents only one side—literally and figuratively—of the *Atom Heart Mother* album. For the album's flip side, Pink Floyd would return to its customary method of working as a self-contained unit. For the second side of the record, each of the band's songwriters—Roger Waters, David Gilmour, and Richard Wright—would provide an original tune. The final track on the album would be a sound collage that hearkened back to part of 1969's live "The Man and the Journey."

Roger Waters's plaintive, gentle, and mostly acoustic "If" features inward-looking lyrics that deal with the nature of human relationships, question whether its first-person protagonist is indeed a good man, and hint at a lyrical theme Waters would soon explore in greater detail. Asking if he would be forced to endure wires in his brain should he go insane, Waters previews the subject matter of *The Dark Side of the Moon*'s "Brain Damage." The folky "If" includes a simple slide guitar solo from David Gilmour; the musical contributions of Richard Wright and Nick Mason are subtle and not central to the song's arrangement. The band would perform the tune on BBC, but "If" never became part of Pink Floyd's live repertoire. In his post–Pink Floyd days, however, Roger Waters would often feature "If," sometimes with extra lyrics and melody.

Keyboardist Richard Wright hadn't had an original song—that is, music and lyrics—on a Pink Floyd album since 1968's "Remember a Day." But with its gentle lead vocal and piano melody, "Summer '68" displays Wright's increased confidence as a songwriter. The tune features a poppy chorus that seems flown in from another song, and in place of a guitar solo, Wright chooses a brief melody—played three times during the tune—performed by the Abbey Road Session Pops Orchestra. The oblique tale of Wright's meeting a groupie on tour, "Summer '68" would be released (in Japan only) as the B-side of a reissued "Julia Dream," itself originally a B-side from 1968. Pink Floyd would never perform "Summer '68" live onstage.

A new composition, David Gilmour's "Fat Old Sun," would become a key part of Pink Floyd's live show. Along with a handful of other tunes—"Cymbaline" and "Green is the Colour" from *More*, and the then-unreleased "Embryo"—"Fat Old Sun" would be reimagined live onstage, transformed from its relatively conventional studio recording into an epic-length work that revealed nuances only hinted at on record. And even on the *Atom Heart Mother* studio version, the underrated "Fat Old Sun" reveals itself as a Gilmour showcase.

"Fat Old Sun" is notable as well as only the second music-and-lyrics composition by the Pink Floyd guitarist after *Ummagumma*'s "The Narrow Way (Part 3)." Gilmour's second composition begins as a return to the pastoral textures of many of the songs on the *More* soundtrack. Gilmour's folky acoustic guitar supports his vocals and lyrics about summer thunder, newly mown grass, evening bird calls, and laughter of children. Waters, Wright, and Mason all provide understated instrumental backing. Gilmour overdubs bits of slide guitar into the arrangement, but the instrument is intentionally placed deep into the mix where it adds subtle texture. Just past the three-minute mark, Gilmour launches into an electric guitar solo over instrumental verses; the final two minutes of "Fat Old Sun" are given over completely to Gilmour on lead guitar with the rest of the band holding down a steady rhythm backing.

The sound of a dripping tap in Nick Mason's kitchen opens the soundscape "Alan's Psychedelic Breakfast." The work is presented as an audio document of an early morning experience of Pink Floyd roadie Alan Styles. In the piece's first of three sections (subtitled "Rise and Shine"), Styles is heard muttering to himself about coffee, toast, and marmalade as he pads about his kitchen. Sections of his vocals are treated to echo and reverberation effects. After a minute or so of this, the band joins in with an instrumental piece built largely over a stately, upbeat piano melody by Richard Wright. David Gilmour adds a countermelody on his guitar, run through a rotating Leslie speaker. Roger Waters's bass is subtle nearly to the point of inaudibility, and Nick Mason provides a time-keeping beat on hi-hat.

The second section of "Alan's Psychedelic Breakfast" ("Sunny Side Up") begins with more ambient sounds of Styles frying an egg; once the title character sits down to enjoy his meal, David Gilmour fades in on multitracked guitars—acoustic and electric slide—providing a melody possessed of a bucolic air. Gilmour is the only musician to play on the "Sunny Side Up" section of the track.

The crackling sound of frying sausages leads into the third and final section, "Morning Glory." After a brief introduction by Richard Wright on piano, the entire band plays a tune vaguely reminiscent of the main theme from *Atom Heart Mother*'s title track. The sound of Styles mumbling to himself about the day to come is overdubbed several times, fading into the band's instrumental.

As unlikely as it would seem, "Alan's Psychedelic Breakfast" was performed live on at least four occasions, all in December 1970, at concerts in the United Kingdom. None of these shows has been documented on an official Pink Floyd release, but the Sheffield concert of December 22 circulates unofficially among collectors. The live "Alan's Psychedelic Breakfast" runs more than twenty-four minutes, nearly twice the length of its studio counterpart. Reminiscent of the previous year's "The Man and the Journey" set piece, the live reading of "Alan's Psychedelic Breakfast" features numerous melodies and solos that are not present on the *Atom Heart Mother* version; Gilmour's guitar work makes extensive use of tape-delay effect, in a very early example of what is known today as "looping." The non-musical parts—performed by Mason, who also cooks a bit and watches television—elicit repeated bouts of laughter from the intimate crowd—roughly 2,000 people—assembled in Sheffield's City Hall.

Atom Heart Mother was released on October 2, 1970, in time for the Christmas holiday buying season, and almost exactly one year after *Ummagumma*'s release. Reviews were mixed. Writing in *Rolling Stone*, Alec Dubro called *Atom Heart Mother* "a step headlong into the last century" and a dissipation of what he considered the band's considerable collective talents. "If Pink Floyd is looking for some new dimensions," he suggested, "they haven't found them here." *Great Speckled Bird*'s Steve Wise dispatched *Atom Heart Mother* as a "Wagnerian piece of classical schmaltz," arguing that the good ("freaky") parts were "ruined by . . . encapsulation in classical garbage."

Despite misgivings—regarding how the piece was completed, what he sees as an unfair diminution of his credit for the work, and frustration with how it was performed—Ron Geesin remains quite proud of his work on the first side of *Atom Heart Mother*. He views it as a moderately successful combination of Pink Floyd's style with something more adventurous. "If you take two seemingly disparate styles and put them together, sometimes they'll make something greater than the original two," he says. "And I think that's what happened with *Atom Heart Mother*."

Geesin has his own ideas as to why Pink Floyd distanced itself from *Atom Heart Mother* shortly after its release. "Radical though they were," he says, "they knew where their bread was buttered. And that is to selling albums." He says that Nick Mason explained the band's disinterest in *Atom Heart Mother* to him more recently in simple terms. "He said to me, 'it was pointing in a direction we did not subsequently want to go.' But Nick's a great diplomat."

Looking back upon *Atom Heart Mother* in later years, the members of Pink Floyd wouldn't express so much as grudging admiration for the work. In 1984, Roger Waters told BBC Radio's Richard Skinner, "If somebody said to me now, 'Right, here's a million pounds, go out and play "Atom Heart Mother,"' I'd say, 'You must be fucking joking. I'm not playing that rubbish.'"

A quarter century after its release, David Gilmour spoke about the album with a writer for *MOJO*. "At the time we felt *Atom Heart Mother*, like *Ummagumma*, was a step towards something or other," he said. "Now I think they were both just a blundering about in the dark."

Though for years Gilmour seemed a bit embarrassed by the track, he would take part in a 2006 live performance of Geesin's "corrected" version, with the orchestration moved a beat. And regardless of what anyone might have thought about the shortcomings of "Atom Heart Mother," it would sharply point the way toward another extended work from the band, one that tops many fan polls as an all-time favorite Pink Floyd song. In terms of melody, length, and structure, "Atom Heart Mother" is a clear antecedent for "Echoes," the centerpiece of 1971's *Meddle*. Mason would acknowledge as much in 1972 when he told *NME*'s Tony Stewart, "I don't think we could have done *Meddle* without doing *Atom Heart Mother*."

By Geesin's measure, *Atom Heart Mother* wasn't a commercially focused release. However, the record charts of 1971 would suggest otherwise: shortly after its release in the UK, *Atom Heart Mother* reached the #1 spot on the British album charts, the first—and, until 1975, the only—Pink Floyd album to climb to the top. And in the United States, where none of the band's first four albums had even made it onto the album charts, *Atom Heart Mother* reached #55, earning a Gold Record award two decades later.

While as an album *Atom Heart Mother* might have been something of a mixed bag—an epic, side-long suite, a handful of short tracks and a pair of slight melodies wedded to the sounds of frying eggs—it did represent a kind of growth for Pink Floyd. From this point forward (until 1979's *The Wall*), the band would produce itself in the studio. Mason credits Ron Geesin for helping the group move in that direction. "The thing that Ron taught us most about was recording techniques, and tricks done on the cheap. We learned how to get 'round the men-in-white-coats and do things at home, like editing," he told *MOJO*'s Robert Sandall in 1994. "It was all very relevant to things we did later."

In between session dates for *Atom Heart Mother*, Pink Floyd continued to play numerous live concerts and festival dates. The band's set began to revolve around a collection of extended songs, some from as far back as *The Piper at the Gates of Dawn*, and some from the soon-to-be released album. A select few dates featured the band joined by brass and choir for "Atom Heart Mother." And as was now Pink Floyd's custom, one of its most notable live performances of this era—one that provided an excellent snapshot of where the band was creatively—was a July session for BBC Radio.

19

BBC THREE

By the time Pink Floyd arrived at BBC Paris Cinema in London on a Thursday in July 1970, the band's live shows had long since coalesced around the presentation of lengthy numbers. Gone was any attempt to present short, concise, hit single-type material for the band's concert audiences. An entire show might only include three or four songs. While the group continued to play selected tunes from its earliest albums—"Astronomy Dominé" from 1967, "A Saucerful of Secrets" from 1968—the focus was on newer material.

One approach the band would find rewarding both creatively and on a practical level was the recasting of some of its shorter pieces into epic-length constructions. That method would be put to effective use onstage, adding extended instrumental breaks and atmospheric passages to what were essentially pop tunes. And beginning in 1970, Pink Floyd's BBC Radio appearances would closely resemble the band's typical live sets.

Generally operated onstage by keyboardist Richard Wright, the group's three-dimensional Azimuth Coordinator immersed the audience within the sonic experience. Quoted in Atlanta, Georgia, underground paper *Great Speckled Bird*, Roger Waters explained the band's ambitions: "We want to throw away the old format of the pop show standing on a square stage at one end of a rectangular room and running through a series of numbers. Our idea is to put the sound all around the audience with ourselves in the middle. Then the performance becomes much more theatrical." That same story noted that the group toured with three tons of gear.

Remarkably, BBC's Radio 1 did not initiate full-time FM stereo broadcast until 1987. But from its inception the radio channel was allowed to use the transmitters of easy-listening Radio 2 for selected programs. The John Peel–hosted *Peel Sunday Concert* was one of those programs; as a result, listeners in 1970—or at least those in the UK with access to an FM receiver—could tune in and hear a high-quality stereo broadcast of a Pink Floyd performance.

"Embryo" is a short piece originally recorded during the *Ummagumma* sessions in 1969; once the group had decided upon the album's live-and-solo concept, there was no place for the track, and it was quietly abandoned. Later—and without the band's consent—Harvest Records included "Embryo" on a 1970 sampler LP called *Picnic*. That recording was a demo, not intended for release in any form. *Picnic* quickly went out of print, and the song went largely unheard for many years until 1983, when US label Capitol—the label that had released some of Pink Floyd's earlier material—released a compilation LP called *Works*, one designed to cash in on the runaway success of 1979's *The Wall* (released on Columbia). *Works* included that short studio recording of "Embryo."

While few record buyers would hear the studio version of "Embryo" in 1970, the song would be a feature of many Pink Floyd concerts for most all of 1970 and 1971. But in concert, the brief tune would be expanded and extended into something well beyond its studio counterpart.

After a warm introduction by its host, the 1970 *Peel Sunday Concert* featuring Pink Floyd opens with "Embryo." While in the context of a regular concert the number could sometimes swell to twenty-five minutes, for the time-constrained BBC broadcast, the group trims the work to a relatively compact eleven minutes. With David Gilmour (and Richard Wright) singing Roger Waters's plaintive, first-person narrative—from the point of view of an unborn child—the dreamy arrangement deftly balances soothing melodic lines and soaring, slashing lead guitar figures. A series of verses and choruses—each followed by a tidy and tightly arranged instrumental break—takes the song to the four-and-a-half-minute mark, at which point Gilmour, Mason, and Wright pull back on their instrumental attack. Roger Waters steps forward musically with an appealing bass guitar melody that runs two measures.

Without warning, the sounds of a cooing, giggling baby enter the mix in prominent fashion. While the BBC's stereo broadcast could not capture the three-dimensional nature of the live performance, in which—thanks to the Azimuth Coordinator—the baby would have made its entrance over the shoulders of concertgoers, even in two-channel audio the effect is remarkable.

Richard Wright doubles Waters's melody a few octaves higher on his organ, while Nick Mason supplies an understated beat. Gilmour provides atmospherics on his guitar. The sounds of children in a playground fade into the mix, and Gilmour introduces a stunning sonic effect. Evoking the songs vocalized by humpback whales, the screaming—yet somehow gentle—sounds emerging from his Fender Stratocaster are achieved by "improper" use of a wah-wah pedal. Gilmour had accidentally discovered that by plugging his guitar signal into the pedal's output jack—and then connecting the input to his amplifier—and turning the pedal backward, he could manipulate the sounds of his guitar in a way that sounded both organic and unlike anything other guitarists were doing. Clearly enamored of his new discovery, the guitarist would incorporate the sounds into a number of live pieces, though the signature use of Gilmour's whale effect would find its home on the landmark "Echoes," from the band's 1971 LP, *Meddle*.

By 1970, the nature of Pink Floyd's extended soundscapes had evolved considerably from the sonic maelstrom of "A Saucerful of Secrets." Much less musically aggressive than earlier works, Pink Floyd's extended set pieces of this era evoke a dreamlike effect, one that doubtless endeared the band to a generation of blissed-out, pot-smoking listeners. The live "Embryo" is perhaps the most successful exemplar of Pink Floyd's refined onstage musical approach of the early 1970s. As the applause for "Embryo" subsides, Peel comments, "I was just thinking about Pink Floyd's music . . . it always makes me feel, at least, very hopeful. It's optimistic music. And that was no exception."

With his confidence as a songwriter growing, David Gilmour would be sole composer of "Fat Old Sun," a relatively brief track from *Atom Heart Mother*. At the time of the BBC broadcast, the album's release was still more than two months away, and the *Peel Sunday Concert* performance would be the live debut of "Fat Old Sun." In time, the five-to-six-minute arrangement would be expanded upon as well—in a 1971 BBC performance, "Fat Old Sun" would run more than fifteen minutes—but for the Peel show, Pink Floyd largely adheres to the studio version.

David Gilmour plays electric guitar on the BBC reading of "Fat Old Sun" rather than the acoustic instrument he would use on the *Atom Heart Mother* studio version; that, plus Nick Mason's more forceful backbeat, gives the live version a heavier feel. Gilmour's wistful lyrics—sung in a high register—are decidedly romantic.

After three minutes of song-proper, Gilmour plays a low-register solo over an instrumental verse. With each repeating of that verse, the guitarist subtly ratchets up the intensity, eventually only to pull back, leaving space for the song to fade into silence. "Is that going to be on the next LP?" Peel asks. An off-mic band member answers in the affirmative; Peel responds, "Great." ("Fat Old Sun" would remain in the band's live sets into the middle of 1971, and in the twenty-first century David Gilmour would sometimes perform the tune on his concert tours.)

Peel continues, "These next two things have already been, in fact, recorded, and you doubtless have the records already." Pink Floyd then begins a medley of two songs, "Green is the Colour" (from 1969's *More*) and "Careful With That Axe, Eugene."

In its studio version, "Green is the Colour" is one of Pink Floyd's more folk-leaning numbers of the era. In concerts beginning in 1969, the song would receive an extended treatment, sometimes running more than thirteen minutes. But by 1970 the band had trimmed the song's arrangement back to something closely resembling the studio original, and would segue directly into "Eugene."

As Gilmour plays the opening chords of "Green is the Colour," Richard Wright adds some very subtle organ that sounds like harmonica. After singing the song's verses, Gilmour plays a guitar solo with a scat vocal doubling the guitar's melodic line. The rest of the band increases the musical intensity under Gilmour's lead, and then the guitarist and Mason drop out suddenly, leaving Richard Wright's quiet, minor-key organ and Roger Waters's two-note bass line to introduce "Careful With That Axe, Eugene."

At a shade over eight minutes, the 1970 BBC Radio reading of "Eugene" isn't remarkably different from the many other documented versions of the piece, but the *Peel Sunday Concert* version shows a band that's much "tighter"—less focused on improvisation and more centered upon a pre-planned reading of the song—than on earlier versions. The loud sections are full of controlled fury, and the quiet sections have a seething undercurrent. After two years of heavy touring and recording, the post-Barrett lineup of Pink Floyd has developed a keen sense of musical interplay.

After introducing the individual members of the band, John Peel sets up the next song, explaining that bassist Roger Waters will be performing on acoustic guitar while Rick Wright plays organ and bass simultaneously (something "well worth watching," he tells the studio audience). A straight reading of *Atom Heart Mother*'s Waters spotlight "If" follows. As Waters sings his melancholy, introspective lyrics, the rest of the band provides understated support. When David Gilmour takes a guitar solo, he adopts a highly distorted, keening tone for his slide guitar, but turns his volume down significantly, giving the solo a faraway feel that seems to complement Waters's lyrics about the "spaces between friends."

After applause for "If," Peel makes a few program announcements, and then introduces the final performance of the day from Pink Floyd. Describing the work as "the high point of the recent and much-discussed" Bath Festival (June 27, 1970), Peel explains that the piece has a working title of "The Atom Heart Mother." The piece—which had previously been known variously as "The Amazing Pudding" and "Untitled Epic"—had only gotten its name minutes before broadcast. "I was present for that," says "Atom Heart Mother" co-composer Ron Geesin. "That was where the newspaper was picked up and the title was found: in the control room of the BBC studio."

Not even counting the several video versions included, the 2016 Pink Floyd box set, *The Early Years*, features audio of no fewer than three previously unreleased recordings of "Atom Heart Mother." One is an early studio version, done before Geesin added the work's signature brass, string, and choral parts. Another is a band-only performance from a Montreux, Switzerland, concert in 1970, without the "classical" elements ("That one should be called 'The Amazing Pudding,'" Geesin insists). The third is a recording from the July 1970 John Peel program and includes choir, cello, and the Philip Jones Brass Ensemble alongside Waters, Wright, Gilmour, and Mason.

Jones's ensemble was a well-established outfit founded in 1951; the ensemble's recent work at EMI on *Atom Heart Mother* was its tenth

documented studio performance. The choir was led by a highly re-
garded conductor and choirmaster, forty-year-old John Alldis. And
Peel's introduction notes that "the arrangements are written by the
Floyd in conjunction with Ron Geesin."

That word *arrangement* still rankles Geesin nearly half a century
later. At the VIP-only opening of a 2017 exhibit of Pink Floyd memorabilia called *Their Mortal Remains* and hosted at London's Victoria and
Albert Museum, Geesin spied a caption card accompanying an original
handwritten score for "Atom Heart Mother." He was incensed by the
wording on the card: "Vocal and instrumental arrangements for *Atom
Heart Mother.*"

"They keep talking about orchestration and arrangement," he says.
"Well, it fucking well isn't orchestration or arrangement; it's *composition.*" Noting that the display features two sheets of the hand-colored
original score for "section i"—the main choir section—Geesin is ada-
mant: "Every note was written by me as an original." It is worth noting
that—Peel's introduction and the V&A display's wording notwithstanding—every copy of the *Atom Heart Mother* album since its 1970 release
has credited the composers of the title track this way: "Mason, Gilmour,
Waters, Wright & Geesin."

And while Geesin—like may composers of ambitious works—has
misgivings regarding the accuracy with which the assembled musicians
and vocalists delivered "Atom Heart Mother" on John Peel's radio program, he is proud of the performance. The fact that the work is performed live for radio would mean that some of the problems with the
studio version—dodgy tempo, limitations of multi-track recording—
were sidestepped. Of course there would be no room for error in a live
concert that featured dozens of musicians. But all involved would turn
in a splendid performance. The BBC recording is a bit "brighter" than
its studio counterpart, and benefits from the interplay—however tightly
structured—among the assembled musicians. In particular, Alldis's
choir members seem to put even more gusto into their vocal parts.
Other than pre-recorded sound effects—presumably horses and motor-
cycles were not welcome on the stage of BBC's Paris Cinema—"Atom
Heart Mother" would be performed and recorded absolutely live, with
no post-production "sweetening." As such, it's a tour-de-force and could
well be regarded as the definitive version of the work.

Returning to working on his own, Geesin would release more than a dozen albums, and immersed himself in "sound installations," compelling and boundary-pushing audiovisual exhibits. Geesin recounts the making of "Atom Heart Mother" in his entertaining and idiosyncratic 2013 book, *The Flaming Cow*. A dedicated collector of wrenches (known "spanners" in British parlance), he wrote and published *The Adjustable Spanner: History, Origins and Development to 1970*. "There was no history," he writes on his website, "so I wrote it."

Though at sixty minutes the July 1970 *Peel Sunday Concert* is a bit shorter than a typical Pink Floyd concert of the era, it stands as one of the best-recorded (and best-performed) concerts by the band from that time. Those who saw the group onstage circa 1970 report similarly impressive performances. Longtime music industry professional Barney Kilpatrick was only thirteen when he saw Pink Floyd play at The Warehouse, a New Orleans concert hall, on May 15, 1970. The band was part of a somewhat odd bill that also included The Allman Brothers Band, and the set list included "Embryo" as well as "Grantchester Meadows" from *Ummagumma*, along with chestnuts like "Astronomy Dominé" and "A Saucerful of Secrets."

"Atom Heart Mother" was performed, introduced on this night as "The Amazing Pudding." On its release, *Atom Heart Mother* would become a favorite of Kilpatrick and his friends, but hearing a live, early version of the tune didn't make a lasting impression. "Whatever they played that night must not have sounded much like what eventually came out on the album," he says.

Kilpatrick was unfamiliar with most of Pink Floyd's music at the time of the show, though he did own and treasure a copy of *Ummagumma*. Referring to a diary he kept from a young age, Kilpatrick says, "I remember being frustrated that I could not see any of the band members, because there was no 'follow' spot[light]. The stage was bathed in murky purple, blue and red for most of the show; It was unlike any concert lighting I can recall from shows I attended around that time." Recalling that the concert was not especially well-attended ("The Warehouse held about 2,000 people when full, but there could not have been more than half as many people at that show"), Kilpatrick recalls that the venue afforded "enough room to lie down on carpet remnants," and that joints were being passed at random among the concertgoers.

But Kilpatrick's most enduring memory—one supported by his contemporaneous note-keeping—is also its most remarkable. Little is known about Pink Floyd's touring personnel of 1970 beyond the names of key crew members, and it's generally accepted that wives and families did not typically join Pink Floyd on tours. Yet Kilpatrick recalls—and his diary notes clearly—that "a woman introduced as 'Jude' was screaming at the top of her lungs during 'Careful With That Axe, Eugene.'"

The week prior to Pink Floyd's two dates in New Orleans included concert dates in Salt Lake City, Utah, and Atlanta, Georgia (the latter on a bill with The Guess Who). It's conceivable that Roger Waters might have overextended his vocal cords on a reading of "Eugene" at one or both of those shows, necessitating an exceedingly rare guest vocal on the song. In 1970, the bassist's wife was Judith Trim Waters, known to her friends as "Jude" (and identified as such in a photo on the inner gatefold sleeve of *Ummagumma*). Assuming Kilpatrick's notes and memory are correct, this May 1970 guest vocal would be the first time a non-band member would join the group onstage to sing, and the last time until performances of a work called *Eclipse*, later to be known as *The Dark Side of the Moon*.

Meanwhile, Pink Floyd was earning admirers in high places. No less a figure than Jimi Hendrix—a skeptic of the Syd Barrett–era lineup's music—would go on the record about the band in two of the last interviews he would give before his untimely death at age 27. Speaking to *Melody Maker*'s Roy Hollingworth, he observed, "They don't know it . . . but people like Pink Floyd are the mad scientists of this day and age." And to *Record Mirror*'s Keith Altham: "Sometimes you . . . lay back by yourself and appreciate them, you know. That's the type of music they're into."

As 1970 tumbled into 1971, Pink Floyd would begin work on its sixth studio album, one which would refine everything the band had learned up to that point. One side of *Meddle* would feature a collection of standard-length songs that showcased everything from folky, pastoral textures to wild, rocking instrumentals; the other would feature the band's most fully realized long-form work, "Echoes."

20

FEARLESS

Amid a UK concert tour dubbed "Atom Heart Mother is Going on the Road," Pink Floyd scheduled dates in early January 1971 to begin work on the band's sixth album. Those sessions at EMI's Abbey Road Studios in London would continue on and off into August, though available reports suggest that the early sessions for what would become *Meddle* were largely unproductive. The band did manage to develop a number of short pieces—none of which would have constituted a song in itself—and began to refer to those snippets as "Nothing."

By April 22, at a concert at the Norwich Lads Club in England, the various "Nothing" bits had been put together in a form the band deemed worthy of performance. Playfully introduced onstage as "The Return of the Son of Nothing," the lengthy work was clearly still in development. But a bootleg recording made three weeks later demonstrates that the song did eventually come together. That earliest known live recording of the piece, eventually known as "Echoes," is a poor-quality audience recording from a show at London's Crystal Palace, billed as "Garden Party" and featuring Pink Floyd on a bill with Mountain, Quiver and the Faces featuring Rod Stewart. That concert finds the band in a very tentative mindset, with several minutes of tuning between each number. The amateur recording renders the vocals somewhat garbled, but it's clear that Roger Waters's lyrics are still in flux, with different words and vocal parts extending over the top of what would eventually be instrumental sections. But this early live performance of "Return of the Son of Nothing" runs between 23 and 24 minutes long—within seconds of the run time of the finished studio "Echoes"—showing that the arrangement was nearly fully formed by April.

On the *Meddle* album, the epic-length "Echoes" would occupy the entire second side of the vinyl disc. The first side would feature five songs of more conventional length and scope.

Some of the most compelling songs in the Pink Floyd catalog would arise out of the musicians' (often accidental) discovery of a new and intriguing sound or sonic texture. That's certainly the case with *Meddle*'s opening track, the instrumental "One of These Days." Credited to all four members of Pink Floyd, "One of These Days" opens with the sound of gale-force winds. Within seconds, that soundscape is joined by a trebly thump on Roger Water's electric bass guitar. But here the bass signal has been routed through a device called the Binson Echorec. The Italian-made device allows users to create and control echoed versions of the sounds emanating from their instruments. But unlike the popular tape-based echo devices of the day (digital echo and reverb technology was still many years in the future), the magnetic drum-based Binson unit was more reliable and provided improved fidelity. As used on "One of These Days," Waters's Echorec-filtered bass guitar sounds take on a distinctive tone unlike anything most listeners would have heard before.

The Echorec had been used to good effect by Syd Barrett on early Pink Floyd tracks including "Astronomy Dominé" and "Interstellar Overdrive," but its use on "One of These Days" is likely the first instance of Pink Floyd applying the Binson effect to bass guitar.

"One of These Days" is constructed primarily around two chords, with a third appearing only occasionally. The work is carried forward on the strength of Roger Waters's throbbing, repeating bass lines, with Nick Mason adding flourishes of drums—including plenty of carefully placed cymbal crashes—as the song unfolds. Richard Wright adds dramatic runs on Hammond organ, and David Gilmour eventually joins in on distorted, careening slide guitar.

The insistent, deeply intense bass-led melody continues; around the two-minute mark, some tape-reversed cymbal hits from Mason can be heard deep in the mix. Seconds later, the drummer lays down a series of forceful floor-tom beats that evoke the sound of a door being knocked by someone in the paroxysms of suppressed rage. As David Gilmour's guitar lines churn and twist, the song's intensity builds to near the breaking point. As the three-minute mark approaches, all instruments, save Waters's bass, drop out of the mix, leaving only the heavily effected instrument to carry the music forward. At first, the other instruments reenter tentatively and subtly, and then Mason's "knocking" drum beat returns. Without further warning, heavily treated spoken vocals from the drummer make a prominent appearance. Reciting the tune's only words, Mason says in a voice redolent of an evil, British cousin of *Sesame Street*'s Cookie Monster, "One of these days, I'm going to cut you into little pieces!"

With that, the song explodes. For the remaining two minutes of "One of These Days," the four musicians careen their way through the instrumental, staying within its arrangement but doing their best to unleash controlled fury. Gilmour's electric guitar is at the head of this effort; Richard Wright has added a straightforward piano part to provide a melodic dimension to the song's rhythmic foundation. "One of These Days" ends abruptly, with David Gilmour's guitar letting out a final, extended groan as the howling wind subsides into the next tune.

From its live concert debut in September 1971, "One of These Days" would become a popular number in Pink Floyd's live set. The song remained in the band's repertoire well into 1974, and in later years the David Gilmour–led band included "One of These Days" in its set lists for years in the 1980s and 1990s. In the twenty-first century, both David Gilmour and Roger Waters would feature the tune in their respective concerts.

With a title that builds literally upon the background sound that introduces it, "A Pillow of Winds" is a Gilmour–Waters co-composition. David Gilmour gently sings Waters's intimate love-song lyrics, marking at least the third mention of eiderdown in a Pink Floyd song. (Popular in England, eiderdown is a duvet or comforter filled with duck feathers.) Gilmour's inventive sequence of chords moves the melody forward as Roger Waters's fretless bass—an instrument he would use only rarely—is confined primarily to a drone-like root note. David Gilmour overdubs at least four guitar parts on the song, including strummed and picked acoustic and electric slide guitars. Richard Wright adds some understated chording on his Hammond organ. Beginning at the song's halfway point, Nick Mason provides a subtle beat with gentle taps on his hi-hat cymbal. Pink Floyd would never play "A Pillow of Winds" live.

A classic country and western feel on David Gilmour's strummed, open-tuned acoustic guitar provides the introduction to "Fearless," the third track on *Meddle*. Nick Mason supplies a solid yet light-touch back-beat, while Roger Waters plays a solid root note figure on his bass. A soaring, gentle slide guitar over the song's chorus leads to the tune's signature ascending melodic guitar riff. Another memorable instrumental flourish in "Fearless" is its repeated yet judicious use of a break (the quickly-played chord sequence C—B♭—G), which imbues the song with a slightly bluesy feel. For the first half of "Fearless," Richard Wright's piano is more felt than actually heard; when it does enter the arrangement, the piano serves as a simple addition to the rhythm section.

David Gilmour overdubs his vocal line, sometimes doubling the melody, other times harmonizing with himself. Roger Waters's lyrics speak—sometimes in first person, other times in third person—of a character who, despite being called an idiot and a fool, rises above circumstances and defies limitations.

Were the ascending riff and break on "Fearless" not memorable enough, for the studio recording, the band decides to add a "field recording" featuring fans of the Liverpool Football Club singing the club's anthem, Richard Rodgers and Oscar Hammerstein III's "You'll Never Walk Alone" from the 1945 musical *Carousel*. Though the song would appear as the B-side of the 1971 "One of These Days" 45-rpm single, there is no record of Pink Floyd having ever performed "Fearless" live in concert or for radio broadcast.

The remaining two songs on the first side of the *Meddle* LP are sometimes considered throwaways, but each has something to recommend it. "San Tropez" is a bouncy, jazz-flavored Roger Waters solo spotlight piece. Solely composed by the bassist, "San Tropez" is a musical cousin to his earlier "Biding My Time," a song featured in 1969's live "The Man and the Journey" suite and finally released (in a studio version) on the rarities collection *Relics* (released in summer 1971). A brief tale of idyllic days spent on the French Riviera, "San Tropez" features a shuffling beat, bits of slide guitar from David Gilmour, and an extended, often single-note piano solo from Richard Wright.

"Seamus" is an acoustic blues song highlighted by bottleneck slide guitar from David Gilmour and acoustic piano from Rick Wright. Sounding as if it were recorded around a campfire, the tune features

"vocals" from a collie dog owned by Humble Pie guitarist Steve Marriott. Gilmour had been dog-sitting the pet while Marriott was on tour,
and "Seamus" (named after the dog) showcases the creature's ability to
"sing" whenever music is played.

Notwithstanding the "Seamus" variant, "Mademoiselle Nob," featured in the *Pink Floyd Live at Pompeii* film, neither of the two songs
that conclude the first side of *Meddle* would ever be played onstage by
Pink Floyd.

Following on from the epic construction of *Atom Heart Mother*'s
album-side-long title suite, "Echoes" is a glacial and majestic twenty-
three-plus minute piece of music that distills all of Pink Floyd's accu-
mulated musical virtues circa 1971 into a fully realized work. The
group-composed "Echoes" begins with a "pinging" opening note, evoking thoughts of a submarine's sonar, a transmission that can be heard
more than 100 miles away. The group achieves the distinctive effect by
means of routing the sound of Richard Wright's grand piano through
two effects in sequence: a rotating Leslie speaker and the Binson Echorec.

Ever so slowly, additional instruments enter the mix; a second, Les-
lie-treated piano plays a series of broken ascending and descending
chords. Around the one-minute mark, David Gilmour enters on single-
note slide guitar. Wright adds Hammond organ to the mix, playing a
two-chord figure. A half minute later, Roger Waters plays the first note
on his bass guitar. As the minor-key arrangement approaches the two-
minute mark, Nick Mason enters with his trademark drum fill. At this
point, the entire band is playing, and repeats the entire opening melodic line, exercising subtlety and restraint.

Seconds shy of three minutes into "Echoes," David Gilmour and
Richard Wright begin their harmonized dual lead vocals. Writing of
albatrosses, rolling waves and coral caves, Roger Waters's lyrics explicitly aim to conjure a dreamy, seafaring ambience. For the next two and a
half minutes, "Echoes" takes the form of a soothing, highly melodic
folk-rock song.

Right around the five-and-a-half-minute mark, the vocals cease, replaced by a soaring David Gilmour lead guitar solo. One of his most
expressive and oft-imitated instrumental breaks, Gilmour's solo flies
above repeated restatings of the verse, adopting its own melodic lines
rather than following the ones used by the vocals. The technique of

switching between minor and major chords adds emotional heft to Gilmour's guitar solo in support of Waters's lyrics.

One of the many distinctive qualities within "Echoes" is its refrain, one that does not feature vocals. Instead, this chorus-of-a-sort is built around a five-note descending melody that leads the underlying chords from C# minor down to A and back again several times, before resolving to E major, then B major, and then—after a passing chord—back to C# minor. Prior to the hit songs on *The Dark Side of the Moon*, the refrain of "Echoes" is among the most enduring and memorable instrumental passages in the Pink Floyd catalog.

With each repeating of that phrase, the band plays with increasing intensity, emphasizing and accenting certain beats. As ensemble performance, this section of "Echoes" represents Pink Floyd playing as a greatly improved, "tighter" musical unit.

Seven minutes in, "Echoes" shifts tone radically. Led by a muscular Roger Waters bass line, Mason and Wright lay down a solid two-chord jam. That jam provides the backdrop for David Gilmour's second guitar solo section, one in which he again soars above the rhythm section. Once again with "Echoes," repeated stating of an instrumental theme finds the band increasing its musical intensity. Wright's heavily distorted Hammond organ adds some grit and texture to the rhythm as well.

After continuing for three and half minutes, the jam sequence fades out, leaving an eerie, desolate soundscape in its place. A howling sound evocative of ocean depths provides a musical backdrop, and David Gilmour introduces his now-refined technique of imitating whales with his guitar and wah-wah pedal. Through the process of overdubbing, Gilmour creates multiple "whale" voices that seem to call out through the depths to one another. This impressionistic interlude continues as the fifteen-minute mark approaches, joined by a lengthy sustained organ chord. At fifteen minutes, the "sonar ping" returns. Using a volume pedal to remove the "attack" of his bass notes, Roger Waters reintroduces the song's earlier chord sequence. Richard Wright adds a two-chord line atop the bass figure, and David Gilmour plays a faraway-sounding, stuttering guitar line.

The guitar sounds moves "closer" (in other words, louder in the mix) as Nick Mason reenters, first on cymbal, then on floor toms. Wright adds a simple yet fetching melody on Hammond. Just past the eighteen-minute mark, David Gilmour adds two electric guitar parts. One is a majestic, slightly distorted, single-note melodic line; the other is a chiming, repeating figure. Roger Waters plays root notes on his bass with great emphasis, leading the band into a brief, dramatic bridge.

Just past nineteen minutes, that bridge leads "Echoes" back into the pop-song part of its construction, with more Gilmour–Wright lead vocals and additional lyrics. The descending riff appears once again, played multiple times (again) with the musical force increasing with each successive run-though.

After the twenty-one-minute mark, "Echoes" engages in liftoff. The rhythmic part of the song falls away, and an ever-ascending whooshing sound seems to lift the song into the skies. Wright's Leslie-effected piano once again plays the song's introductory broken chords, and eventually all sounds disappear into the sonic mist, leaving behind only the "ping." And with that, *Meddle* concludes.

Pink Floyd's now extensive experience creating music for films— specifically the development of musical passages that fit into a defined span of time—may well have influenced the making of "Echoes." It's remarkable that—as outlined above—many of the work's changes from one musical section to another tend to occur right around a minute or half-minute mark in the song. Moreover, the architectural education background of Waters and Mason—with its emphasis on tidiness, order, right angles, and level construction—may have subtly manifested itself within the twenty-plus minutes of "Echoes." The song would endure as a centerpiece of Pink Floyd's live set well into the 1970s, and would be resurrected—albeit briefly—in 1987 when the Waters-less lineup of Pink Floyd embarked on a world tour in support of *A Momentary Lapse of Reason*.

Meddle was released worldwide on October 31, 1971. While it charted impressively in the United Kingdom (#3) and the Netherlands (#2), in the United States the album reached only #70 on the *Billboard* 200. But after the runaway success of *The Dark Side of the Moon*, many listeners delved into Pink Floyd's earlier work, and *Meddle* would become one of the most popular items in the band's catalog; the album would eventually be certified Double Platinum (more than two million copies sold).

Initial sales notwithstanding, critical reaction to *Meddle* was decidedly positive. In a review that began by reminding readers that *Atom Heart Mother* had been "nothing short of disaster," *Rolling Stone*'s Jean-Charles Costa enthused about "One of These Days" and "Echoes" and summed up *Meddle* as "killer Floyd start to finish." Recognizing that it represented a progression, *NME*'s Tony Stewart wrote, "'Echoes' was only possible because of [*Atom Heart*] *Mother*, and it expressed more." Writing with the hindsight gained over more than three decades, BBC's Daryl Easlea wrote in 2007, "'Echoes' dominates the entire work. It has a majestic grace, filling every one of its 23 minutes with the sophisticated mystery that came to define everything about Pink Floyd; slightly obscure; extremely special." He went on to characterize *Meddle* as "everything right about progressive rock; engaging, intelligent and compelling."

The members of Pink Floyd knew that the epic track that grew out of meandering, exploratory experiments was something special indeed. For his part, Roger Waters would look back upon "Echoes" as a turning point in his development as a songwriter. "It was the beginning of all the writing about other people," he observed in an interview for a 2003 documentary. "It was the beginning of empathy, if you like. There's a sort of thread that's gone through everything for me ever since then, and had a big eruption in [*The Dark Side of the Moon*]." David Gilmour commented on "Echoes" in the same documentary. Speaking about Pink Floyd's experimental nature, pushing musical boundaries while retaining melody, he said, "When you get to *Meddle*, quite clearly 'Echoes' shows the direction that we're moving in."

Pink Floyd fan, expert, and host of the syndicated radio show *Floydian Slip*, Craig Bailey sees *Meddle* as a key moment in the band's history. He characterizes the 1971 album as "the point where things really began to gel into what was going to become the type of music that they would put on *The Dark Side of the Moon*."

By the time *Meddle* landed on retail shelves, Pink Floyd was on tour in the United States. Set lists from that period included "Echoes" and "One of These Days" plus older material, and encores often took the form of twelve-bar blues instrumentals. Two weeks before the start of that American tour, the band had traveled to Italy to film a live "concert" in the desolate, unoccupied ruins of a coliseum in Pompeii. A month after the release of *Meddle*, Pink Floyd was back in the studio, developing ideas for a new stage show to be called "Eclipse." In time, that work would come to be known as *The Dark Side of the Moon*.

Part VI

Burning Bridges (1971–1972)

21

BBC FOUR

Pink Floyd would be busier than ever in 1971. The band played at least seventy concerts, at venues in England, Europe, and the United States. The band performed "Atom Heart Mother Suite" on a number of occasions with local brass ensembles, orchestras, and choirs. And the year found the group touring for the first time ever in Australia and Japan. In addition to the numerous studio recording sessions for *Meddle*, Pink Floyd traveled to Italy to film sequences for a music performance film directed by British filmmaker Adrian Maben. With that schedule, there would be less time for the band to schedule a visit to BBC's Paris Cinema. In 1971, Pink Floyd performed for BBC Radio only once, on September 30. Most of that concert would be broadcast at 10 p.m. on Tuesday, October 12, on the *Sounds of the Seventies* radio program. One track performed, "Blues," would not be broadcast. The concert—sans the missing "Blues," which does circulate among collectors—is included on Pink Floyd's massive 2016 box set, *The Early Years*.

Until 1988, Musicians' Union rules in the United Kingdom enforced a so-called needle time policy that limited the amount of pre-recorded music that could be broadcast on the BBC. The original impetus for the rule was to keep records from putting live performing musicians out of work. Even in 1971 such a rule may have seemed quaint, but in retrospect, the policy would mean that many otherwise undocumented live rock and pop performances would be recorded and preserved for the enjoyment of future generations. Not counting rare interviews and a 1974 concert broadcast recorded at London's Wembley Arena (featuring *The Dark Side of the Moon*), the September 1971 appearance would be Pink Floyd's final concert for the BBC.

Once again, popular deejay John Peel would be the host for Pink Floyd's BBC show. Introducing the program to an in-house audience coached ahead of time to cheer after each phrase, Peel jokingly scolds those in attendance: "No, you blew it. You did it all wrong. Anyway, the Pink Floyd!" The quartet immediately launches into *Atom Heart Mother*'s "Fat Old Sun." Unlike the version played for BBC Radio a little more than a year earlier, the 1971 performance of the song extends beyond fifteen minutes. From its opening strains, this arrangement is quite different than the previous one. Richard Wright introduces the song with a simple, melancholy pattern of two minor chords on his organ. The entire band joins in, but Wright's organ takes a larger role in moving the melody forward than on the studio or earlier BBC versions wherein the organ part is quite subtle. When David Gilmour reaches the "sing to me" bridge, Wright's organ carries the tune completely, with that same two-chord break imbuing the song with a dolorous ambience.

After a second verse that closely follows the arrangement of the first—and as "Fat Old Sun" approaches the five-minute mark—David Gilmour tears into a rousing solo on his electric guitar. Gilmour continues for a full minute, with Waters, Wright, and Mason playing at full strength behind him. At that point, all musicians scale back the intensity of their playing, beginning a hushed and understated interlude that restates the song's verse structure. The band plays quieter and quieter still for another minute, until only Richard Wright's organ remains.

After the briefest of silences, Wright effectively restarts "Fat Old Sun" with the same two-chord figure on his organ. As the entire band enters the arrangement, David Gilmour plays a slashing rhythmic figure, leaving space for Wright to turn in an extended, percussive organ solo of his own. Once again, the band reaches the heights of instrumental intensity. Right at the nine-and-a-half-minute mark, the song changes radically into a funky, laid-back, and hypnotic three-chord blues jam, with breaks for both Wright and Gilmour to take turns at solos. The musical bed of the jam's second half has a feel quite like the ending moments of *Meddle*'s "Echoes."

Right before the twelve-minute mark, the band seamlessly returns to the core melody of "Fat Old Sun," and David Gilmour sings through the verse and "sing to me" refrain one more time. After a bit of Gilmour's wordless vocalizing, the song touches down for a landing, to rapturous applause. Host John Peel makes the observation that the song has "changed quite a bit during the last twelve months."

Peel introduces "One of These Days," quoting Roger Waters. "'It's a poignant appraisal of the contemporary social situation.' Err . . . you can make what you will of that!" He also teases the audience, letting them know to expect the vocal debut of drummer Nick Mason. "Although," he cautions, "at no time will you see his lips move . . . which is something of a technical tour-de-force." This would be the public debut of "One of These Days," a month ahead of its release as part of the *Meddle* LP. The live performance of the song differs from its studio counterpart in only one significant way: after the playback of Mason's ring modulator-treated phrase, the band continues with the existing musical phrases for a few more beats before launching into the more "explosive" section of the song. In light of the effectiveness of the vocal's timing on the LP, it's safe to assume that the premature triggering of the tape onstage was a mistake. For good measure, once the song ends, the spoken-word tape playback is activated a second and final time.

The 1971 performance of "Embryo" for BBC Radio is something of a curiosity. The arrangement of the song doesn't differ significantly from that of a year earlier, but the song's most distinctive feature—the taped sounds of a cooing baby followed by children playing outdoors— are conspicuous in their absence. Peel's introduction does make clear that Pink Floyd was quite displeased at the studio version having been released on Harvest's *Picnic* sampler LP, but it's unknown why the band would leave out such a crucial component of the live arrangement on the occasion of a radio performance. Waters, Wright, Mason, and Gilmour are all in fine form for this reading, but the performance seems skeletal without its remarkable extra-musical sounds.

A radio performance of "Echoes" demonstrates the degree to which Pink Floyd has worked out an extended piece that began its life as a collection of short pieces. In a live context and without the benefit of overdubbing, the BBC Radio recording of "Echoes" is an authentic document of the manner in which the band would present the work in concert. Save the absence of additional guitar and keyboard parts featured on the *Meddle* studio recording, the live reading of September 1971 is nearly identical to its studio counterpart, and to the version performed in the ruins of a Pompeii, Italy, coliseum for *Pink Floyd Live at Pompeii*, filmed less than a week after the BBC date.

American underground publication *Great Speckled Bird* often covered Pink Floyd album releases and concerts, and writing for the paper, Steve Wise observed, "Pink Floyd possesses a remarkable sense of how discordant elements and sound effects can be fitted together and made, believe it or not, melodic." But despite the band's burgeoning popularity in the United States, Pink Floyd remained a cult band. In a 1971 interview with a KPPC-FM disc jockey, Richard Wright admitted as much: "It's possible we haven't reached the stage yet where we could fill up huge sports stadiums anyway in America, and that's why we are in small halls." The cost of the band's live presentation—massive amounts of gear, a custom quadraphonic audio system, lights and other visual effects—meant that touring would not yet be a lucrative proposition.

And despite the addition of a handful of new pieces, the band members realized that it was time once again for new material. The set list had not changed appreciably in several months, and critics were beginning to pick up on that reality. In that same KPPC interview, Nick Mason observed, "you can get trapped by your own greatest works, like 'Interstellar Overdrive.'" On the prospect of new music, he said, "Every time we finish an album we say, 'Right. Now, let's do another one, and we'll have two a year.' [But] we've never managed it yet."

But a creative breakthrough lay just over the horizon. By November, Pink Floyd would begin working on musical ideas that would eventually take form as *The Dark Side of the Moon*. By the end of 1972, that album would be nearly complete, as would another album, the soundtrack LP *Obscured by Clouds*. And in between those projects, the group would perform ninety-three concerts in 1972, as well as involve itself in an ambitious project that aimed to combine rock music and ballet performance.

22

CHILDHOOD'S END

In an unprecedented burst of creative flowering, Pink Floyd spent the better part of the first three weeks of January 1972 at Abbey Road Studios in London. The band's recent commercial success with *Meddle*, however modest when viewed on a global scale, would mean that Pink Floyd could afford to book time in one of London's most in-demand studios, simply to develop and write material for a forthcoming album. By the middle of the month, an embryonic stage presentation was readied with three days of rehearsals at the Rainbow Theatre; the live premiere of *The Dark Side of the Moon* took place on a Thursday night, January 20, at the Dome, a popular venue fifty miles south of London in the English seaside resort town of Brighton. Though technical problems plagued the premiere, the following night's show in Portsmouth went much more smoothly, as did most of the remaining dozen shows, all in England.

Three days after the mini-tour, Pink Floyd left for Strawberry Studios at Château d'Hérouville, near Paris, for the first of two one-week recording sessions. (Days earlier, Elton John had recorded his fifth studio album at Strawberry; he named the album *Honky Château* in honor of the studio.) Putting aside for the moment all of the band's new material from *The Dark Side of the Moon*, Pink Floyd instead set about the task of recording music for another motion picture. Once again working for director Barbet Schroeder, the group would come up with ten brand-new songs, this time for a film set in the lush jungles of Papua New Guinea and called *La Vallée*. Breaking mid-project for a five-night run of concerts in Japan, the band would return for a second week-long recording session in France. Save for a few days of post-production mixing back in London, the twelve days spent at Château d'Hérouville provided all of the music Schroeder needed for his film. They also yielded a new Pink Floyd album—one not explicitly marketed as a soundtrack—called *Obscured by Clouds*.

For the sessions, Pink Floyd brought along a recent acquisition, a VCS 3 synthesizer built by London-based Electronic Music Studio and bought used from the BBC Radiophonic Workshop. Primitive by twenty-first-century standards, the VCS 3 was but a year old in 1970, and represented cutting-edge synthesizer technology. The device is controlled not by a traditional organ-style keyboard, but by a cluster of knobs and fader tabs. The wide palette of otherworldly sounds within the VCS 3 would be a prominent feature of *The Dark Side of the Moon* and used, in more sparing fashion, during the sessions for *Obscured by Clouds*.

The film itself—described as a chronicle of the lead characters' journey of self-discovery—finds Westerners interacting with the Mapuga tribe of native peoples. Beyond their titles and some notable sound effects, the songs composed and recorded for Schroeder's second directorial turn (after 1969's *More*) bear little if any lyrical connection to the onscreen action or dialogue. But as mood pieces, Pink Floyd's ten songs for *La Vallée* are effective at helping to create specific moods.

Obscured by Clouds is characterized by a wealth of instrumental numbers. The album opens with the title track (credited to Waters and Gilmour), introduced by a low, extended bass-note hum courtesy of the band's new VCS 3. Nick Mason joins in with a simple drum pattern, eventually layering percussive complexity atop it. More VCS 3 lines are added, and after nearly a minute, David Gilmour enters on slide guitar, with Waters joining on bass. As Gilmour plays a straightforward solo, his band mates hold down the rhythmic backing, with Wright and Waters never diverging from the single note (A) that they're playing. Pink Floyd would perform the tune a number of times live onstage in 1972–1973.

As "Obscured by Clouds" fades toward silence, a crisp Nick Mason snare drum introduction kicks off "When You're In." Beginning with the same note, and in the same key, as the track that precedes it, "When You're In" eventually unfolds into a tune with more standard chord changes. An insistent, vaguely martial melody, the second instrumental on *Obscured by Clouds* features a traditional verse-and-chorus structure, with Rick Wright's organ and David Gilmour's lead guitar often playing the signature melody in unison. Wright also adds occasional, subtle keyboard fills as flourishes. The group-credited "When You're In" takes a longer than customary amount of time to fade out. Pink Floyd included the song in its live performances around the time of the album's release.

The 3/4 time signature is often called "waltz time." The traditional dance designed to accompany music in that time signature is also called the waltz. But while "Burning Bridges" (credited to Richard Wright and Roger Waters) is nominally in 3/4, the glacially paced tune is perhaps better thought of as being in 6/8, as the pattern and melody do not conform to the waltz "feel." Richard Wright's Hammond organ melody forms the basis of the gentle tune. Gilmour and Wright take turns singing lead and backing each other with vocal harmonies. Gilmour's quiet, shimmering guitar melody supports Wright's organ part, and the guitarist adds two distinctly different solos mid-song, plus a third as the tune fades out. "Burning Bridges" would never be performed live by Pink Floyd or any of its individual members.

Most every Pink Floyd soundtrack project features at least one hard rock song. *More* had "The Nile Song," and *Zabriskie Point* would have had several had Antonioni used the material the band provided. "The Gold It's in The . . ." is *Obscured by Clouds'* entry in that category. Like "The Nile Song," it feels awkwardly out of place within the band's catalog—the tune is as unfinished as its title—but considered on its own merits, it's a reasonably successful album track. With a boogie-rock feel, it's a slice of somewhat clichéd lyrics ("You go your way; I'll go mine") and a rote melody. Lacking a traditional chorus, each verse ends in a way that leaves the listener expecting a few more measures of music and words; instead, a Nick Mason drum fill—the term *fill* is especially appropriate here—appears to bridge the tune into the next verse. David Gilmour does his enthusiastic best with the under-written lyrics (the final word of the line "All I have to do is just close my eyes" is extended uncomfortably over four beats). "The Gold It's in The . . ." redeems itself somewhat with a blistering electric guitar solo from Gilmour. The solo takes up the better part of two out of the song's three minutes. Not surprisingly, "The Gold It's in The . . ." would never be performed onstage by Pink Floyd.

The group's practice of using odd titles for tunes on *Obscured by Clouds* continues with a Waters–Gilmour song, "Wot's . . . Uh the Deal?" With a pastoral, country-ish feel that places David Gilmour's acoustic guitar and Richard Wright's acoustic piano at the center of the mix, it's one of Pink Floyd's prettiest melodies. Waters's melancholy lyrics concern having a chill in one's soul, fear of aging, and the frustrations of keeping up with the rat race; all of these themes would seem to have been in the forefront of the bassist's thoughts, as all would figure prominently in the lyrics of the temporarily suspended *The Dark Side of the Moon* project. Some fetching "round" singing (courtesy of Gilmour's overdubbed voice) adds a pop quality not often found in the band's work. A subtle yet rousing chorus leads into a pair of lovely solo breaks from Rick Wright and David Gilmour, respectively. The tune's dour lyrics are more than offset by the lilting melody and sublime instrumental work. Like most of the songs from *Obscured by Clouds*, "Wot's . . . Uh the Deal?" would never become part of a Pink Floyd live set, but in 2006, David Gilmour performed the song on multiple dates of his *On an Island* tour. Those performances included Richard Wright on piano, and represent some of his final concerts before his death in 2008.

Though it's credited to David Gilmour and Richard Wright, the instrumental "Mudmen" is very close in both melody and arrangement to the Wright–Waters composition "Burning Bridges." The first minute and a half of the song features Wright's organ as its central instrument, with some understated vibraphone accompaniment deep in the mix. David Gilmour adds a soaring guitar solo, after which the melody breaks down, with Mason's drums exiting. A VCS 3 sound bed provides backing for a second Gilmour solo, this time on slide guitar. Mason and bassist Waters eventually rejoin, and the tune's final minute features all four musicians playing with gusto (albeit at an exceedingly measured pace). There are no known live Pink Floyd performances of "Mudmen."

The second side of the *Obscured by Clouds* LP opens with perhaps the album's strongest tune, "Childhood's End." Solely composed by David Gilmour, "Childhood's End" would be only the fourth tune written by the guitarist on his own while in Pink Floyd. (It would also be his last solo composition for the band until reforming Pink Floyd without Roger Waters in the mid-1980s.) The song opens with an extended fade-in featuring Rick Wright's organ and VCS 3. Via overdubbing, the synthesizer produces multiple sounds; one of these is a thumping, percussive sound that provides a beat for the song prior to Nick Mason's drum part. The distinctive VCS 3 percussion for "Childhood's End" would soon appear again on a Pink Floyd record, this time as a prominent feature of "Time" from *The Dark Side of the Moon*.

As that extended introduction begins to fade out, the full-band arrangement of "Childhood's End" is faded in, first featuring Gilmour's acoustic guitar, followed by electric guitar, bass, drums, and a vibrato-laden Hammond organ from Rick Wright. Gilmour's lyrics had been inspired by the Arthur C. Clarke science fiction novel of the same name. A minor-key blues with some dramatic flourishes, "Childhood's End" would be featured prominently in Pink Floyd concerts beginning in 1972 and continuing into the next year. Following a favored band practice, those live performances often extended the song to twice the length of its studio version. None of these performances have been released officially, but many audience recordings circulate among collectors.

Viewed within the context of Pink Floyd's body of work, Roger Waters's "Free Four" is atypical. Displaying the sardonic gallows humor he had exhibited in songs as early as "Take Up Thy Stethoscope and Walk" from 1967's *The Piper at the Gates of Dawn*, the bassist weds a jaunty, singalong melody to dark lyrics. In the tune—which has six verses but no chorus—Waters contrasts life as "a short, warm moment" and death as a "long, cold rest," and refers to an angel of death, burial, and a funeral drum. The song, which features peppy hand claps throughout, briefly comments on the perils of the music industry—a theme to which Roger Waters would return in some detail on Pink Floyd's 1975 LP, *Wish You Were Here*—and begins and ends with lyrics that suggest that everyone will "talk to yourself as you die." An uptempo David Gilmour guitar solo and a rumbling bass note—courtesy the VCS 3—are the distinctive sonic elements of "Free Four." Pink Floyd never played the song live, but Capitol Records did release the song in the United States as a single in 1972. It did not chart.

Richard Wright's melancholy "Stay" is the final vocal track on *Obscured by Clouds*. After Wright enters on grand piano, David Gilmour joins in on slide guitar played through a wah-wah pedal. The rhythm section of Roger Waters and Nick Mason plays a straight, understated part in the song. Rick Wright harmonizes with himself on the song's vocals. The tone and style of "Stay" would be a preview of the songs Wright would write and record six years later on his solo debut album, *Wet Dream*. David Gilmour's guitar solo employs the wah-wah pedal effect in even more emphatic fashion, and continues in understated style as the song concludes.

Obscured by Clouds closes with an instrumental track, "Absolutely Curtains." The song opens with a quiet flourish on Nick Mason's cymbals, joined by a long-held organ chord and a brief piano figure. At the one-minute mark, Rick Wright's Farfisa organ makes an appearance, as do some quiet tubular bells and electric piano. Tack piano and celeste are subtly woven into the mix of what is essentially a one-chord, impressionistic piece. Wright's Hammond organ fades in and then drones on. Pink Floyd fades out, leaving behind the sound of a "field recording" of a chant featuring the Mapuga tribe (from the film). That field recording continues for nearly two minutes, and then *Obscured by Clouds* is over.

Pink Floyd's seventh studio album was released June 2, 1972. Between the end of the album's recording sessions and its release date, Pink Floyd had embarked upon a US tour, and then crossed the Atlantic to play a pair of festivals (2nd British Rock Meeting in West Germany, and Amsterdam Rock Circus in the Netherlands). While the regular concert dates had featured the still-developing *The Dark Side of the Moon* in its entirety, for the shorter festival set, Pink Floyd reverted back to earlier set lists that included tunes from older albums, with "A Saucerful of Secrets" as an encore.

Critical response to *Obscured by Clouds* was measured. Atlanta underground publication *Great Speckled Bird*'s Steve Wise wrote, "The old Floyd that I knew and loved just isn't here . . . The album's pleasantness will simply not compensate for its lack of dynamism." With the benefit of hindsight, many latter-day reviewers would praise the album as an underrated gem in Pink Floyd's catalog. The 2016 box set, *The Early Years*, includes a new remixed version of the album in its entirety as part of the massive package.

Because of disagreements with director Barbet Schroeder's production company, Pink Floyd and EMI chose not to market *Obscured by Clouds* as a soundtrack film to *La Vallée*. But hoping still to capitalize on the band's connection to the film, when it was released to theaters in August 1972, the film was titled *La Vallée/Obscured by Clouds*. Meanwhile, Pink Floyd continued work on *The Dark Side of the Moon*, and in between sessions continued efforts on a planned ballet performance for which the band had committed to write new music.

23

POMPEII AND BALLET

After the band's September 30, 1971, live concert recorded for BBC Radio's *Sounds of the Seventies*, Pink Floyd headed for Pompeii, Italy. The group had agreed to take part in the making of a concert film. But *Pink Floyd Live at Pompeii* would be no ordinary rock show movie. Director Adrian Maben had decided to avoid the typical approach of filming a band at a show, with cuts between onstage action and an adoring live audience. For his film, Maben chose an unusual venue: the Amphitheatre of Pompeii, the oldest surviving structure of its kind (and the earliest known to have been constructed of stone). Constructed around 70 BCE, the Amphitheatre of Pompeii would serve as a model for modern-day stadiums.

Odder still was the choice—agreed upon between the director and Pink Floyd—to stage a concert with no audience. So for four days in early October, Pink Floyd set up all of its audio gear (but not its lighting rigs or other visuals) and was filmed performing a selection of new and older material. The band had performed an entire "concert without audience" for film in 1970, but that session—done for San Francisco's public television station KQED—took place in a studio (the KQED session finally received home video release as part of 2016's *The Early Years* box set).

For the film, Pink Floyd performed six songs: "Careful With That Axe, Eugene," "A Saucerful of Secrets," and "Set the Controls for the Heart of the Sun" (all originally recorded in 1968), "One of These

Days" and "Echoes" (both originally heard on 1971's *Meddle*), and one new song, "Mademoiselle Nobs."

By this point in the band's career, all of the songs in the *Pompeii* set (save "Mademoiselle Nobs") were concert staples, and the arrangements were quite well established. As such, the live performances in the film differ little from standard concert versions of the time. Though Richard Wright had not yet begun to bring a grand piano on tour, for *Pink Floyd Live at Pompeii* the keyboardist would have access to one, and his acoustic piano is a prominent part of the band's reading of "A Saucerful of Secrets" in particular.

A slight, offhand track, the country blues "Mademoiselle Nobs" is a variation on *Meddle*'s "Seamus," featuring a different dog providing vocalization, and without human vocals. Notably, when a 5.1 surround sound version of *Live at Pompeii* finally received sanctioned released in 2016 (as part of *The Early Years* box set), "Mademoiselle Nobs" was not included.

Additional recording and filming for *Pink Floyd at Pompeii* would take place in mid-December in Paris's Studio Europasinor. There, the band did some overdubbing and fixing of vocal tracks, as well as transflex filming (a technique that allows post-production superimposition of other images, similar to modern-day "green screen" video techniques used for special effects and weather reports). The film received limited release in 1972, with wider distribution on its 1974 re-release. Capitalizing on Pink Floyd's massive success with 1973's *The Dark Side of the Moon*, that second release added footage of the band working on recordings at Abbey Road Studios.

Pink Floyd Live at Pompeii received positive reviews. Writing about the film in 1974, *Great Speckled Bird*'s Ward Silver noted that "'Careful With That Axe, Eugene,' perhaps the most viscerally terrifying music they have ever done on record, is light years more powerful when director Adrian Maben cuts from Roger Waters' mind-wrenching scream to Vesuvius' overflowing lava." The movie became a staple of weekend midnight movies across the United States in the late 1970s and early 1980s, and sold well on its VHS release. Director Maben put together a "Director's Cut" of *Pink Floyd Live at Pompeii in 2003*, adding modern-day computer graphics, stock footage, and outtakes from the original filming sessions. For his part, David Gilmour didn't think much of that third revised version; in a *Record Collector* interview, he sarcastically referred to it as "a new, groovier version," explaining that Maben had made "footage of ludicrous architectural designs of what Pompeii might have looked like." Making it clear that the 2003 edit was not approved by him, he offered his opinion: "Just stick with the original!"

Nick Mason wrote about the original film in his Pink Floyd history, *Inside Out*, noting that "the elements that seem to make it work—none of which we had thought much about during the filming in October 1971—were the decision to perform live instead of miming and the rather gritty environment created by the heat and the wind." He summed up *Pink Floyd Live at Pompeii* succinctly as "a surprisingly good attempt to film our live set."

The quietest member of the band, Rick Wright wouldn't provide many on-the-record comments about *Pompeii*. But in a 1989 conversation with band biographer Nicholas Schaffner, he seemed to hold a positive view of the film. "The only problem," he said, "was the director!"

In 2014, *Rolling Stone* placed the film at #12 on its list of greatest rock documentaries, noting its place in history as "the ultimate document of psych-rock's transition" into progressive rock. And with fond memories of the original 1972 experience, David Gilmour returned to the Amphitheatre of Pompeii in 2016 to film a concert of his own—this time with an audience in attendance—for a one-night-only worldwide theatrical screening in September 2017.

In some ways, *Pink Floyd Live at Pompeii* seems destined to take its place as the film that will never die. In early 2017, Adrian Maben announced plans for yet another revised version of the film—bringing the total to four—for release in November 2017. In an Italian-language interview with news website repubblica.it, he teased interviewer Michele Chisena about the discovery of long-lost outtake footage, saying, "Wait and see for the answer." Pressed on the motivation for releasing yet another cut of the 1972 film, he explained, "I'm a bit like a nineteenth century French painter, Pierre Bonnard, who used to retouch and paint his paintings in later years when they were still in the Louvre. And the museum officials were furious!"

"We're writing a ballet for Roland Petit which will be in Paris next June," Roger Waters told *Georgia Straight*'s Mike Quigley in October 1970. "And the sky's the limit for that."

As the wryly self-effacing Nick Mason would write in his Pink Floyd chronicle, *Inside Out*, the band's motivation for exploring a combination of rock music and ballet performance was borne of the band's "quest for upmarket artistry." In 1970, the band members met with acclaimed French ballet company director and choreographer Roland Petit to discuss the prospect of collaboration.

Petit had long since earned a reputation for cutting-edge productions: rather than yet another production of *The Nutcracker Suite* or *Swan Lake*, Petit had begun his choreography career staging *Guernica*, a work inspired by Pablo Picasso's antiwar painting of the same name and based loosely on William Shakespeare's *Romeo and Juliet*. The adventurous Petit staged many other works, including 1967's *Paradise Lost*, based upon John Milton's epic poem published three hundred years earlier.

The ideas explored over a series of conversations ranged widely; as the concept progressed, it would become less and less ambitious, more conventional. One idea floated was the staging of a ballet production of Marcel Proust's 1913 novel, *À la recherche du temps perdu* (*Remembrance of Things Past*). Early plans called for ballet icon Rudolf Nureyev to star in the lead, and for the troupe to be backed by Pink Floyd plus an orchestra featuring more than 100 musicians. And Pink Floyd would write all new music for the production. That wildly ambitious idea—based as it was upon a book often described as dense and impenetrable—received a cool reception from Pink Floyd.

Subsequent concepts discussed and discarded included a version of *Arabian Nights*, Mary Shelley's *Frankenstein*, and, courtesy of director Roman Polanski, who was in on some of the informal meetings, making a pornographic film. "It was a complete joke because no one had any idea what they wanted to do," Roger Waters told *ZigZag*'s Connor McKnight in 1973.

"It just went on for two years, this idea of doing a ballet," Nick Mason explained to McKnight in that same interview. The discussions were characterized by "no one coming up with any ideas, us not setting aside any time because there was nothing specific." Eventually Petit took charge. "In a desperate moment, Roland devised a ballet to some existing music, which I think was a good idea," Mason explained.

In November 1972, a series of shows was staged in Marseilles, France. Petit served as choreographer and artistic director for Les Ballets de Marseilles, and the production starred ballerina Maïa Plissetskaia, formerly of Moscow's famed Bolshoi Theatre. The program was in three parts, the third of which was titled *Le ballet Pink Floyd*. A four-movement work, that ballet had as its soundtrack five songs from the Pink Floyd catalog, played live by the band on a raised stage behind the dancers. Two days of rehearsals were followed by five shows at Marseilles' Salle Valliers sports complex.

A second season of *Le ballet Pink Floyd* would be staged in Paris in January 1973; this time, after a two-day rehearsal, the work was presented twice a day over four succeeding weekends, for sixteen performances total. The band played live for the first eight; recordings of Pink Floyd would be used for the remaining performances.

Even though the band was playing songs that had been in its repertoire for some time—"Careful With That Axe, Eugene," in particular—the demands of choreography meant that there was no room for deviation, much less improvisation. The music and dance had to be closely synchronized, and that meant that performances of the songs ("Eugene," plus "Echoes" and "One of These Days" [from *Meddle*] and "Obscured by Clouds" and "When You're In" from the just-released album) would have to be played exactly the same way each time. As such, musical spontaneity would not be a feature of the concerts. But as surviving film clips (included on DVD and Blu-ray in *The Early Years* box set) illustrate, the overall effect is still quite breathtaking. The dancers are in fine form and deliver expressive movement that corresponds (after a fashion) to the music being performed live.

The experience of playing to a tightly choreographed program in *Le ballet Pink Floyd* may have provided a foundation for the group when, seven years later, the band would embark upon a three-city tour (London, New York, and Los Angeles) to perform *The Wall*, another work that required live performance that mandated adherence to painstakingly precise timings.

Though when asked about the project in 1998, David Gilmour told *MOJO* that the whole thing was little more than "a bit of old ballet danced to a bit of old music," its legacy would quietly endure. Forty-plus years after *Le ballet Pink Floyd* staged its final performance, the Corps de Ballet of the Teatro dell'Opera in Rome, Italy, would stage an updated version of Petit's work, using additional (pre-recorded) music from Pink Floyd's catalog. The program described Petit's ballet as a "masterpiece" and went on to note that its "great impact is due to the psychedelic effects of the music, the clever lighting and the choreographed movements which unite cultured dance with rock."

Part VII

On the Run (1972–1973)

24

QUIET DESPERATION

Amid other high-profile activities—namely the Roland Petit ballet project, filming of *Pink Floyd Live at Pompeii,* and a concert schedule that included no fewer than ninety dates in 1972—the four members of Pink Floyd channeled their creative energies into the creation of their newest work. The group's live performances would be essential to development of that project. In the past, the band had routinely developed new material onstage before committing it to tape (the epic compositions "Echoes" and "Atom Heart Mother Suite" being the readiest examples), but in 1972 Pink Floyd would refine and polish an entire album's worth of music, start to finish, onstage.

Originally (and provisionally) titled "Eclipse," the album-length work was first presented in January. Thanks to an anonymous and intrepid audience member who secreted a portable recorder into the Brighton Dome concert venue, an audio document of the first-ever performance of "Eclipse" has been preserved for history. The illicit recording provides an illustrative example of the work in its most inchoate stage: here it is remarkably close in many ways to the final form that would be recorded as *The Dark Side of the Moon,* but a number of key elements are yet to be refined.

As captured on that recording, "Eclipse" opens with a tape playback simulation of a beating heart. After more than a minute, some ominous, droning notes—likely courtesy the VCS 3 the band had recently purchased—are added to the mix. Baffled laughter can be heard among the audience; few if any would have any idea what lay in store. The synthesizer note is bent upward, and the audience begins to clap; likely this is the point at which the band appears onstage (or at least becomes visible to the audience).

As the "heartbeat" continues, Pink Floyd launches into a new song, "Breathe." Built around a simple yet irresistible two-chord motif, "Breathe" had grown out of informal jam sessions earlier in the month. Interviewed in the DVD *Classic Albums: The Making of* The Dark Side of the Moon, Roger Waters wryly recalled the tune's genesis: "Let's play E and A minor for an hour or two. All right, that'll take up five minutes."

After a minute and a half meditation on that two-chord vamp, David Gilmour enters with plaintive vocals. The lyrics for the song—like all of the words created for *The Dark Side of the Moon*, written by Waters— are still in development here. But the songwriter's general idea—setting a scene based upon an individual—is already fully in place. Even in its early form, Waters's lyrics explore the potential and, more important, the challenges and limitations of a human life. The subtle differences between the words in this January 20 concert and the lyrics on the finished album are striking: here Gilmour sings the final line of "Breathe" as "you stumble toward an early grave." On the LP, it's "race toward . . ."

On *The Dark Side of the Moon*, the sequence of songs slides seamlessly from "Breathe" into "On the Run." But on this January 1972 live recording, the latter has yet to be developed. In its place is a piece known as "The Travel Sequence." A somewhat formless jam, it's nonetheless more conventionally musical than the abstract set pieces Pink Floyd had introduced onstage just a few years earlier. Built around a single chord, "The Travel Sequence" allows David Gilmour space to riff on his electric guitar; rather than play soaring single-note lead runs, he chooses to play chugging, melodic chord sequences redolent of the improvisational sections of *Tommy*, the Who's own 1969 conceptual set piece. Arguably, Gilmour's playing style on "The Travel Sequence" owes more to the style of Who guitarist-composer Peter Townshend than his own.

Simultaneous with Gilmour's guitar riffing, Richard Wright plays an extended solo on Rhodes electric piano. As the jam unfolds, both men play with increased intensity. Meanwhile, drummer Mason and bassist Waters hold down a solid—if intentionally unspectacular—rhythmic foundation. As the seven-minute mark passes, the jam dissolves into silence.

After that extended period of silence, a ticking clock—or an audio facsimile of one—is heard. "Time" has begun. Unlike its eventual studio counterpart, this early version of "Time" does not feature Nick Mason playing rototoms, one of the song's most distinctive features. Instead, a basic, two-note intro—with long spaces between the notes—unfolds. This version of the song has a dreamy feel, with little of the ferocity of the studio recording. It's nearly three minutes before the vocal line begins, and when it does, the dual lead (David Gilmour and Richard Wright) has a languid, almost lazy texture. When Wright takes his solo vocals, he sings of "lying supine in the sunshine."

David Gilmour's lead guitar solo on "Time" is quite similar to the one he would eventually record for *The Dark Side of the Moon*, but in the context of the understated arrangement of "Time" here, it feels somewhat out of place. The song ends live onstage as it would on the album, with Wright and Gilmour harmonizing on one of Roger Waters's best and most evocative lyric lines ever: "Hanging on in quiet desperation is the English way / The time is gone, the song is over; thought I'd something more to say."

"Breathe (Reprise)" follows, as it would on the album. But instead of Roger Waters's lyrics, here the song features a bluesy David Gilmour lead guitar solo, accompanied by scat vocals that follow the same melodic line.

On *The Dark Side of the Moon*, the song "The Great Gig in the Sky" comes right after "Breathe (Reprise)." But for the debut performance of "Eclipse," the song sequence features something quite different: an embryonic version of a Richard Wright instrumental known at the time under a number of titles, including "The Mortality Sequence." Though it's not clearly audible on the Brighton recording—other bootlegged shows from 1972 would capture the performance in improved fidelity— "The Mortality Sequence" includes tape playback of a man reading Bible verses from the Book of Ecclesiastes, and clips of speeches from British author and conservative religious activist Malcolm Muggeridge. The band's most keen enthusiast of tape manipulation, Nick Mason had created loops of the spoken-word bits; the finished tape has a disorienting, psychedelic feel to it. As the tape plays, Rick Wright contributes a hymn-like melody on his Hammond organ. Just past the three-and-a-half-minute mark, a loud hissing sound begins; it's considerably louder than the music being made onstage. A loud "thud" is heard. Wright wraps up the forlorn melody.

The sound of clanging coins and banging cash registers begins, but along with it is the sound of a second recording that sounds as if it's spinning out of control. The second tape is playing a wobbling sound, and while it would have been difficult for the assembled audience to ascertain whether this was part of the show—Pink Floyd had long since developed a reputation for incorporating unusual sonic elements into its onstage performances—listening to the recording today, it's clear that something has gone terribly wrong.

Nonetheless, Roger Waters gamely launches into the signature 7/4 bass line of what would go on to become one of Pink Floyd's most well-known tunes, "Money." Here, against the backdrop of the tape mal-functions—and taken at a dreadfully sluggish pace—the song is just short of a disaster. With little choice, since Waters has begun, Gilmour, Wright, and Mason join in for a stomping, near-metallic reading of the new song. Gilmour is either not singing at all, or his microphone is malfunctioning as well. Around the two-minute mark, the band suc-cumbs to the inevitable and stops playing. The loud hissing continues unabated. Someone somewhere finds a way to turn it off, and after a few seconds of confused silence, the audience offers tepid applause.

While what would follow onstage isn't captured on the bootlegger's tape, a number of reporters were in attendance that night and docu-mented in writing what had taken place. In a show review, *NME*'s Tony Stewart quoted Waters's announcement to the audience: "That wasn't pretty. We'll fix that." And after conferring with band mates and road crew, the bassist returned to the stage, announcing, "Due to severe mechanical and electric horror, we can't do any more of that bit. So we'll do something else." Abandoning the evening's plans, Pink Floyd would launch into its old set list, playing "Atom Heart Mother Suite," and then after a break, continue with "Careful With That Axe, Eugene," "One of These Days," and "Echoes." For an encore, the band would perform a four-year-old tune, "A Saucerful of Secrets."

"Basically it was a big disappointment to use old stuff," Nick Mason told Stewart backstage after the concert had ended. "But it couldn't be helped. I think probably it was better to do that." And while the *NME* reporter noted that some among the audience seemed unmoved by the concert, he came away impressed. "At no time during the performance were Floyd untogether," he wrote. "The musicians go together like salt and vinegar on fish and chips—it is that sort of tasteful relationship."

Stewart's enthusiasm wasn't shared by Andrew Means of rival music paper *Melody Maker*, who was also in attendance. "What their music lacked in framework and conception," he wrote, "it seemed to be trying to compensate for with volume and aural clarity."

The band would attempt *The Dark Side of the Moon* again the following night in nearby Portsmouth. This time, technical problems would be greatly diminished. And once again an audience member would make a recording of the entire performance.

25

ANY COLOUR YOU LIKE

The technical problems of the previous night's concert had not diminished Pink Floyd's resolve. From the opening moments of the Friday night show at Portsmouth's Guildhall, the band would be in control of the electronics and effects so critical to the new set piece. The second attempt at performing *The Dark Side of the Moon* in its entirety would proceed far more smoothly than the first.

An unreleased (and unauthorized) audience recording of the Portsmouth concert captures the entire performance for posterity, and it shows the band playing in a more assured manner than it had done the night before. The set opens with the "heartbeat" tape, proceeds into "Breathe," giving way to "The Travel Sequence" and "Time." But toward the end of "Time," the instrumental reprise of "Breathe" has been altered; it now features lyrics in place of David Gilmour's lead guitar and scat vocal of the night before. At this point in the development of *The Dark Side of the Moon*, the band is still tinkering with the music and arrangement, and Roger Waters is still writing and refining the work's lyrics.

"The Mortality Sequence" (also sometimes known at this stage as "The Religion Song") is a bit shorter for its second night. Richard Wright's organ playing is assured as ever, but while the texture of the piece is appealing—and suitably evocative of a church-going experience—the melody itself is unremarkable. As Wright's organ fades to silence, the taped cash register sounds that introduce "Money" play through the band's PA system.

At this stage, "Money" still begins with Roger Waters's unaccompanied bass guitar. But for the second night, the tapes are playing at the correct speed; serving in the role of a drumbeat, the cut-and-pasted sounds of coins and cash registers had been assembled to provide the song's 7/4 time signature, and the musicians follow along. The jagged time signature adds an off-kilter feel to what is, at its core, a blues-based chord progression.

The instrumental midsection of "Money" features a searing David Gilmour lead guitar solo laid atop a stomping rhythm section. This part of the song builds upon the riff Pink Floyd developed as "Moonhead" and performed on BBC television for the 1969 moon landing. Fourteen months before its release on *The Dark Side of the Moon*, all of the elements that would make "Money" one of Pink Floyd's most memorable songs are fully in place.

Without missing a beat, the band segues from "Money" directly into the world premiere of another new song, "Us and Them." Richard Wright had composed the piano-based melody years earlier; an instrumental version had been recorded for use in Michelangelo Antonioni's film *Zabriskie Point*, but it was not used. Originally known as "The Violent Sequence," the tune would remain unused for nearly two years before being repurposed—with lyrics added by Roger Waters—as a centerpiece of *The Dark Side of the Moon*. "It's sort of amazing to me now that we had that piece of music in 1969 when we recorded the music for *Zabriskie Point*," said David Gilmour in a 2003 documentary. "And throughout *Atom Heart Mother*, *Obscured by Clouds* and the *Meddle* album, we didn't dig it out and use it." Calling it "a lovely piece of music," he observed that "Us and Them" was "obviously waiting to be reborn" on *The Dark Side of the Moon*.

Illustrating the work-in-progress nature of Pink Floyd's new stage presentation, in this early live version of "Us and Them," it's Waters who takes the lead vocal, not David Gilmour. The melody lies near the top-end of the bassist's vocal range, but he does a creditable job with the song.

In its undeveloped state at the Guildhall concert, "Any Colour You Like" is a brief (under two minutes) piece—more an interlude than a song—that showcases David Gilmour on lead guitar and scat vocal. Musically it's quite similar to the previous night's instrumental version of "Breathe (Reprise)."

The debut of "Brain Damage" reveals a tune based precariously upon a taped percussion part that feels quite out of place. Roger Waters's lyrics, however, are fully developed. Taped voices fade in and out of the mix as the song nears its end. A careening synthesizer tone leads into a squealing, free-form instrumental that concludes the first complete performance of *The Dark Side of the Moon*. The song "Eclipse"— which would close the album in dramatic fashion—has not yet been written, and thus would not be featured as part of Pink Floyd's live performance in Portsmouth and other dates around that time.

The 1972 shows featuring the still-developing *The Dark Side of the Moon* concert set piece would be remarkably well-documented by bootleggers. No less than forty-five concerts were illicitly recorded, providing a nearly show-by-show chronology of the work's ongoing refinement. But *Dark Side* came together into something resembling its final form rather quickly: while the set ended with sound effects following "Brain Damage" for the earliest performances, by February 12—three and a half weeks after the Brighton premiere—"Eclipse" had been added to *The Dark Side of the Moon*.

"When you're working in a band and you're performing something willy-nilly, it develops and changes," Roger Waters said in an interview for the 2003 documentary *Classic Albums: The Making of* The Dark Side of the Moon. Nick Mason concurred, noting that it was a truly collaborative endeavor. "All four of us were there, and there was a discussion about putting the album together and making it into this themed—what is now called a concept—album."

The work would continue to evolve across numerous live performances throughout the year. But significant progress would be made within days of the premiere. "Since their Brighton tour opener, Floyd have tightened up a lot of their numbers," wrote Tony Stewart in *NME*. He noted that the sound effects had changed a great deal in the two weeks between the premiere and a February 3 set at the Lanchester Polytechnic College Arts Festival. Calling *The Dark Side of the Moon* "a superbly constructed number," Stewart went on to observe that at Lanchester, the band "managed to get right through it without technical hitches."

Though it would not always be played, *The Dark Side of the Moon* was most often the centerpiece of Pink Floyd's 1972 concerts. When the band headed to Japan in March, *Dark Side* was performed in its entirety at all six shows. And when the band mounted a two-leg North American tour—all of April and most of September—*The Dark Side of the Moon* would be the centerpiece of those shows, though for the first leg the work was titled "Eclipse (A Piece for Assorted Lunatics)."

The changes and refinements made to the onstage performances would inform the concurrent studio sessions for the album, and vice versa. By most accounts, audiences appreciated the opportunity to hear new material from Pink Floyd, even if it wasn't fully developed. But not everyone was impressed. Writing for *Great Speckled Bird*, Steve Wise reviewed the band's April 18 concert at Atlanta's Symphony Hall. "Their first set featured, as far as I could tell, all new material," Wise wrote. "But the band seemed a bit out of synch, and their usual power and intensity was dulled."

By November, a number of changes had been made to *Dark Side*, bringing it closer to its final form. While "The Travel Sequence" would still be an extended jam, a recording (created by audio engineer Alan Parsons) of clocks would open "Time," and the song would be played faster, with David Gilmour adopting a slightly more aggressive vocal tone. "The Mortality Sequence" was now completely replaced by an instrumental of breathtaking beauty, Richard Wright's "The Great Gig in the Sky." The signature wordless vocal line that would be featured on the album had not yet been conceived; an audience recording from a Hamburg, West Germany, concert (November 12, 1972) shows that tapes of spoken-word recitations would be played along with Wright's piano-centered melody. "Any Colour You Like" often took the form of an extended, bluesy reading alternating between subtle and musically intense sections.

Pink Floyd's last live performance of *The Dark Side of the Moon* prior to the record's March 1973 release would take place on December 10, 1972, at Palais des Sports, in Lyon, France. An audience recording shows that "The Travel Sequence" has developed into a more cohesive piece (one that would go unused on the finished album). "Any Colour You Like" has mushroomed into a nine-minute piece. In the time between the Lyon concert and the end of February, Pink Floyd would complete recording sessions and post-production mixing for its eighth studio album.

26

THE GREAT GIG IN THE SKY

In the thirteen months between the live premiere of *The Dark Side of the Moon* and its release on LP, cassette, and 8-track tape, tens of thousands—perhaps even hundreds of thousands—of concert-going fans had heard the developing work in its entirety. A heavy touring schedule took the band to concert dates in England, the United States, Canada, Japan, Australia, West Germany, the Netherlands, Denmark, Switzerland, France, and Belgium. At those shows, Pink Floyd would perform the extended work known variously as "Eclipse," "A Piece for Assorted Lunatics," and *The Dark Side of the Moon*, plus a second set of songs from the band's seven-album back catalog.

But that which fans heard onstage and what they would find on the record released worldwide on Thursday, March 1, 1973, were two very different things. The band's extensive performance schedule and count-less hours in the studio had yielded a finished piece that—while it would preserve and reflect all of the stage performance's best qual-ities—represented a far more refined, nuanced, and deeply textured work.

The changes from the stage show would become clear to listeners mere seconds after the needle dropped onto the spinning vinyl record. Taking a cue from classical overtures—but applying the ideas in a de-cidedly modern manner—Pink Floyd opens *The Dark Side of the Moon* with a brief piece that sonically references and previews most, if not all, of the album's themes in the space of just over one minute. Titled

"Speak to Me," the instrumental soundscape is a heady, dizzying mé-lange of sounds compiled by Nick Mason.

"Speak to Me" fades in from silence to open with the simulated heartbeat sound that introduced *The Dark Side of the Moon* to concert-going audiences. Thirty seconds in, the sound of a ticking clock is added to the mix, followed by another clock. Seconds later, a man's voice speaking in malevolent, threatening tones can be heard, boldly declar-ing that he's "been mad for fucking years." A ringing cash register can be heard. Another man states matter-of-factly that he's "always been mad." A third man speaks, but his words are obscured by the cacophony of the assembled sounds. A fourth voice enters the mix, but rather than speaking, this man breaks out in maniacal laughter. A droning, mechan-ical sound—created by the band's VCS 3 synthesizer—enters the soundscape as all of the other elements continue to increase in volume and intensity. The whirring of the mechanical sound—along with the sinister laughing—begins to drown out all of the other sounds. Deep from within the mix, a minor chord from Richard Wright's organ begins to emerge. A woman's voice lets out a series of four terrified wails. *The Dark Side of the Moon* has begun.

"Speak to Me" tumbles straight into "Breathe," a tune credited joint-ly to Roger Waters, David Gilmour, and Richard Wright. With the benefit of context and hindsight, it's quite clear what each man has brought to the song. The two-chord pattern upon which the song is built had arisen during the earliest work sessions for what would be-come *The Dark Side of the Moon*; as E minor and A major are two of the most effortless chords to play on a guitar—and because they natu-rally go together—it's likely that guitarist Gilmour came up with the pattern. "A lot of the musical ideas just came up just jamming away" in a rehearsal room in Bermondsey, London, Gilmour said in a 2003 inter-view filmed for a documentary about the album.

Like all of the songs on *The Dark Side of the Moon* (and the four albums that would follow it over the next decade), the lyrics of "Breathe" are from the pen of Roger Waters. Beginning with the kernel of an idea that began during the sessions for an outside project, the collaboration with Ron Geesin on the soundtrack for *The Body*, Waters builds a set of lyrics around the phrase "breathe in the air." Following on to his recently developed focus on writing with empathy—an inter-est that had begun with *Meddle*'s "Echoes"—Waters crafts lyrics that speak of opening oneself to others ("Don't be afraid to care"), and self-determination ("Choose your own ground"). The song also expresses need and vulnerability ("leave, but don't leave me"). And while "Breathe" displays guarded optimism ("Long you live and high you fly"), that point of view is quickly tempered by an admonition that to succeed, one must play by society's rules, and further, that in the end, death is the inevitable outcome.

Waters would be justly proud of his lyrics for "Breathe," though in interviews he would sometimes speak self-deprecatingly of his words for the song. "It always amazes me that I got away with it, really," he said in a 2003 interview, suggesting that the words to "Breathe" are typical of what a high-schooler might write. "It's so sort of 'lower sixth,'" Waters said. In that same interview, he shed some light on the song's meaning, or at least how it might be received by listeners. "In context with the music—and then in context with the piece as a whole—people are prepared to accept that simple exhortation to be prepared to stand your ground and attempt to live your life in an authentic way."

Meanwhile, keyboardist Richard Wright's musical contribution to "Breathe" should not be overlooked, as it's a crucial one that helps the song rise above a standard-issue two-chord jam. Noting that his musical background was jazz, Wright explained what he created for the song when interviewed for the 2003 documentary, *The Making of* The Dark Side of the Moon. Wright had devised a transitional chord sequence that connects the end of the song's first verse with the start of the second (there's no chorus as such), and the idea came from a surprising source: it is, he says, "totally down to a chord I actually heard on a Miles Davis album, *Kind of Blue*." That jazz influence upon the song—and others on *Dark Side* as well—would be one of several qualities to take the album beyond the musical areas explored by its predecessors; doing so would widen Pink Floyd's appeal.

Over the course of *The Dark Side of the Moon*'s development as a unified work, "The Travel Sequence" had been a frustrating sticking point for the band. Onstage, it took the form of a simple, relatively formless instrumental that featured Gilmour's guitar solo and some electric piano fills from Richard Wright. "We'd been playing it live that way for some time as a guitar jam sort of piece," Gilmour recalled in a 2003 interview for the *Making of* . . . documentary. "I think that we were—none of us—that happy with it as a piece," he said.

So for the album, Gilmour and Waters co-composed a new piece that would use the sonic textures of the VCS 3 (also known as the Synthi) synthesizer as a starting point. Debuting in 1969, the VCS 3 was one of the earliest available synthesizers, and unlike similar devices from American companies led by inventors Robert A. Moog and Don Buchla, the British-made VCS 3 had been designed as a relatively light-weight, portable machine housed in a suitcase.

The new instrumental piece, "On the Run," begins with a droning bass note that provides linkage with the final notes of "Breathe." That droning sound is followed immediately by what sounds very much like Nick Mason playing a remarkably fast percussion pattern on his hi-hat cymbal. In fact, the relentless beat is a product of the VCS 3. A swirling organ note—run through a rotating Leslie speaker—adds a bit of organic musical character to the increasingly electronic soundscape.

A low-frequency, gurgling pattern of notes fades into the mix; it, too, has been created using the VCS 3 and its built-in sequencer, a feature that allows a melody to be pre-programmed into the machine and then played back at the triggering of a switch. With that sequence playing on its own (so to speak), David Gilmour's hands are free to further manipulate the sound, adjusting the treble, bass, and other sonic qualities, effectively in real-time.

Around the thirty-second mark of "On the Run," a female voice can be heard; her words are indecipherable, but her tone suggests the slightly officious demeanor of someone announcing a flight departure schedule at an airport. The urgent feel of the hi-hat percussion and the ceaseless sequence of notes from the VCS 3, coupled with the added sounds of running footsteps, only reinforces the notion of someone struggling to keep up with a schedule and timetable devised and maintained by other, unseen forces.

Additional aural textures from the VCS 3 evoke mental pictures of spacecraft descending ominously toward the unnamed running everyman. Gilmour and Waters continue to manipulate the controls of the synthesizer, varying the tone color and character as the electronic "rhythm section" continues unabated. One of the male voices from "Speak to Me" returns; it, too, is unintelligible. But the portentous laugh that follows leaves little question that some kind of danger—or at least the dark unknown—lies close ahead.

A squalling sound—again from the VCS 3—seems to fly across the aural landscape. The unknown spacecraft makes several passes overhead, each time veering ever closer to its intended target. At the three-minute mark, a loud explosion is heard, followed by its rumbling aftermath. But the protagonist has survived to live another day; he can be heard running and breathing heavily as the after-effects of the booming sound recede into the sonic distance.

Recording the many sounds that would make up "On the Run" would be merely the first step in creating the track. Crafting the densely textured tapestry of sounds for "On the Run" would involve pushing the capabilities of the recording console to its limit; all four members of Pink Floyd along with engineer Alan Parsons took part in the final mixing of the track, at which time the various sonic components would be faded in and out of the piece in real time as a completed recording was made. "A mix in those days was a performance, every bit as much as doing a gig," David Gilmour observed in 2003.

The calm atmosphere created by the near-silence that follows "On the Run" is joined by the sound of a few gently ticking mechanical clocks. That reverie is jarringly punctured by the sudden clamor of countless timekeeping devices striking their alarms, chiming the top of the hour, and so forth. "Time" has come. As that racket begins to subside, a different kind of ticking is heard. Once again it's the mechanical, percussive tones of the VCS 3 synthesizer, joined by the "heartbeat" sound; the two are in sync.

More than forty seconds into "Time," a single, low-register note (E) is struck simultaneously on David Gilmour's guitar, Roger Waters's bass, and the VCS 3. Explicitly making use of the concept of time, the band waits a full eight seconds before hitting the next note (F♯). The effect of the long pause—four measures in musical notation—is to convey the tension associated with waiting; the long space between notes suggests the manner in which anticipation (and/or dread) can cause one to perceive that time is moving slowly, or even approaching a standstill. The subtle fills on Richard Wright's electric piano do nothing to relieve the tension.

Nick Mason adds some inventive percussion to the extended introduction of "Time." Using rototoms—small, rack-mounted drum heads with steel frames that can be rotated on the fly, thus tuning to specific (and generally high-pitched) musical notes—he colors the sonic palette, adding even more tension in the process.

Taken at a pace ever so slightly quicker than Pink Floyd's original live versions of a year earlier, this "Time" is nonetheless far more dramatic, thanks to an overall sharper attack on the instruments, even in the introduction before the song-proper has begun. After the bass notes establish the basis for the song's chord structure a few times—joined by ever-busier rototom work—Mason signals the beginning of the main section of "Time" with a familiar drum fill.

David Gilmour enters immediately on lead vocal. Where the earlier live readings of "Time" had featured dual lead vocals (Gilmour and Wright), with the two gently harmonizing, here Gilmour initially sings alone, adopting a much harder, more aggressive vocal demeanor.

As the guitarist sings Roger Waters's lyrics about the dullness of everyday existence ("You fritter and waste the hours in an offhand way"), he adds bluesy, inventive fills on guitar in the spaces between vocal phrases. The synthesizer's excellent ability to generate deep and sustained low-frequency notes helps provide an even more solid bottom-end to the song than Waters's bass alone could ever provide. The feeling of anticipation created by the introduction is made explicit as Gilmour sings of "waiting for someone or something to show you the way."

As he has done in the live version of "Time," Rick Wright takes a solo lead vocal for the next few lines, the song's "bridge" ("Time" has no chorus in a traditional sense). Waters's lyrics have been changed from "lying supine in the sunshine" to the more direct "tired of lying in the sunshine." Meanwhile, another new sonic element has been added: for the first time ever on a Pink Floyd record (save for the choral sections on 1970's "Atom Heart Mother Suite"), female vocals are used. Four session singers—Barry St. John, Liza Strike, and Lesley Duncan, all from Great Britain; plus American rhythm and blues singer Doris Troy—lend their talents for a variety of soulful, harmonized "ooh"s and "aah"s, all filtered through effects on engineer Alan Parsons's recording console. The net effect of the female vocals is to introduce an earthy soul and jazz sensibility to the music. When Wright reaches the third line of lyrics, David Gilmour joins on harmony vocal as the two sing of time having slipped by without notice, taking opportunities with it: "You missed the starting gun."

Gilmour once again takes the lead vocals, singing Waters's words that express the seemingly inevitable frustration of losing the battle against time's relentless march forward, as the sun is "racing around to come up behind you again." In the end, Roger Waters's lyrics assert, each day will find you "shorter of breath and one day closer to death."

In a plaintive voice, Richard Wright voices Waters's further observations in a resigned, mournful tone, singing of plans coming to naught. After the memorable lyrics about the English character trait of "quiet desperation," Wright resignedly sings, "The time is gone, the song is over, thought I'd something more to say."

After an inventive series of chords that transitions out of "Time," a reprise of "Breathe" begins. Here, David Gilmour sings—in a slightly more hopeful tone—of home fires and resting one's bones. After Waters's lyrics about a distant iron bell tolling, people dropping to their knees to pray, and magic spells being spoken, the brief reprise of "Breathe" ends.

At this point in the original stage presentation of *The Dark Side of the Moon*, the band had played Richard Wright's instrumental "The Mortality Sequence," featuring tape playback of religious-themed speeches. Wright played a "churchy" sounding Hammond organ melody, and the rest of the band would provide subtle, understated musical support. For the finished album, all of these elements have been discarded in favor of a completely new song and arrangement from the band's keyboardist.

A stately piano melody, "The Great Gig in the Sky" was written by Richard Wright sometime in 1972, and the basic musical track was recorded at Abbey Road Studios in June of that year. The song would replace "The Mortality Sequence" in the live *The Dark Side of the Moon* around that same time. Wright's grand piano is the central instrument in the song's arrangement; he plays a lengthy series of "jazzy" chords (that is to say, chords with voicings more complex than standard major and minor combinations of notes, and often making use of four or even five notes in the right hand). The melody is somber and contemplative, with few of the quasi-religious musical trappings so prevalent in "The Mortality Sequence."

"The Great Gig in the Sky" opens with Wright playing alone. Subtly, David Gilmour joins in on pedal steel guitar, and Waters plays bass guitar. Taped voices ruminating on death and dying ("You gotta go sometime") are folded into the mix. At the one-minute mark, Nick Mason begins keeping time with clicks on his drum sticks, and after two introductory hits on his snare drum, the song's vocals begin.

But "The Great Gig in the Sky" features no ordinary vocals. The wordless performance is by a session vocalist, Clare Torry, who was paid £30 (the equivalent of about $475 today), double the standard EMI rate because the session took place on a Sunday. After a few tries at singing along to a playback of the finished backing track, Torry had found herself at a loss as to what the band wanted. In a 2005 interview with author John Harris, Torry recalled the minimal direction she was given: "Well, they did say, 'Be more emotional.'" Torry turned in a wholly unexpected, searing, and deeply sensual vocal performance, the like of which she had never done before. She related to Harris what happened next. "I said, 'I hope that's alright.' And they said, 'Yeah, lovely; thank you.' And I left."

Torry's vocals on "The Great Gig in the Sky" are a landmark in the Pink Floyd catalog. While session vocalists had been used before, the idea of ceding lead vocal duties to someone outside the band was highly unusual for the group. Certainly no member of Pink Floyd could have brought forth a vocal performance remotely similar to what Torry had recorded in a mere three attempts. Richard Wright's original concept for the song did not include female vocals. But Torry's performance on "The Great Gig in the Sky" stands as one of the most remarkable vocals ever to be found on a pop album. Prior to her one-off session date for Pink Floyd, Torry had made her living providing vocals on budget-priced "sound-alike" records featuring anonymous musicians covering the hits of the day. After the *Dark Side* session, Torry would go on to work on sessions for Alan Parsons, Meat Loaf, Johnny Mercer, Culture Club, Tangerine Dream, and many others, including Roger Waters's 1987 solo album, *Radio K.A.O.S.* She toured as a member of Waters's post–Pink Floyd band, and sang with the David Gilmour–led lineup of Pink Floyd at a live concert in 1990. Some years later, Torry would lobby successfully for a composer's co-credit on "The Great Gig in the Sky."

As the breathy final notes of Clare Torry's bravura performance fade away, Richard Wright plays the song's final chord on his Steinway grand piano. Those notes are left to decay into silence, and as they do, engineer Alan Parsons manually adjusts the tape speed, bending the note upward and then downward again. With that, the first side of *The Dark Side of the Moon* comes to a close.

27

ALL YOU CREATE

Pink Floyd had flirted with unusual time signatures before *The Dark Side of the Moon*. But most of the songs written by Roger Waters, David Gilmour, or Richard Wright or some combination thereof had been in either rock-standard 4/4, or in a meter based around a three- or four-count. "Echoes" is in 12/8, but its beat doesn't feel odd to most listeners because the beat is based on multiples of four. Even a rhythmically unusual (for Pink Floyd) song like "Burning Bridges" (from 1972's *Obscured by Clouds*) is in "waltz time," 3/4. Not since the days of Syd Barrett had Pink Floyd traded in unconventional—within the confines of pop music—time signatures on songs like *A Saucerful of Secrets'* "Jugband Blues," which shifts between 3/4, 4/4, 5/4, and 6/4, all in the space of three minutes.

Simply stated, there would be little precedent in the Pink Floyd catalog for a song such as "Money," the opening track on the second side of 1973's *The Dark Side of the Moon*. But from his earliest home demos for "Money," Roger Waters had applied a 7/4 beat to his fairly conventional, blues-based chord progression. The song opens like no other song in recording history, with a tape-based audio construction made of sound snippets (coins falling, cash registers, tearing paper meant to represent bank notes) put together to establish both the song's motif and its time signature.

After the taped sequence runs through two measures, Waters joins in on bass guitar. David Gilmour comes in on guitar with Nick Mason on drums; Rick Wright adds electric piano fills in between Gilmour's lead guitar phrases. Gilmour sings lead, voicing Roger Waters's cynical, first-person lyrics about grabbing that "cash with both hands" and extolling the pleasure of automobiles, caviar, and owning a football (soccer) team.

In the song's second verse, Gilmour continues the ironically self-centered lyrics by threatening those who would want some money for themselves. He wishes for a Lear jet, and dismisses charity as "do goody good bullshit." All of these lyrics are set against the backdrop of the tune's stomping 7/4 beat.

The third verse of "Money" introduces yet another Pink Floyd first: a saxophone solo. Dick Parry had been a member of Jokers Wild with David Gilmour, and by 1972 had played on a half dozen album sessions by various American and British recording artists. For "Money," Parry delivers a full minute-long, rhythm and blues–flavored solo that's heavy on memorable melodic lines and complementary to David Gilmour's electric guitar solo that follows.

As Gilmour leans into his solo, the band—Waters, Wright, Mason, and Gilmour himself playing rhythm guitar on a separate track—breaks from the 7/4 meter into a straight 4/4, playing a spirited version of the "Moonhead" melody developed some two years earlier. After forty-five seconds or so, the rhythm section brings the intensity down, allowing more sonic space for Gilmour. In turn, he shifts his soloing style to a series of sparse, bluesy licks with as much silence as sound; the spaces between his notes serve to further emphasize the guitar melody. After a descending full-band melodic line that recalls Syd Barrett's favored approach, the spirited arrangement returns, with Gilmour resuming his soaring, slashing, heavily reverberating guitar solo. That solo emphasizes the highest notes that the guitar is capable of achieving. As a whole, the instrumental section of "Money"—Dick Parry's sax solo plus David Gilmour's three consecutive solos—takes up three full minutes. Not a second is wasted.

Gilmour returns to the vocal mic to sing Roger Waters's final verse, quoting the biblical wisdom of 1 Timothy ("Money . . . is the root of all evil today"), but inserting a qualifier ("so they say") into the middle of the aphorism, and concluding that anyone asking his or her boss for a raise (a "rise" in British parlance) should not be surprised to learn that "they're giving none away."

As the strains of "Money" fade away, taped voices—creepy laughter and random comments about being "in the right" in a physical altercation—lead into an ethereal, church-like organ with a character reminiscent of the final "Celestial Voices" section of Pink Floyd's 1968 track "A Saucerful of Secrets."

Roger Waters's lyrics for "Us and Them" sit atop the piano melody Richard Wright had composed for *Zabriskie Point* back in 1969; the instrumental was then known as "The Violent Sequence," as it was created to accompany the film's footage of police crackdown on protest marches and similar conflicts. But because director Michelangelo Antonioni chose not to use the piece—or, for that matter, most all of the other music Pink Floyd custom-created for his movie—Wright's melody was ripe for its re-purposing as a key part of *The Dark Side of the Moon*.

After a thirty-second organ introduction, the shimmering rhythm section joins in. Waters's understated yet assured bass line supports Wright's piano, while David Gilmour picks the individual notes of chords. Nick Mason provides a subtle backbeat. After another thirty seconds, Dick Parry enters on saxophone, playing a smoky, romantic lead. Parry takes full advantage of Wright's jazz-inflected piano chord shadings to explore "blue" (non-standard pitch) notes on his sax.

David Gilmour's vocals on "Us and Them" are a thing of beauty: dreamy yet concise, yearning yet somehow assured. Roger Waters's lyrics focus on the spaces between people and the often futile nature of modern existence ("in the end it's only round and round"). The repeating-effect delay applied to the end of each of Gilmour's vocal phrases ("us . . . us . . . us") provides an aural representation of the emotional distance between individuals.

One of the unique qualities of Roger Waters's lyrics for *The Dark Side of the Moon* is his complete avoidance of traditional vocal chorus/refrains. Other than restatement of a key word or phrase—"Money," for example—his lyrics move forward in each song, never circling back upon themselves in the manner of most conventional pop songwriting. "Us and Them" stands as a key example of this: the title phrase appears at the beginning of Gilmour's vocals, never to be repeated. The chorus (as such) of "Us and Them" features not a refrain but a new set of lyrics each of the three times it comes around. And the massed vocals on that chorus—Gilmour, Wright, and the four-woman ensemble of singers—

sing Waters's words in glorious, close harmony. Waters's belief that citizens, most especially those in the military during time of war, are often mere pawns in a game controlled by others is vividly given voice with this line: "'Forward!' he cried from the rear, and the front rank died."

Calling attention to one specific example of Rick Wright's inventive flourishes on "Us and Them" creates the danger of overstating its importance, but it's worth mention nonetheless. For the first and third word in each verse ("Us and them," "Me and you," "Black and blue," etc.) a repeating, "echo" effect is applied to David Gilmour's vocals, emphasizing the sense of empty spaces, distance, and loneliness. The few bars that follow musically have "holes." That is to say that the absence of new sounds is intentional, and itself part of the music.

But during the phrase "Up and down," Richard Wright playfully adds the tiniest bit of filigree. As he has been doing, in the first lines of each verse, Wright is playing a melody based on a D major chord, leaving space after the vocal phrases. But in the sonic emptiness after Gilmour sings "Up," Wright's right hand jumps up a full octave, playing a quick D major chord. It's a literal musical expression of the concept of "up," the kind of sentimental filigree one might not expect on a rock record. But its judicious use—a single time on the record—makes its application inspired, and those familiar with the song would likely find it odd if Richard Wright's decorative "up" chord were missing.

As "Us and Them" winds its way toward a conclusion, the vocal chorus delivers one of Roger Waters's bleakest, least-hopeful lyrics ever, one that shines a light upon humankind's selfish tendencies: "For want of the price of tea and a slice the old man died."

Holding to *The Dark Side of the Moon*'s seamless continuity, there is no break between "Us and Them" and the album's third instrumental work (or fourth, if one considers the wordless "The Great Gig in the Sky" an instrumental). One of Nick Mason's signature drum fills links directly to "Any Colour You Like." A funky beat and celestial, highly melodic synthesizer work from Rick Wright characterize the tune, credited to Wright, Gilmour, and Mason. Wright's keyboard textures here, realized on a then relatively new and compact analog synthesizer called the Minimoog, preview the keyboardist's further sonic explorations on Pink Floyd's next album, 1975's *Wish You Were Here*. "Any Colour You Like" also features a kind of call-and-response between multiple tracked versions of David Gilmour's heavily effect-laden electric guitar. In its musical structure, "Any Colour You Like" follows "Breathe" quite closely, right down to Rick Wright's jazz-flavored ending transitional phrase. But this time, that transition leads the listener into "Brain Damage."

Lyricist and bassist Roger Waters takes his first solo lead vocal on *The Dark Side of the Moon* with "Brain Damage." As part of a suite of songs concerning the pressure of everyday life, "Brain Damage" is perhaps the most explicitly dour, concerned as it is with insanity. That condition would have been one that hit remarkably close to home for Roger Waters and his Pink Floyd band mates; at the time of *The Dark Side of the Moon*'s release, the band's original leader and songwriter Syd Barrett had been gone from the group for more than five years. Though the band's first musical attempts after Barrett's departure took the form of self-conscious attempts to follow in his musical style, Pink Floyd soon established a new musical identity of its own. Yet the shadow of Barrett remained with the band, and each of the three albums that would follow *The Dark Side of the Moon* would deal with his memory in its own way.

"The lunatic," as Roger Waters sings in each of the three verses of "Brain Damage," is never very far away at all. First he is "on the grass," then "in the hall" ("in *my* hall," Waters sings the second time, making the personal connection even more direct), and finally "in my head." The solutions offered to deal with the "lunatic" are unsatisfying: brain surgery is suggested, as is solitary confinement. But nothing provides a suitable resolution, as Waters writes and sings, "you shout and no one seems to hear." In *The Dark Side of the Moon*'s most direct reference to Syd Barrett—who is never named on the record—Waters sings, "the band you're in starts playing different tunes," a nod to the situation in which Syd Barrett found himself in late 1967.

David Gilmour's whistle-like fills on slide guitar punctuate Waters's vocal phrases; as the song progresses, the singer is joined by Gilmour on harmony vocals. And while *The Dark Side of the Moon* is no Broadway musical, the stagecraft technique of bringing cast members back to the spotlight as the production nears its end is used to good effect on "Brain Damage." In between lyrical phrases, members of the female chorus sing soulful, wordless moans, and all join in on the song's final line: "I'll see you on the dark side of the moon."

"Eclipse" closes *The Dark Side of the Moon* in grand fashion. The song has the feel of a credits-roll, with its cascading lines of vocal harmonies, tumbling one after the other with some twenty-four lyric lines before a resolution. "Eclipse" enumerates a litany of things that a person can observe or experience through one's senses (touch, see, taste, feel), emotions (love, hate, distrust), actions (save, give, deal, buy, "beg, borrow or steal," create, destroy, do, say, eat, meet, slight, fight). Gathering together all of the album's vocalists (save Clare Torry)—David Gilmour, Roger Waters, Richard Wright, Lesley Duncan, Barry St. John, Liza Strike, and Doris Troy—*The Dark Side of the Moon* concludes by asserting how very small each individual truly is in the grand scheme of the universe. Everything that currently exists, everything in the past and the future, and "everything under the sun is in tune," in the words of Pink Floyd lyricist Roger Waters, but inevitably "the sun is eclipsed by the moon."

As the album's signature heartbeat fades to nothingness, the doorman from EMI's Abbey Road Studios, Gerry Driscoll, gets the final word: "There is no dark side of the moon, really. Matter of fact, it's all dark."

The Dark Side of the Moon was released worldwide on March 1, 1973. It reached the top spot on album charts in the United States, Canada, and Austria, making it to the number two spot in Australia, the United Kingdom, Norway, and the Netherlands. Remaining on the U.S. charts for a staggering 741 consecutive weeks, it finally slipped off the *Billboard* 200 during a year in which the chart was dominated by the *Dirty Dancing* film soundtrack and releases by George Michael, Van Halen, Guns N' Roses, and U2. The songs on *The Dark Side of the Moon* quickly became a staple of rock FM radio stations, and remain popular on classic rock radio to the present day.

On its release, *The Dark Side of the Moon* would be recognized as a significant leap forward for Pink Floyd, and a landmark album in the history of popular music. Critics far and wide remarked upon its virtues. "Probably this is Floyd's most successful artistic venture," wrote *NME*'s Tony Stewart, noting the album's "development in form and structure" over Pink Floyd's previous efforts. Observing the widened musical scope afforded by the intelligent use of the vocal ensemble, soloist

Clare Torry, and saxophonist Dick Parry, Stewart likened Pink Floyd's new vocal approach to that of the Moody Blues. Before ending his review with a few quotes from the album, Stewart suggested that *The Dark Side of the Moon* is "designed for late-night listening."

In America, *Rolling Stone*—a publication that had on occasion been at odds with Pink Floyd—offered a more measured response. Reviewer Loyd Grossman felt that "The Great Gig in the Sky" went on too long, and called David Gilmour's vocals "sometimes weak and lackluster," yet still lauded *Dark Side* as "a fine album with a textural and conceptual richness that not only invites, but demands involvement." Praising the record's grandeur and ambition, he wrote that *The Dark Side of the Moon* had "true flash . . . that comes from the excellence of a superb performance."

Time has only increased the stature of Pink Floyd's 1973 album. At the end of the 1970s, when *Rolling Stone* published its book-length *Record Guide*, *The Dark Side of the Moon* earned five stars (defined as "Indispensable: a record that must be included in any comprehensive collection"). While he had savaged some of the band's previous efforts—*More* and the *Relics* compilation each got one star, and *The Piper at the Gates of Dawn* earned only two—critic Bart Testa was unequivocal: "*Dark Side of the Moon* is Pink Floyd's masterpiece." Praising Waters's lyrics and the album's "rich lyricism" (and calling out the important contributions of Dick Parry and Clare Torry), Testa called the record's songs "perfect vehicles" for the group's "instrumental procedures." *MusicHound Rock* awarded *Dark Side* five "bones" (its highest rating), calling the work "essential . . . a seamless and inventive song cycle bolstered by a three-dimensional soundscape of instruments and special effects," but made sure to mention the high-quality songwriting as well.

Most every poll of rock fans places *The Dark Side of the Moon* at or very near the top of best-album lists. The United States Library of Congress holds a copy of the album in its National Recording Registry, noting it as a recording that is "culturally, historically or aesthetically significant." Several of the tracks on the album have topped polls for best guitar solo, and in 1974 the album won the NME Awards for Best British Album and Best World Album.

Even before its release, the members of Pink Floyd seemed to have realized they had created something truly remarkable in *The Dark Side of the Moon.* And with the benefit of hindsight, the members were able to articulate their thoughts on what it all meant. Speaking for the 2003 documentary DVD, *The Making of* The Dark Side of the Moon, Roger Waters summed up the album's meaning as succinctly as he ever had, saying, "*The Dark Side of the Moon* was an expression of political, philosophical, humanitarian empathy that was desperate to get out." Elsewhere in the same interview, Waters offered what he believed to be one of the album's central themes: "At any point you can grasp the reins and start guiding your own destiny." Commenting upon its near-universal appeal, Waters said *The Dark Side of the Moon* is "driven by emotion; there's nothing plastic about it. There's nothing contrived about it. And I think that's . . . maybe one of the things that's given it its longevity."

In that same DVD, the generally reticent Richard Wright commented on the unity of purpose that characterized the album's creation. "It felt like the whole band were working together," he said. "It was a very creative time." Nick Mason agreed, observing, "It was one of those really good moments that bands do experience where everyone is onside, and everyone likes the idea, and there's some sort of agreement as to more or less who's going to do what." He also noted that *Dark Side* contained "a lot of ideas, compressed onto one record."

In a 1988 interview for *Musician Magazine* with Pink Floyd biographer Nicholas Schaffner, guitarist David Gilmour connected some of the dots. "If you take 'A Saucerful of Secrets,' the track 'Atom Heart Mother,' then 'Echoes,' all lead quite logically towards *The Dark Side of the Moon*." Commenting in 2003 upon the album's continued lyrical relevance—and looking back several decades—David Gilmour recalled thinking, "My God, we've really done something fantastic here." In a sentimental moment, Gilmour added, "I would love to have been a person who could sit back [and listen] with his headphones on, the whole way through, for the first time." Noting that he never had that experience with *The Dark Side of the Moon*, he admitted, "it would have been nice."

Thematically unified, seamlessly produced, and engineered with the utmost attention to detail, *The Dark Side of the Moon* would set the 1970s-and-beyond standard for albums as entities unto themselves. Certainly there were unified-concept releases before *Dark Side.* Some held together better as narratives, but none equaled Pink Floyd's eighth studio album in terms of sonic continuity: *The Dark Side of the Moon* was (and remains) a movie for the ears. Oddly enough—especially as the product of a group that had been employing quadrophonic (four-channel) sound in its concerts since the late 1960s—*The Dark Side of the Moon* was never issued in quadrophonic sound. First marketed in the United States in May 1972, "quad" was trumpeted by is proponents as the ultimate in sonic reproduction. Though many quad releases were in the "easy listening" or soundtrack categories, estimates suggest that well over 150 rock albums received quadraphonic release. The track "Money" would, however, be remixed from the master tape into quadrophonic sound in 1976 for a various-artists demonstration record, *Quadrafile.* And engineer Alan Parsons had created a quad mix of *The Dark Side of the Moon* in 1972, but it was deemed unsatisfactory and was not released. For the album's thirtieth anniversary in 2003, producer James Guthrie created a new 5.1 surround sound mix (the modern-day successor to the long-abandoned quadraphonic format), released on the Super Audio Compact Disc (SACD) medium.

Since the departure of founding member Syd Barrett, it had taken Pink Floyd the better part of five years, seven albums, and hundreds of concerts (not to mention film projects and ballet performances) to progress to the point at which the band would create a masterpiece. With *The Dark Side of the Moon*, the quartet of David Gilmour, Nick Mason, Roger Waters, and Richard Wright had done just that. Richard Wright would look back upon the making of Pink Floyd's eighth album as "a very, very happy and creative and enjoyable time." And Nick Mason—always an astute observer of his band's situation—called the *Dark Side* sessions "probably the most focused moment in our career in terms of all of us working together as a band."

But in their spare moments, the four members of Pink Floyd might have wondered to themselves, "What now?" Looking back upon the success of *The Dark Side of the Moon*, the period when Pink Floyd broke through, David Gilmour noted the situation in which the band found itself. "It certainly did the trick, and it moved us up into a super league, I suppose you might say. Which brought with it some great joy, some pride, and some problems." Richard Wright admitted, "Of course it changed our lives; we were now a big rock 'n' roll band playing in stadiums." Gilmour observed that with that kind of success, "You don't know what you're in it for any more. You know, you were in it to achieve massive success, and get rich and famous and all these other things that go along with it. And when they're all suddenly done, you're going, 'Well, hmm. Why? What next?'"

Part VIII

Playing Different Tunes

28

THINGS LEFT UNSAID

The legacy of Pink Floyd—especially as manifested on *The Dark Side of the Moon*—would prove indelible in future years. Beyond the album's durability as a commercial juggernaut, *Dark Side* would continue to invite study, analysis, and appreciation decades after its debut. A year after its release, *NME*'s Ian MacDonald attempted to describe the album's meaning. "What happened to idealism, anti-materialism, and the brotherhood of man?" he asked rhetorically. "*The Dark Side of the Moon* is Roger Waters' stab at answering such questions."

Aiming to explain the album's success on both artistic and commercial levels, he noted that "Waters' own troubled conscience is, broadly speaking, successfully transformed into the troubled conscience of us all. It's a record about *unease*." Calling *The Dark Side of the Moon* "a passively compassionate view of the world," he added, "but it's also record-company 'product.'"

In 1978, *Trouser Press*'s Kris DiLorenzo attempted a somewhat more scholarly analysis of the album. "*The Dark Side of the Moon*'s format could be seen as a reincarnation cycle," he wrote. Pink Floyd "employ the trappings of ceremony in liturgical-sounding chants, angelic chorales, confessional passages and unmistakably Christian imagery, but the essence is entirely different: Pink Floyd are talking about a purer form of spirituality, a 'cosmicconsciousness' without denomination."

Writing in 1976 not so much about *Dark Side* but more about the band in general, Miles penned an essay for *NME*, proudly proclaiming,

"The Floyd were the *loudest* band anyone had ever heard at that time. They were also the *weirdest*. And they were without doubt the *hippest*. We all dug them. They were our band." And Pink Floyd would become "our band" for countless music fans, including many who had never even heard the music the band made with Syd Barrett.

"My eldest sister was a bit of a hippie," says Jason Sawford. "She came home with *The Dark Side of the Moon*. I was thirteen years old, and I was hooked instantly. I think I was searching for things in life to make sense of everything," he says. He viewed *Dark Side* as "thinking man's music." Fifteen years later, keyboardist Sawford would co-found The Australian Pink Floyd Show, a massively successful tribute band.

Group co-founder Steve Mac was a bit older when he first heard *Dark Side*, but it made a similarly indelible impression. "I liked the way the album *The Dark Side of the Moon* was a work of art in its own right," he says.

Both men would grow to appreciate the subtleties of Pink Floyd's music—especially *The Dark Side of the Moon*—as they delved into learning to play songs from the group's catalog. "I think there's a kind of simplicity and grace in the music," Sawford says, "that brings out the lyricism without getting overly complicated. Their songs are so sculpted to perfection that you couldn't think of doing it any better."

Guitarist Mac singles out David Gilmour's instrumental work as a key to Pink Floyd's appeal. "He certainly does some very imaginative, creative, and intelligent things. Where other guitarists may try to show off their skills, David Gilmour is more about enhancing the song for the listeners," he says. "There's a lot of skill and talent to be able to do that." He characterizes Gilmour's guitar style as one that takes the willing listener on "an emotional journey."

"Pink Floyd weren't trying to copy anyone else," Sawford notes. "Their own style evolved, and it became very influential." He believes that the group's balance of sophistication and simplicity "speaks to people all over the world." Mac affords special praise to what he calls Roger Waters's "timeless lyrics" as well. "Even in today's world, you can relate to the lyrics as if they were written today, *for* today."

The Australian Pink Floyd Show has long had a fan of their own in David Gilmour; the guitarist hired the band to play at his fiftieth birthday party in 1996. "He got in touch and asked if we could come play to him and his 500 guests," says Steve Mac, beaming. "Which we did," he adds. "It was terrifying, but fantastic . . . such an honor indeed."

With drummer Tahrah Cohen, American guitarist Joe Pascarell co-founded a Pink Floyd tribute band of his own, the Machine, in 1988. He, too, had been a fan of the band for many years. And like countless others, *The Dark Side of the Moon* was his introduction to the band's music.

"I have a very, very cool older brother who loves music," Pascarell says. "And in 1973 all I knew was the Beatles. My brother brought home *The Dark Side of the Moon*, and when I was 13 years old he actually took me to see them; that was in 1974." Hooked for life, Pascarell would go on to see the band on all of its subsequent American tours.

Band mate and longtime keyboardist for the Machine, Scott Chasolen got into Pink Floyd when he discovered *The Dark Side of the Moon* in his dad's record collection. "There's no other music that puts you in that space," he says.

Joe Pascarell hears in David Gilmour's guitar playing a blues influence. "Every note is important: when the note begins, when it ends, how long it lasts. It's never noodling, or riffing, or showing off." Contrasting Gilmour's style with that of "shredder" guitarists, Pascarell says, "he seems to get the most out of the least notes." And like many others of his generation, discovering *Dark Side* would lead Scott Chasolen to explore the rest of the band's catalog on his own.

Pascarell would learn to play guitar by listening to Pink Floyd records. "I sat there for hours and hours and hours trying to figure it out: 'When I put this note in, why doesn't it feel like when [David Gilmour] plays that note?' That's how I learned all of it. I 'osmosed' the music," he says with a chuckle. Scott Chasolen emphasizes that he was influenced greatly by the keyboard playing of Richard Wright long before he joined the Machine. Wright "wasn't particularly blues-based," Chasolen says. "He spoke his own musical language."

Pascarell describes the trademark Pink Floyd songwriting style as "patient. The music sits there for a very long time, and really allows you to get inside of it," he says. Pascarell points to the song "If" from 1969's

Ummagumma as the first significant Roger Waters composition. "It's very simple—it's a young songwriter learning how to write—but it has hints of the beautiful things that were to come." David Gilmour's early composition "Fat Old Sun" from *Atom Heart Mother* also earns praise from Pascarell. Chasolen adds that "Pink Floyd's music doesn't make you feel inferior if you didn't understand it; it's not intimidating. It's spiritual *and* it's cerebral. It has a life of its own. When music is created from the right place, it never dies."

While he makes it clear that he's not comparing the music of Pink Floyd to that written by Wolfgang Amadeus Mozart, Pascarell does see some similarities in the respective musical legacies. "There's a reason that 200-plus years after he's dead, people line up to hear Mozart's music," he notes. "And Pink Floyd's music isn't driven by fad or fashion; it's really honest music. I think if you can make honest music like that, and present it in a honest way, *that's* when it becomes timeless. And that's what happened with the music of Pink Floyd."

Yogi Lang's RPWL started out as a Pink Floyd tribute band, but soon evolved into a group playing its own original material. But as the German group's 2016 album *RPWL Plays Pink Floyd's "The Man and the Journey"* illustrates, the band has never forsaken its Pink Floyd–focused origins. "You don't play Pink Floyd's music by notes," Lang says, attempting to get to the heart of the group's sound. "You don't even play it by chords. It just . . . flows."

The keyboardist recalls a watch-phrase that he'd keep in mind when playing Pink Floyd songs: "Keep it simple. It's not a mystery; it's just about bringing your feelings [forth] on the keys." Reflecting on the music of his favorite group, Lang says, "When the music and the story are together—and the story is told—it's enough."

Though his professional association with Pink Floyd ended in 1968 when he and Andrew King chose to manage Syd Barrett as a solo artist, Peter Jenner would continue to follow the band's progress. And though in 1968 he viewed Barrett as the artist with the greater potential, he would be quite impressed with the music Pink Floyd made after its founding guitarist had left the band. He admits that in 1968, he thought, "Don't they realize they can't do it without Syd? And they can't do it without *me!*" But he soon revised his thinking. "I was dead wrong. Couldn't be more wrong; I'm full of admiration," he says. "The extraordinary thing for me is that Roger and Dave were able to make such great records, subsequently."

On first hearing *The Dark Side of the Moon*, however, Jenner was less than impressed. He recalls thinking to himself, "Where are the tunes? Where are the songs?" But he says that he soon "grew to love it." He maintains some reservations on a personal level—today he describes Roger Waters as "no great lovable human being"—but readily and enthusiastically gives Waters the credit he believes he is due. "Roger took an idea and built on it. Everything they did subsequently was there in what they did with Syd. And they built an empire on those foundations."

When Steve Howe had his near-miss experience of almost sitting in for a missing Syd Barrett, the guitarist was in the band Tomorrow. By 1970, he had taken Peter Banks's spot as guitarist in Yes, a position he still holds today. And Howe recalls that Pink Floyd would often be referenced during Yes recording sessions. "There was a marvelous cliché," he says. "In the '70s when Yes were twiddling around on something and worrying about money, we'd say something like, 'Pink Floyd just did that in a day!' We always thought of them as a very big band who projected their style of music, and never stopped living up to expectations."

Howe notes the progress that Pink Floyd made in the years between Syd Barrett's departure and the making of *The Dark Side of the Moon*. "They learned as they went along," he says. "They got more confident, and they continued to be able to team up on ideas. I guess that's what musicians do: they make it look easy, and then they keep on doing it."

Drummer Willie Wilson has as close to an insider's perspective on Pink Floyd as anyone outside the core group. He played with David Gilmour in Jokers Wild, worked on sessions for both of Syd Barrett's solo albums, played on Gilmour's solo albums, and served as the drummer in the "surrogate band" on Pink Floyd's *The Wall* live dates. He was also present for countless Pink Floyd studio sessions over the years. Today, he and David Gilmour remain good friends.

As such, Wilson is less focused on Pink Floyd as a band, and more on its members as living, breathing people. Unlike bands such as the Who and Led Zeppelin—both legendary for destroying hotel rooms, driving cars into swimming pools, throwing televisions out of high-rise windows, and such bored-rock-star antics—he says that Pink Floyd "weren't living the rock and roll lifestyle as such. There's not a lot of dirt to dig on them, really."

Longtime host of the syndicated radio program *Floydian Slip*, Craig Bailey has his own ideas about the group's appeal. "There is a mystery surrounding Pink Floyd," he says, having to do with "the fact that you rarely saw them on their album covers. Not to mention the fact that their music often times played with your head."

Remarking on the creative journey the group followed in its post–Syd Barrett incarnation, he observes, "If I didn't know anything, and you played me something from *The Piper at the Gates of Dawn*, and then you played me *Dark Side of the Moon*, I would have no reason to believe that that was the same band."

He sees *Meddle*'s side-long "Echoes" as a turning point in Pink Floyd's development. Noting that the work began as a series of unconnected "nothings," he points out that "eventually it evolved into this huge epic, where one piece flows into the next into the next. And that's very much like the second side of *The Dark Side of the Moon* and the way that it behaves."

Bailey has produced and broadcast more than 1,100 episodes of *Floydian Slip*. In the years since his program debuted, he's had time to ponder the enduring popularity of Pink Floyd's music, but the specifics remain elusive. "There's a certain 'secret sauce' that no one can quite put their finger on" about the group, he says. He does point to the timeless quality of the group's 1973 album. "If I had never heard *The Dark Side of the Moon* and you played it for me," he says, "I would think that's something that was made today."

And it's Roger Waters's lyrics for *Dark Side* that come in for special praise from Bailey. "If you take the time to listen to the lyrics, they're universal and timeless," he says. "They deal with huge issues that anybody can understand. No matter your gender, your race, what age you grow up in, what part of the world you grow up in, we all understand 'Us and Them.' We understand money, we understand the fact that time is passing and time is finite. All of these—the broad issues of *The Dark Side of the Moon*—are eternal."

Robyn Hitchcock prefers the Syd Barrett–era music of Pink Floyd to the music they would make after his departure, but he appreciates some of the latter's qualities. "Once they'd got rid of Syd—or Syd had got rid of himself—they started performing songs in a more organized, less psychotic or intense way," he says. Hitchcock cites what he calls the "very listenable" live version of "Astronomy Dominé" on *Ummagumma* as an example.

"They just straightened it all out as everything itself was straightening out," Hitchcock says. "People were realizing their limitations with psychedelics, and discarding the hype decidedly." Pink Floyd "should have changed their name after Barrett went, because what they did was so different," he says. *"The Piper at the Gates Of Dawn* doesn't appear to be an ancestor in any way of *The Dark Side of the Moon*, though Barrett himself is obviously a key inspiration for it." With his trademark faculty for memorable phrases, Robyn Hitchcock describes Syd Barrett as "part of Pink Floyd's acceleration; he was the rocket booster that got Pink Floyd off into the stratosphere and then just fell away."

Hitchcock places Pink Floyd into context of the popular and political culture in which it existed. "The counterculture had this enormous momentum between 1966 and '69," he says. "Then it kind of coasted, and then Blue Meanies counter attacked; [UK Prime Minister] Margaret Thatcher got in and everything got darker and darker and darker. And so we now have Donald Trump and Theresa May. And the journey from liftoff to dystopia was chronicled by no other act as acutely as by Pink Floyd."

29

OH, BY THE WAY

With a keen sense of self-awareness—in light of the fact that all of Pink Floyd's music in the coming decade would bear the overwhelming stamp of his (as opposed to the group's) personal creative vision— Roger Waters said in 2003 of the group's post–*Dark Side* output, "It's not to say we didn't do some good work, but the good work that we did was actually all about a lot of the negative aspects of what went on after we'd achieved the goal."

In the wake of *The Dark Side of the Moon*, Pink Floyd truly did find itself creatively spent. The extended period of time developing *Dark Side* as a stage presentation and then a studio album had left little time for initiating other new compositions. So while the band would have no problems from a live performance standpoint—"Time" and "Money" are what fans were paying good money to see and hear, after all—the idea of a studio project was more daunting.

A long-gestating project called *Household Objects* was initiated but eventually abandoned due to its ponderous and time-intensive nature. Simply put, the concept behind *Household Objects* was to create music without the use of musical instruments. This was an age long before the advent of sampling; recording and sculpting the sounds made from rubbing wine glasses, tapping on spoons, stretching rubber bands, and the like took countless hours. More frustrating was the fact that once these sounds were bent toward musical purposes, they ended up sounding rather ordinary. Bits of the *Household Objects* tapes would appear as bonus tracks on subsequent reissues of 1970s-era Pink Floyd albums, and one notable section formed the basis for part of "Shine On You Crazy Diamond," the epic centerpiece of 1975's *Wish You Were Here*.

Another project explored but not taken on was the idea of returning to work on film soundtracks. Alejandro Jodorowsky, director of *El Topo*, had secured the rights to make a motion picture adaptation of Frank Herbert's 1965 science fiction novel *Dune*. Initial meetings between the director and Pink Floyd were not successful, and the idea was abandoned. In the end, Jodorowsky—the second director to attempt to tackle the book—would be unsuccessful in his efforts to complete the film. His rights to the work lapsed in 1982, and a David Lynch–directed *Dune* would be released in 1984.

The music created by Pink Floyd in the post–*The Dark Side of the Moon* era would overwhelmingly reflect the sensibility and larger concerns of bassist Roger Waters. The success of *Dark Side*—and the ongoing need for new material—meant that Waters's position as Pink Floyd's sole lyricist was now ironclad. While there's no denying the poignancy and weight of much of Waters's post–*Dark Side* lyrics, the creative center of gravity within Pink Floyd had shifted. Many critics point to 1975's *Wish You Were Here* as musically superior to its predecessor, and the album certainly draws upon the lessons learned from earlier projects. The nine-part "Shine On You Crazy Diamond"—split across both sides of the original LP—is a sonic odyssey full of many of the elements that had made *The Dark Side of the Moon* such a success: Richard Wright's deeply textured keyboards (with a growing use of synthesizers), soaring, extended guitar solos from David Gilmour, and generous amounts of Dick Parry's soulful saxophone. And *Wish You Were Here* would be a massive success in the marketplace, though not on the level of the groundbreaking album that came before it.

Curiously—in light of *Wish You Were Here*'s reputation as an ode to Syd Barrett—Pink Floyd sound engineer Brian Humphries asserted in a 1975 interview that the band wished to distance itself from Barrett's legacy. "As far as Syd goes," he told *Circus*'s Alan Betrock, "the band really want to let the past lie. That was then and now is now."

The members of Pink Floyd would grow farther apart as individuals in the years after making *The Dark Side of the Moon*. Doubtless part of that would have been a product of the group's staggering financial success. As they all approached their thirtieth birthdays, the members of Pink Floyd were settling into adulthood, with families and interests beyond the group. And into a situation that at times resembled a creative vacuum, the fertile mind of Roger Waters would fill that space.

In its own way, 1977's *Animals* would be Pink Floyd's answer to the burgeoning punk rock scene. Still very much in line with the band's earlier music in terms of theme and sonic textures, *Animals* is possessed of a harsher, more metallic, and sinister demeanor in both its music and subject matter. Waters's lyrics metaphorically divide all of humanity into three categories: pigs, sheep, and dogs. While David Gilmour would continue to sing lead on much of the band's material—paving the way in later years for his billing as "the voice and guitar of Pink Floyd"—there would be a sense of disconnect between Waters's artistic vision for the band and the concerns and interests of Wright, Mason, and Gilmour. Put simply, the music that Pink Floyd made in the post–*The Dark Side of the Moon* era feels less like the product of a band, and closer to the fruit of one man's artistic vision, with expert help from some exceedingly talented and creative assistants. While that often made for some richly textured and compelling music, it would not be a recipe for harmony within the group. (It's worth noting that at no time since Roger Waters's departure from the band in the early 1980s has David Gilmour ever performed so much as a single note from *Animals* live onstage.)

In the late 1970s, perhaps owing at least in part to Roger Waters's growing dominance of Pink Floyd, two of the group's other members would each venture outside the group to make a solo album. Released in 1978, *David Gilmour* features the guitarist's longtime friend Willie Wilson on drums, along with bassist Rick Wills. Around the time of the album's release, Gilmour told *Circus*'s Shel Kagan that he felt the need to step out from behind the shadow of Pink Floyd. "A lot of people tend to cling together and say 'we live for the group' and at the beginning you need that. But later on you need other things."

Richard Wright's *Wet Dream* would be released in September 1978, four months after *David Gilmour*. Six of its ten tunes are instrumentals. The musicianship—featuring guitarist Snowy White, an auxiliary live player on Pink Floyd's 1977 *Animals* tour—is first-rate, and Wright's songs have a jazz-leaning ambience. *Wet Dream* is largely downtempo, and the keyboardist's vocals have a consistently melancholy air.

After the solo album side projects, the four members of Pink Floyd would reconvene to begin work on the band's eleventh studio release.

But despite the staggering success of 1979's *The Wall*, that double-album is even less of a creatively collaborative work than were *Wish You Were Here* or *Animals*. Working with an outside producer (for the first time since the *Ummagumma* and *Meddle* era a decade previous), Bob Ezrin, Waters had assumed nearly total control of Pink Floyd. Of the twenty-six tracks on the album, David Gilmour receives co-writer credit on but three; most of the album features both music and lyrics by Roger Waters (one track, "The Trial," is a co-write between Waters and producer Ezrin). None of Nick Mason's tape experiments would find a place in Waters's start-to-finish conceptual story line, and—in a set of circumstances that illustrated the degree to which the rest of the band had abdicated responsibilities—keyboardist Richard Wright had been summarily fired from the band by Waters during the making of the album.

Recorded around the same time as *David Gilmour* and *Wet Dream* but held for release until 1981, *Nick Mason's Fictitious Sports* is easily the oddest solo outing from a Pink Floyd member. Arguably, it's not a Mason album at all: jazz pianist Carla Bley composed the album's eight songs and co-produced the album with Mason. (The drummer had previously ventured briefly into outside production, working in the studio control room for *Music for Pleasure*, the 1977 album from punk rock tricksters The Damned.) *Nick Mason's Fictitious Sports* sounds nothing like Pink Floyd, but should be of interest to fans of avant-garde jazz.

1983's portentously titled *The Final Cut* would, for a time, signal the end of Pink Floyd. A Roger Waters solo album in all but name, *The Final Cut* finds the participation of drummer Nick Mason and guitarist David Gilmour reduced even further than had been the case on *The Wall*. With Richard Wright gone from what remained of the group, session players would handle the keyboard parts. Other than a handful of standout tunes—"Southampton Dock," "Two Suns in the Sunset"—*The Final Cut* is short on melody. Its production values are stunning, and Waters's lyrics are compelling, but there remains a hollow core at the musical heart of the album. There would be no tour to promote the disc, and the group effectively ceased to exist upon release of *The Final Cut*.

In 1984, David Gilmour would release his second solo album, *About Face*. That well-received disc showed the guitarist in a situation not unlike the one George Harrison had found himself in back in 1970 with *All Things Must Pass*: with his own songwriting contributions largely unwelcome within his band, Gilmour had a surfeit of quality material from which to create a solo album. Gilmour would tour with a band of his own in support of the album.

That same year, Waters released his solo debut, *The Pros and Cons of Hitchhiking*. Despite the presence of master guitarist Eric Clapton, *Hitchhiking* is most notable for its lack of memorable tunes. Arguably even more ponderous than *The Final Cut*—though meticulously produced—*Hitchhiking* suggested to Pink Floyd fans of that era that although Roger Waters may have been the band's guiding lyrical light for nearly a decade, Gilmour's music made for a much more enjoyable listening experience.

That perspective was not lost on Gilmour himself; amid legal wrangling (and very public disputes with Waters), the guitarist decided to reactivate a Waters-less Pink Floyd with the pointedly titled *A Momentary Lapse of Reason* in 1987. That album featured Gilmour and Mason, with Wright returning once again as a paid employee. A large cast of session musicians was also employed. While *AMLOR* would be criticized as a too-self-conscious-by-half attempt to revive the Pink Floyd "sound," there would be no denying its success in that regard. The album top-tenned all over the globe, and a massive world tour would follow.

Pink Floyd's live band in 1987 was quite large, an early example of a trend in rock music of assembling a massive musical cast so as to be able to re-create every nuance of the studio versions. The band's visuals were second to none, and—unlike *The Wall* dates—the band played not only most of its latest release but material from earlier albums as well.

Seven years would pass before Pink Floyd would release another studio album. *The Division Bell* was a notable improvement on all levels: Gilmour's songwriting skills had grown further, thanks in no small part to the collaboration with his girlfriend (later wife), Polly Samson. Wright was back in tow as a full member and involved himself in writing Pink Floyd music for the first time in a decade. Drummer Mason sank his creative teeth into the album's soundscapes. Another tour followed—Pink Floyd's last, as it would turn out—and it met with even larger-scale success.

Meanwhile, Waters continued his solo career; *Radio K.A.O.S.* had been released in 1987, followed by 1992's *Amused to Death*. Though he would tour with his own band—performing large chunks of Pink Floyd's back catalog—*Amused to Death* would be the last new rock studio album from Waters for nearly a quarter century, until 2017's *Is This the Life We Really Want?*

Pink Floyd did seem to bury the hatchet in 2005, though. Moved by Bob Geldof's efforts to combat world poverty, the massive Live 8 concert festival was staged in July of that year, with simultaneous concerts in nine cities across the globe. An undisputed highlight of the London concert was a reunion of Waters, Wright, Gilmour, and Mason, who took the stage to play five songs from the 1970s part of their catalog. While every other act would be introduced before performing, the briefly reunited Pink Floyd truly needed—and received—no introduction.

Live 8 would be the final time that Pink Floyd's longest-running and most well-known lineup would come together. Mason would occasionally appear at a Gilmour show; Wright would play on Gilmour's albums and tour as his keyboardist until his death in 2008 at age sixty-five. Waters continued to tour, mounting modern-day performances of *The Wall*, often with all-star musical casts. Gilmour and Waters even played a few songs together at shows in 2010 and 2011.

All was quiet on the Pink Floyd front for many years, until the 2014 release of *The Endless River*. Back around the time of release of *The Division Bell*, Mason had mentioned in an interview the existence of near-finished music that didn't make it onto that album. Describing the music as "ambient" in nature, Mason predicted it would eventually see release in some form. That release did come, albeit two decades later, as *The Endless River*.

2016 brought perhaps the biggest and most unexpected surprise in the now half-century history of Pink Floyd. A sprawling twenty-five-hour set (including CDs, DVDs, Blu-ray discs, and memorabilia), *The Early Years 1965–1972* shone a light on the band's least-explored period. And the existence of *The Early Years* helped emphasize the previously overlooked development of Pink Floyd's music in the years between Syd Barrett's 1968 departure and the creation of 1973's landmark *The Dark Side of the Moon*. Viewed in hindsight, that musical development seems at times to be quite linear: Pink Floyd progressed from strength to strength, learning from its mistakes and building upon its creative successes. Live concert set pieces like "The Man and the Journey" whetted the group's appetite for long-form works that would hang together conceptually. Epic compositions such as "A Saucerful of Secrets," "Atom Heart Mother Suite," and "Echoes" demonstrated Pink Floyd's skill at linking discrete pieces of music into a larger sonic framework. The more personal writing style that lyricist Roger Waters would develop beginning with *Ummagumma*'s "Grantchester Meadows" and "If" signaled a growing understanding of the value of meaningful lyrics. Though they could not have known so at the time, all of these qualities would serve to move Pink Floyd along on the creative timeline that culminated in 1973's *The Dark Side of the Moon*.

BIBLIOGRAPHY

Alterman, Lorraine, "Lorraine Alterman on Pop Records," *Detroit Free Press*, November 5, 1967.

Altham, Keith, "Jimi Hendrix: The Final Interview," *Record Mirror*, September 11, 1970.

Barrett, Syd, et al., Interview by Nancy Bacal, Canadian Broadcasting Company, January 1967.

Berendt, Joachim, *The Jazz Book*. New York: Lawrence Hill & Co., 1975.

Betrock, Alan, "Pink Floyd: More Gritty, Less Giddy," *Circus*, October 1975.

Boltwood, Derek, "'We Feel Good' Say the Pink Floyd," *Record Mirror*, October 21, 1967.

Chisena, Michele, "Adrian Maben, il regista di 'Pink Floyd at Pompeii,'" *Repubblica*, January 10, 2017, http://www.repubblica.it/spettacoli/musica/2017/01/10/news/adrian_maben_il_regista_di_pink_floyd_a_pompei-155046915/.

Cohen, John, "Pink Floyd Visionary Syd Barrett Dies at 60," *Billboard*, July 22, 2006.

Costa, Jean-Charles, "Pink Floyd: *Meddle*," *Rolling Stone*, January 6, 1972.

Cushing, Charlie, "Passionate Pink," *Great Speckled Bird*, May 25, 1970.

DiLorenzo, Kris, "Pink Floyd: But Is it Art?" *Trouser Press*, May 1978.

Dubro, Alec, "Pink Floyd: *Atom Heart Mother*," *Rolling Stone*, December 10, 1970.

Fitch, Vernon, *The Pink Floyd Encyclopedia*. Burlington, Ontario: Collector's Guide Publishing, 1998.

Geesin, Ron, "The Adjustable Spanner," http://rongeesin.com/all-the-latest-news/71-the-adjustable-spanner/

———, *The Flaming Cow: The Making of Pink Floyd's Atom Heart Mother*. Stroud, United Kingdom: History Press, 2013.

Gilmour, David, "My Moon-Landing Jam Session," *The Guardian*, July 1, 2009.

Graff, Gary, and Daniel Durchholz, editors, *MusicHound Rock: The Essential Album Guide*. New York: Schirmer Trade Books, 1999.

Green, Richard, "Richard Green Spends a Hectic Weekend with NICE in Paris," *New Musical Express*, January 31, 1970.

Grossman, Loyd, "Pink Floyd: *The Dark Side of the Moon*," *Rolling Stone*, May 24, 1973.

Grow, Kory, "40 Greatest Rock Documentaries," *Rolling Stone*, August 15, 2014.

Easlea, Daryl, Interview with David Gilmour, *Record Collector*, May 2003.

———, "Pink Floyd *Meddle* Review," *BBC*, 2007. http://www.bbc.co.uk/music/reviews/wnbd/.

Harris, John, *The Dark Side of the Moon: The Making of the Pink Floyd Masterpiece*. Cambridge, MA: Da Capo Press, 2005.

Hendrix, Jimi, Interview by Steve Barker. London, January 1967.

Hibbert, Tom, "Syd Barrett: *The Madcap Laughs/Barrett/Opel*," *MOJO*, July 1994.

Hollingsworth, Roy, "Hendrix Today," *Melody Maker*, September 5, 1970.

Jones, Nick, "Freaking Out with the Pink Floyd," *Melody Maker*, April 1, 1967.

———, "Pink Floyd: All Saints Church Hall, London," *Melody Maker*, October 20, 1966.

———, "The Who, The Move, Pink Floyd: The Roundhouse, Chalk Farm, London," *Melody Maker*, January 7, 1967.

Jones, Nick, and Chris Welch, "Who's Psychedelic Now?" *Melody Maker*, January 14, 1967.

Kagan, Shel, "Atom Heart Brother Floyd Guitarist David Gilmour's First Solo LP Finds Him in the Pink," *Circus*, August 1978.

Kent, Nick, "The Cracked Ballad of Syd Barrett," *New Musical Express*, April 13, 1974.

Kopp, Bill, "Album Review: Pink Floyd – *The Dark Side of the Moon* (Experience Edition)," *Musoscribe*, April 18, 2012. http://blog.musoscribe.com/index.php/2012/04/18/album-review-pink-floyd-the-dark-side-of-the-moon-experience-edition/.

———, "Get Me to the Copyright Lawyer on Time," *Musoscribe*, July 9, 2012. http://blog.musoscribe.com/index.php/2012/07/09/get-me-to-the-copyright-lawyer-on-time/.

———, "A Look Back at Pink Floyd's 'Point Me at the Sky,'" *Musoscribe*, December 18, 2013. http://blog.musoscribe.com/index.php/2013/12/18/a-look-back-at-pink-floyds-point-me-at-the-sky/.

———, "Pink Floyd," *Trouser Press*, 2001. http://www.trouserpress.com/entry.php?a=pink_floyd.

Lewisohn, Mark, *The Complete Beatles Recording Sessions: The Official Story of the Abbey Road Years*. London: Bounty Books, 2005.

MacDonald, Ian, "Pink Floyd: *Dark Side of the Moon*," *New Musical Express*, February 23, 1974.

Marsh, Dave, "Pink Floyd: *Relics*," *Creem*, November 1971.

Marsh, Dave, and John Swenson, editors, *The Rolling Stone Record Guide*. New York: Random House, 1979.

Mason, Nick, *Inside Out: A Personal History of Pink Floyd*. San Francisco: Chronicle Books, 2005.

Mason, Nick, and Richard Wright, interview by Ted Alvy, KPPC-FM, October 16, 1971.

McKnight, Connor, "Notes Towards the Illumination of the Floyd," *ZigZag*, July 1973.

Means, Andrew, "Pink Floyd: The Dome, Brighton," *Melody Maker*, January 29, 1972.

Miles, Barry, *Pink Floyd: The Early Years*. London: Omnibus, 2007.

———, "Pink Floyd: Games for May," *New Musical Express*, May 15, 1976.

———, *Pink Floyd*. New York: Delilah/Putnam, 1980.

———, "Pink Floyd: *A Saucerful of Secrets*," *International Times*, July 26, 1968.

Miller, Jim, "Pink Floyd: *A Saucerful of Secrets*," *Rolling Stone*, October 26, 1968.

Palacios, Julian, *Syd Barrett & Pink Floyd: Dark Globe*. London: Plexus Publishing, 2010.

Pink Floyd. *Classic Albums: The Making of* The Dark Side of the Moon. DVD. Directed by Matthew Longfellow. London: Eagle Rock Entertainment, 2003.

Povey, Glenn, *Echoes: The Complete History of Pink Floyd*. Chicago: Chicago Review Press, 2010.

Quigley, Mike, "An Interview with Pink Floyd," *Georgia Straight*, October 14, 1970.

Rolling Stone editors, "Eric Clapton: The *Rolling Stone* Interview," *Rolling Stone*, May 11, 1968.

Sandall, Robert, "Pink Floyd: The Third Coming," *MOJO*, May 1994.

Schaffner, Nicholas, "Repent, Pink Floyd Idolaters!" *Musician Magazine*, August 1988.

———, *Saucerful of Secrets: The Pink Floyd Odyssey*. New York: Delta, 1991.

Stewart, Tony, "Chuck Berry, Pink Floyd, Billy Preston, Slade: Locarno Ballroom, Coventry," *New Musical Express*, February 12, 1972.

———, "Pink Floyd: *Dark Side of the Moon*," *New Musical Express*, March 17, 1973.

———, "Pink Floyd: Electric Chaos, But Just Great," *New Musical Express*, January 29, 1972.

———, "Pink Floyd: Simple But Not Banal," *New Musical Express*, February 19, 1972.

Sutcliffe, Phil, and P. Henderson, "The True Story of *Dark Side of the Moon*," *MOJO*, March 1998.

Turner, Steve, "Syd Barrett, a Psychedelic Veteran," *Beat Instrumental*, June 1971.

Valentine, Penny, "Pink Floyd: They're All in the PINK!" *Disc and Music Echo*, April 8, 1967.

Walsh, Alan, "Hits? The Floyd Couldn't Care Less," *Melody Maker*, December 9, 1967.

Waters, Roger, Interview by Richard Skinner, "Saturday Live," BBC 1, June 9, 1984.

Watkinson, Mike, and Pete Anderson, *Crazy Diamond: Syd Barrett & the Dawn of Pink Floyd*. London: Omnibus, 2001.

Welch, Chris, "The Great Pink Floyd Mystery," *Melody Maker*, August 5, 1967.

———, "Pink Floyd: Royal Albert Hall, London," *Melody Maker*, July 5, 1969.

———, "Syd Barrett: Confusion and Mr. Barrett," *Melody Maker*, January 31, 1970.

Wink, Roger, "Chubby Checker Pink Floyd And Ramones Inducted Into National Recording Registry," *Noise11*, March 22, 2013. http://www.noise11.com/news/chubby-checker-pink-floyd-and-ramones-inducted-into-national-recording-registry-20130322.

Wise, Steve, "Pink Floyd," *Great Speckled Bird*, May 1, 1972.

———, Review of *Meddle* and *Relics*, *Great Speckled Bird*, November 15, 1971.

———, Review of *Obscured by Clouds*, *Great Speckled Bird*, July 3, 1972.

Wright, Richard, "Awards History—1974." *New Musical Express*, http://www.nme.com/awards-history/1974-606205.

———, "Everything Is There, and Even More," *Rock & Folk*, November 2016.

———, Interview by Mark Blake, EMI Records Ltd., 1996.

———, "Pink Floyd," *Beat Instrumental*, January 1970.

———, "Pink Floyd," *Top Pops & Music Now*, September 15, 1969.

———, *Pink Floyd Anthology*. New York: Warner Brothers Publications, 1980.

———, "Pink Floyd: A Saucerful of Secrets," *Melody Maker*, August 10, 1968.

———, "Platter Chatter: Albums from the Doors, Sopwith Camel, Beach Boys, Procol Harum and Pink Floyd," *Hit Parader*, February 1968.

———, "Syd Barrett Speaks," *Beat Instrumental*, March 1970.

INDEX

ABOUT THE AUTHOR

Bill Kopp is a lifelong music enthusiast, musician, collector, and, since the 1990s, music journalist. His writing has been featured in music magazines including *Bass Guitar*, *Prog*, *Record Collector*, and *Shindig!* (all in Great Britain), as well as *Billboard*, *Electronic Musician*, *Goldmine*, *Living Blues*, *Trouser Press*, *Ugly Things*, and more than a dozen alternative weekly newspapers. He is the Jazz Desk Editor and Prog Editor at BLURT online, and has written liner note essays for twenty albums, including titles by Julian "Cannonball" Adderley, Larry Coryell, Edgar Winter, Rick Wakeman, The Ventures, Ben Folds, Dave Mason, and Iron Butterfly. He has interviewed several hundred musicians and music industry figures of note, and his musoscribe.com blog has featured new content—thousands of music reviews, essays, interviews, and features—every business day since 2009. He lives in a nearly century-old house in Asheville, North Carolina, with his wife, two cats, many thousands of vinyl records, and perhaps too many synthesizers and guitars. He's active on social media on Facebook (www.facebook.com/reinventingpinkfloyd/) and Twitter (@the_musoscribe).